Praise for *The Ghost Ships of Archangel*

"In this gripping history, Geroux recounts the fascinating story of multinational convoy PQ-17, which sailed through treacherous ice-filled waters to deliver tanks, explosives, and other supplies to support the Soviet WWII effort. . . . WWII aficionados, and anyone else who likes a good story, will find this well-written adventure tale a real pleasure."

—*Publishers Weekly* (starred review)

"An important but overlooked point in World War II . . . A nightmarish story of survival in the ice fields of the Arctic; an engaging read for fans of military history."

—*Library Journal*

"This book is sheer enjoyment. . . . A riveting saga . . . Using marvelous accounts from first-person perspectives, Geroux crafted a history to be enjoyed by naval enthusiasts, mariners and World War II fans. This is not one to miss!"

—*The Virginia Gazette*

PENGUIN BOOKS

THE GHOST SHIPS OF ARCHANGEL

William Geroux wrote for the *Richmond Times-Dispatch* for twenty-five years. His writing has appeared in *The New York Times*, the Associated Press, Smithsonian.com, and Time.com and various regional magazines. His previous book is *The Mathews Men*. A native of Washington, D.C., and a graduate of the College of William and Mary, he lives in Virginia Beach, Virginia.

THE
GHOST
SHIPS OF
ARCHANGEL

THE ARCTIC VOYAGE
THAT DEFIED THE NAZIS

WILLIAM GEROUX

PENGUIN BOOKS

PENGUIN BOOKS
An imprint of Penguin Random House LLC
penguinrandomhouse.com

First published in the United States of America by Viking,
an imprint of Penguin Random House LLC, 2019
Published in Penguin Books 2020

Illustration credits appear on p. 318.

ISBN 9780525557487 (paperback)

THE LIBRARY OF CONGRESS HAS CATALOGED THE
HARDCOVER EDITION AS FOLLOWS:
Names: Geroux, William, author.
Title: The ghost ships of Archangel : the Arctic voyage that defied the Nazis /
William Geroux.
Description: New York, New York : Viking, [2019] |
Includes bibliographical references and index. |
Identifiers: LCCN 2018049389 (print) | LCCN 2018055894 (ebook) |
ISBN 9780525557470 (ebook) | ISBN 9780525557463 (hardcover)
Subjects: LCSH: World War, 1939–1945—Naval operations. |
World War, 1939–1945—Arctic Ocean. | Naval convoys—History—20th century.
Classification: LCC D771 (ebook) | LCC D771 . G436 2019 (print) |
DDC 940.54/50916324—dc23
LC record available at https://lccn.loc.gov/2018049389

Printed in the United States of America
3 5 7 9 10 8 6 4

BOOK DESIGN BY LUCIA BERNARD
MAPS BY JEFFREY L. WARD

For Kema, Sarah, Nick, and Cody

Death barred the way to Russia, but you crosst.

—JOHN MASEFIELD, "For All Seafarers"

CONTENTS

MAPS

PROLOGUE

THE SPINNING NEEDLE

Jim North could not tell exactly what was happening, but in the pit of his stomach he knew the fate of convoy PQ-17 had taken a calamitous turn. All around him, the thirty merchant ships in the convoy were veering off in different directions through the icy Arctic waters, abandoning the tight defensive formation that had kept the German bombers and U-boats at bay since the convoy left Iceland a week before. Every ship's signal lanterns blinked messages nonstop. On the bridge of North's vessel, the freighter *Troubadour,* the Norwegian captain and the first officer held a terse discussion in their native tongue, punctuated by vile curses. North understood only the curses, but there was no mistaking the tone of their voices. A fresh crisis had overtaken convoy PQ-17 on its misbegotten voyage to Arctic Russia.

It was the Fourth of July 1942, a little past 9:30 p.m., although the time of day meant nothing to the men on the ships because the Arctic sun never set in July. The convoy was less than 800 miles from the North Pole. Earlier in the day, the American vessels forming the core of the convoy had celebrated Independence Day by hoisting brand-new U.S.

flags into the fog and scudding clouds. Soon afterward, the Allied warships protecting the convoy had fought off an attack by twenty-three German dive-bombers. Three ships had been sunk but the mariners considered the battle a victory, an encouraging sign that they might yet reach the Soviet Union alive. Some of the men were still congratulating one another when the new crisis—whatever it was—engulfed them.

North was still trying to figure out what the Norwegians were saying when he was startled by the blare of another ship's claxon. A small British escort vessel approached the *Troubadour,* and a British officer shouted through a bullhorn, repeating an extraordinary message that had been sent to all the ships by signal flags. Convoy PQ-17 was breaking up. The powerful warships protecting it were already racing away. The *Troubadour* and the other merchant ships—all of them hopelessly slow and packed with TNT and other explosive cargo—were supposed to find their own way, alone and unprotected, across hundreds of miles of the remote Barents Sea to Russia.

The convoy already was surrounded by U-boats, which had been shadowing it, probing for gaps in its defenses. Now there would be no defenses. The twenty-four-hour Arctic daylight offered no respite from the German bombers, more of which were certainly on the way. Worst of all, perhaps, convoy PQ-17 faced a possible attack by the German battleship *Tirpitz,* the world's most formidable warship. The *Tirpitz* had guns that could hurl devastating shells for a distance of twenty-two miles—from beyond the horizon. It could sink lesser ships like the *Troubadour* before they even saw it coming. Men on some Allied ships called the *Tirpitz* the "Big Bad Wolf."

"Sorry to leave you like this," the commander of a departing British destroyer shouted across the water to a friend on one of the merchant ships he was leaving behind. "Looks like a bloody business. Good luck."

The scattering ships would need a great deal of luck, not only against the Germans but against the Arctic itself. The convoy's route skirted the edge of the polar ice field extending down from the North Pole. The water was full of icebergs and floes with razor-sharp edges. Though it was midsummer, the ocean was still cold enough to kill a person in minutes, and the air temperature often dipped below zero degrees Fahrenheit. Clouds and fog could persist for days, leaving navigators unable to fix their ships' positions by the sun. The nearness of the Magnetic North Pole rendered vessels' magnetic compasses useless.

At twenty, Jim North was the youngest and greenest deckhand on the *Troubadour*. He had never been to sea before and knew little about the Soviet Union except that "it was a big country fighting the Germans like we were." After the convoy had repelled the German dive-bombers, North had felt cocky, indestructible. Now, as he watched the convoy dissolve, he wrote, "I was scared shitless."

THOUSANDS OF MILES AWAY in Washington, D.C., London, and Moscow, President Franklin D. Roosevelt, British prime minister Winston Churchill, and Soviet dictator Joseph Stalin were testing the limits of their fraught alliance against Adolf Hitler. The Soviet Union was fighting for its survival against Nazi Germany in a war of medieval savagery that already had claimed millions of lives—far more than America and Britain together would lose in the entire course of World War II. America and Britain were merely watching the slaughter from the sidelines. Stalin was furious. But Roosevelt and Churchill did not think their troops were ready yet to compete with German troops on the battlefield. For the time being, the only help they were willing to give Stalin was to send convoys of war supplies across the ocean to the reeling Red Army. Whether that was enough help to keep Stalin on the Allied side was in doubt. But Roosevelt and Churchill were determined to keep the convoys sailing.

Roosevelt, Churchill, and Stalin were usually too busy to pay much attention to individual convoys. But they would all have cause to remember convoy PQ-17.

Amid the chaos on the *Troubadour*'s bridge, the Norwegian captain,

George Salvesen, quickly regained his unruffled demeanor. He had a plan. Salvesen did not think the lumbering *Troubadour* could survive an 800-mile run across open water with the Nazis already upon it. Instead, he would take the ship north, into the polar ice field, and hide there until the German attacks subsided. The captain ordered North to steer northwest into the ice—the opposite direction of most of the other fleeing vessels. The ice field was a treacherous place for a ship. The captain hoped it was the last place the logical Germans would think to look.

North did as he was ordered. The *Troubadour* had to dodge floes as it approached the ice barrier, a low wall of brilliant white stretching all the way across the northern horizon. A cold, gray fog swirled around the ship. A startled polar bear scrambled away from the *Troubadour* across a pressure ridge, where two floes had slammed together with crushing force. The *Troubadour* was about to become a Ghost Ship. The bridge had fallen into an uneasy silence. The captain called out "Steady as she goes," trying to sound reassuring. But North was far from reassured when he glanced at the compass to note the ship's bearing. The needle of the useless compass was spinning around and around.

CHAPTER ONE
THE ENEMY OF MY ENEMY

The stark beauty of Iceland was mostly lost on the men who took part in convoy PQ-17. By the middle of May 1942—six weeks before the convoy sailed to Arctic Russia—most of them had already spent weeks on their ships in a bleak anchorage on the coast of Iceland. The place was named Hvalfjord, which was Icelandic for "Whale Fjord," reflecting the waterway's long history as a whaling center. But to some of the Allied mariners, Hvalfjord felt more like an accursed realm out of Norse mythology.

U.S. Navy ensign Howard Carraway gazed up from the chill waters to see "high, barren, almost terraced mountains on either side . . . hovering over us like great black ghosts." A massive crag named Botnsulur loomed above the other mountains, its peaks wreathed perpetually in clouds. The constant sun broke through the gloom occasionally out of sheer persistence.

A cold wind blew relentlessly through the fjord, keening and moaning in the ships' rigging and often rising into a scream. "For 24 hours, the wind has blown steadily from the north at unbelievable velocity, a steady rising and fading howl, vicious and cold," Carraway wrote. At times, it blew hard enough to yank anchors out of the muddy bottom and send ships careening through the harbor. A storm in January with 100-mile-per-hour wind gusts had blown the 13,000-ton American heavy cruiser USS *Wichita* into two other vessels before the warship finally ran aground. At times the wind abruptly ceased, leaving a silence so profound that ducks could be heard plopping down onto the water's surface a half mile away. Seals cavorted among the ships, performing twists and rolls. But the mariners had grown to resent the animals' carefree play. Nothing else about Hvalfjord was carefree.

The ships were gathered at the end of a long, deep fjord north of the capital of Reykjavik. Hvalfjord was empty except for a few scattered farms and the rudimentary British and American naval bases. The bases consisted of fuel tanks, docks, and Nissen huts—prefabricated shelters of corrugated metal—offering supplies and cheap beer. The anchorage was crowded with more than a hundred cargo ships, flying the flags of a dozen Allied nations. They had been rushed to Hvalfjord to sail to the Soviet Union. The vessels ranged from brand-new Liberty ships, freshly launched from American shipyards, to rusting old tubs from the previous world war. Each ship had a crew of civilian volunteers to sail it and a military gun crew to defend it.

The two-thousand-mile voyage from the United States to the North Russia ports of Murmansk and Archangel, which mariners dubbed "the Murmansk Run," was notorious for the severity and variety of its dangers. Those included not only German bombers and U-boats but the extreme Arctic weather. Prime Minister Winston Churchill called the Murmansk Run "the worst voyage in the world." Seafaring men usually avoided it unless they knew no better or had no choice. Ensign Carraway fit into both those categories.

Carraway was one of the many Americans at Hvalfjord for whom convoy PQ-17 was to be a first taste of war. He jokingly referred to himself as the Great American Chicken, although events would prove otherwise. Carraway stood five foot nine, with blue eyes and sandy-brown hair. He spoke softly in a South Carolina drawl that stopped short of a twang. Carraway had grown up on a tiny farm in rural Olanta, South Carolina, near Florence, where his parents eked out a living growing tobacco and cotton. Money was so tight that Carraway, one of seven children, spent two years living with relatives to spare his parents the cost of feeding him. Carraway hated farm work but loved books. He worked his way through Furman University, graduating with a degree in English in the spring of 1941. A few months later, with America on the brink of war, he and his three brothers agreed they all should enlist before they got drafted. Each brother chose a different branch of the armed forces. They may actually have drawn straws, since Carraway, whose nautical experience consisted of rowing a skiff around a farm pond, ended up joining the U.S. Naval Reserve.

Carraway was assigned to the Navy Armed Guard, a branch of the sea service created to man the guns installed on merchant ships to protect them from enemy submarines and planes. Though he probably did not know it, the Armed Guard was widely regarded in the Navy as an undesirable and hazardous posting. No matter how capable the Armed Guard crew was, guns on freighters and tankers provided scant protection, particularly against U-boats, which often struck without warning. Merchant ships were the primary targets of U-boats, whose main mission was to cut the Allied supply line. The Navy Armed Guard's official motto was "We aim to deliver!" but its unofficial motto was "Sighted sub, glub, glub."

If Carraway was disappointed at being posted to the Armed Guard, he did not express it—at least not until he was assigned to the *Troubadour*.

The *Troubadour* was floating evidence of America's desperate need for cargo vessels early in the war. The ship was an old, coal-burning freighter, 415 feet long, with space for 6,000 tons of cargo in six holds, and a dubious past. Built in England in 1920, the ship had changed names and owners three times by 1940, when as the *Confidenza* she hauled scrap iron for an Italian company. The vessel happened to be docked in

Jacksonville, Florida, in 1940 when Italy, following Germany's lead, declared war on Britain and France. Although America was still a neutral nation, U.S. authorities held the ship in port to prevent it from serving Italy or Germany. The *Confidenza* sat rusting at the pier for almost a year before her Italian crew received a coded message to sabotage it so the Allies could not use it either. The Italians dry-fired the ship's boilers— heating them without water in order to melt and warp the turbines and steam pipes—until the U.S. Coast Guard saw what was happening and seized the ship. The damage was severe, but the crippled *Confidenza* was turned over to the U.S. War Shipping Administration, the federal agency in charge of wartime shipping. The boilers were repaired and the vessel was fitted out with guns. The agency decided to sail the *Troubadour* under the flag of Panama rather than the U.S. flag, which exempted the vessel from stringent Coast Guard inspections and allowed the hiring of foreign mariners at low pay.*

As a result, the *Troubadour* was manned by a polyglot crew. Its thirty-four-year-old captain, George J. Salvesen, and all its officers were Norwegian. They had been at sea on other ships when the Nazis seized Norway in 1940, and had been forced to live at sea or in temporary lodgings in Allied or neutral nations. They were stateless men, and angry ones. The third mate, Sigurd Olsen, choked up when he talked about his wife and children, living under the Germans' thumb in the coastal city of Bergen. Olsen longed for them and the fjords and the shimmering aurora borealis. He vowed to take revenge on the Germans. If necessary, he would wait until after the war. When German tourists returned to Bergen's cobblestoned streets, he told Carraway, he would make them suffer for his years of exile at sea.

The *Troubadour*'s crew consisted of forty-six merchant mariners, all of

---

* Such "flags of convenience" are still widely used today by shipowners to avoid Coast Guard regulations, taxes, various legal requirements, and the necessity of paying union wages to American mariners.

them civilians who had joined the ship only for this one voyage to Russia. They came from seventeen different countries, including the United States, England, Norway, South Africa, Uruguay, Latvia, Estonia, Honduras, Holland, Sweden, Poland, Portugal, Spain, Belgium, and Grand Cayman Island. Some had been recruited from immigration camps in the United States, where they were given a choice of sailing with the *Troubadour* or being deported. Their level of experience varied widely. So did their dedication to the Allied cause.

One of the ten Americans on the *Troubadour* was James Baker North III of Bucks County, Pennsylvania. North had quit high school soon after the Japanese attack on Pearl Harbor on December 7, 1941. He was "red hot" at the Japanese and feared nothing except that the war would end too soon for him to fight in it. At age twenty, North was five foot ten and 125 pounds with "bad tonsils and a loud mouth," as he put it. He wanted to be a pilot, but his inflamed tonsils caused both the Navy and Army air forces to reject him. A friend advised North that the U.S. Merchant Marine would not care about his tonsils and would offer him "easy money" while he served his country. Like Carraway, North knew nothing about ships. He concocted a tale about having worked on a shrimp boat, and one of the maritime unions—which were as desperate for mariners as the government was for ships—accepted North as an ordinary seaman, the lowest rank of deckhand. At the union hall in Philadelphia, North heard that a ship named the *Troubadour* needed crew for a voyage to Russia with a five-hundred-dollar bonus. North had never heard of the Murmansk Run, and five hundred dollars was more money than he had ever seen. He could not think of any reason not to hurry down to the docks and sign on with the *Troubadour*.

North's hope of easy money was quickly dashed. Soon after he joined the ship, a tough character in the crew grabbed him and started pounding his head on the deck out of pure meanness. Another tough shipmate watched the pounding for a while and then slugged North's tormentor. The two brawlers exchanged a flurry of wild punches. Then they shook hands with each other and with North. North had made his first "friends" on the *Troubadour*. He would make others over the course of the voyage, but he gave some of his shipmates a wide berth. North was especially wary of two big redheaded brothers from Liverpool who worked as firemen, shoveling coal into the *Troubadour*'s flaming boilers to keep up the steam. The brothers apparently had been staring into fires too long and something was wrong with their eyes. They got right up in a person's face when they talked. That was too close for North, who always expected them to assault him.

The only men on the ship North actively disliked, however, were Carraway and his eight Navy Armed Guard men. North regarded them as self-important fools. Carraway in turn considered North and the other civilian mariners lazy, unreliable, and very likely disloyal. "They're Trotskyite Reds and rowdy as all hell," Carraway wrote. When a valve on the ship was left open, allowing the sea to flood the Armed Guard's ammunition, Carraway was convinced the crew had done it on purpose. North thought that was absurd: What mariner would disarm his own ship before a hazardous voyage?

On her way to Hvalfjord, the *Troubadour* had stopped in New York and Glasgow, Scotland, to take aboard weaponry, munitions, and supplies for the Soviets. The ship's main deck was crowded with crates, trucks, and three M-3 General Lee tanks, lashed by steel wire to ringbolts in the deck to keep them from being washed overboard. Originally, the deck cargo had included hundreds of metal drums of ethylene gas. But the drums had started breaking free and bouncing around the deck during a storm off New England, and the captain had ordered all of them thrown overboard to prevent a disaster. Even without the drums, the *Troubadour*'s deck was so congested that the crew had to build a wooden catwalk above the cargo so the Navy Armed Guard men could reach their guns quickly.

The *Troubadour*'s newly installed guns consisted of four .30-caliber

Lewis machine guns, which Carraway suspected lacked the firepower to damage either planes or U-boats; and a single 4-inch, 50-caliber cannon, mounted on a platform on the ship's stern, with a barrel as long as a telephone pole. The "4-50" cannon was formidable but could not be elevated higher than 45 degrees, which severely limited its use against planes. None of the guns seemed to have enough ammunition. Carraway wondered what the people who had armed the *Troubadour* had been thinking. At least the *Troubadour* was better armed than another convoy PQ-17 vessel, the Liberty ship *Christopher Newport,* whose guns included an old cannon that had been plucked out of retirement in a public park in Baltimore.

Carraway, a romantic at heart with a wry, cynical side, felt his innocence quickly falling away. His transformation was obvious in a diary he kept of the voyage, in violation of naval regulations. He wrote the diary as an ongoing love letter to his new bride, Avis, a petite, green-eyed beauty he had married just before joining the ship. In every entry, he addressed Avis as "Angel" and chronicled the day's events in detail so he could share the experience with her when he got back home—if he got back home. Well before the *Troubadour* reached Hvalfjord, Carraway had begun referring to the ship in his diary as a "piece of refuse" and "this gawd-damned old seagoing latrine." When a pigeon took up residence on the *Troubadour,* Carraway wrote, "He must have been badly mistreated in his former home to seek refuge on this scow."

Carraway was determined to overcome all obstacles and keep the *Troubadour* afloat long enough to deliver its cargo. He knew the Soviets needed help badly. Still, like most Americans in Iceland, he had grown up believing the Soviet Union was a malevolent threat to the free world. There was something strange about risking his life to help a secretive, totalitarian state run by the brutal Joseph Stalin. Carraway would have found it stranger still if he had known about the history and the high-level political maneuvers surrounding convoy PQ-17.

———

FOR MOST OF AMERICA'S HISTORY, its relations with Russia had been friendly if not close. The Russian empress Catherine the Great was the first world leader to recognize the United States after the American Revolution—although she did so mainly to weaken Britain, Russia's maritime rival. During the War of 1812, Russia offered to mediate between the United States and Britain. While the American Civil War was raging, Russia expressed support for the Union side while Britain and France leaned toward the Confederacy. After America was reunited, Russia sold Alaska to the United States for a negotiated price of $7.2 million. The United States and Russia maintained a steady level of trade, mostly through the port of Archangel on the White Sea, until the Bolshevik Revolution in 1917.

The Bolsheviks fed on resentment among Russian soldiers over the demoralizing defeats they kept suffering at the hands of the Germans in World War I. Once the Bolsheviks seized power, they quickly made peace with Germany, ceding vast stretches of territory and pulling Russian troops from the battlefield. The Russians' withdrawal enabled the Germans to shift hundreds of thousands of troops to the western front to launch an offensive against the British and French. The result was a longer and bloodier war that eventually drew in the United States. As the fighting was finally ending in 1918, the British landed a small military force by sea at Archangel to try to stop the Bolsheviks from cementing their control of Russia. President Woodrow Wilson augmented the British forces with 5,500 American doughboys, most of them raw recruits from Michigan and Wisconsin who had expected to be defending French soil against Germany. Under British command in Archangel, the American troops fought an undeclared war against small bands of Bolsheviks in remote forests and mosquito-infested bogs south of the city. The Americans built log forts and held off raiding parties, like pioneers in America's Old West. The fighting continued for ten months, spanning the severe winter of 1918–19, when temperatures plunged so far below zero that blood from gaping wounds froze instantly, which actually saved lives in a few cases. Before the Americans left Archangel in June 1919, they had lost 244 men to combat or illness. They had fought well against the nascent Red Army, but their small-scale intervention had failed to slow the Bolsheviks, who had begun calling themselves Communists. To this day, the doughboys of Archangel are the only American troops to have confronted Russian troops on the battlefield.

As the last of the British forces withdrew from Archangel in early 1919, ardent anti-Communists in Britain—led by Churchill, who was then minister of munitions—called for the mustering of a large international force to stop the Bolsheviks. But Wilson and other leaders of the victorious Allied nations, who were still counting the dead from the supposed "war to end all wars," had no stomach for a new war in the vastness of Russia. Wilson refused to send any more troops into Russia. Churchill warned at the time that the Western nations would regret not listening to him: "The day will come when it will be recognized without doubt throughout the civilized world that the strangling of Bolshevism at birth would have been an untold blessing to the human race." Churchill's passionate opposition to Communism would complicate his dealings with Stalin and Roosevelt in World War II and become part of the story of convoy PQ-17.

The short-lived Allied intervention in Russia in 1918–19 was quickly forgotten in the United States, but not in Russia, where it would stoke resentment for generations and sour U.S.-Soviet relations during the Cold War. In 1959, Soviet premier Nikita Khrushchev told an audience in Los Angeles, "We remember the grim days when American soldiers went to our soil headed by their generals to help . . . combat the new revolution. . . . [A]ll the capitalist countries of Europe and of America marched upon our country to strangle the new revolution. . . . [N]ever have any of our soldiers been on American soil, but your soldiers were on Russian soil. These are the facts."

As the Western democracies watched from the sidelines after World War I, the Communists consolidated their control of Russia. In 1924, Stalin succeeded Vladimir Lenin as leader of the Soviet Union. Over the next twenty-eight years, Stalin would prove the accuracy of Churchill's dire warning. Stalin was born Ioseb in a rural village in the southern Soviet state of Georgia, where he was regularly beaten by his father, a drunken cobbler. The boy excelled in school but was expelled from a religious seminary and gravitated toward a violent gang of Bolsheviks, for whom he organized bank robberies and spent time in prison. Although Stalin never served in the military, he wore military-style clothing, including a peaked cap, tunic, and long boots. He carried a gun, affected a martial bearing, and adopted the surname of Stalin, from the Russian word *stal,* meaning "steel."

Stalin's administrative skills had made him indispensable to the fledgling Communist Party. He traded on those skills to rise to power despite a lifelong reputation for casual cruelty that unsettled even the fanatical Leon Trotsky—whom Stalin eventually would have assassinated with an ice pick to the skull. People who dealt with Stalin often mistook him for a reasonable man with whom they could work. Many of them would pay for that mistake with their lives as Stalin transformed the Soviet Union through brute force and terror.

After World War I, Stalin believed he had to transform the Soviet Union from a rural backwater into a modern power, or its hostile neighbors would carve it up during the next war. History suggests he was right about that, but his strategies took little account of human life. Stalin ordered millions of peasant farmers to surrender their land so the state could establish a vast system of collective farms to feed the Soviet Union. The peasants were uprooted and relocated to new factories and industries. Those who objected were murdered or herded into a fast-growing network of prison camps, collectively known as the Gulag. The collective farms struggled under their inexperienced new overseers, and food grew scarce. Stalin blamed thieves, hoarders, and other enemies of the state.

He dispatched his secret police, the NKVD—a Russian acronym for the People's Commissariat for Internal Affairs—to maraud through the countryside and ferret them out, while the food shortages worsened into a famine. By 1934, the Gulag swelled with inmates ranging from Stalin's political foes to outspoken artists to thoroughly loyal citizens who had been falsely accused by friends or relatives under intense pressure to accuse *somebody*. A mind-boggling 6 to 8 million Soviet citizens had died of starvation, illness, or gunshots to the back of the head—the signature of the NKVD executioners.

Amid the death and suffering, Stalin's transformation of the Soviet Union took hold. The famine ended. Industrial production soared. The Red Army grew into a large, well-armed force. The Gulag evolved into a source of slave labor that built dams, canals, and other enormous public works projects. Millions of young peasants whose parents had never dreamed of being anything *but* peasants received formal education and found opportunities in industry and the military. All they knew was the Soviet system. If they were lucky enough to avoid the NKVD, they could tell themselves this was progress.

No one in the Soviet Union, however, was ever truly safe. In 1936, Stalin set in motion a series of purges he insisted were necessary to snuff out a conspiracy against the Soviet state from within. The secret police murdered or imprisoned more than a million people, ranging from Stalin's old Bolshevik comrades to Soviet government officials and military officers. Torture produced false confessions, followed by show trials at which hapless defendants confessed to elaborate crimes they had not committed and denounced other equally innocent people. Even the most slavishly loyal Russians lived in terror of a knock at the door. The purges became known as the Great Terror. But an even greater terror loomed to the west.

Stalin quickly recognized the threat the Nazis posed to the Soviet Union. Hitler had called Bolshevism a creation of the Jews he despised, and he declared Germany needed *Lebensraum*—living space—where the

Nazi "master race" could propagate and flourish. Hitler certainly meant Soviet territory. Stalin set out to try to avoid a war with Nazi Germany, or at least to delay it. The purges of the Great Terror had claimed more than forty-eight thousand Soviet military officers, leaving the Red Army and Soviet Navy in disarray.

Stalin looked first for an alliance with Britain and France. In April 1939, he proposed that the three nations craft an agreement to defend any independent nation from the Baltic Sea to the Mediterranean. But leaders of the British and French governments wanted nothing to do with Stalin. Two of the nations most threatened by Hitler, Poland and Romania, refused to allow Soviet troops on their soil even to defend it from the Nazis. The Poles and Romanians "did not know whether it was German aggression or Russian rescue that they dreaded more," Churchill wryly observed. Britain and France left Stalin's offer dangling. Stalin decided to pursue a pact with Hitler.

Stalin did not think a treaty with Germany would stop Hitler from attacking the Soviet Union eventually. But he believed it could buy time for the Red Army to prepare. And while the treaty was in effect, Stalin reasoned, the Nazis and the Western democracies might tear each other to pieces, leaving the Soviet Union stronger than any of them.

Hitler was just as eager for a deal with Stalin. After Germany occupied Czechoslovakia in 1939, Hitler wanted to invade Poland. He knew such a step might lead to war with Britain and France, and he was prepared to fight them. But if the Soviet Union sided with them, the Germans would have to fight on two fronts. In May 1939, Hitler sent out feelers to Stalin, and a deal came together quickly. Officially, it committed Nazi Germany and the Soviet Union to not attacking each other for ten years. But the heart of the deal was a secret bargain that would ignite World War II. Stalin agreed not to intervene when Hitler invaded Poland. Hitler agreed that the Soviet Union could occupy the eastern third of Poland as well as the Baltic states of Latvia, Lithuania, and Estonia.

Stalin further agreed to provide Germany with grain, oil, wood, copper, and manganese for hardening steel.*

The German-Soviet nonaggression pact was signed on August 23, 1939. In Moscow, Stalin drank a toast to Hitler's health. In Berlin, the teetotaling Hitler allowed himself a sip of champagne and is said to have declared, "Now Europe is mine." Amid the smiles and flowing alcohol, Stalin quietly told his trusted lieutenant Khrushchev, "I know what Hitler's up to. He thinks he has outsmarted me, but actually it is I who have outsmarted him." News of the pact between the dictators stunned the Western allies. "The sinister news broke upon the world like an explosion," Churchill wrote. Even so, Churchill believed the Soviet-Nazi partnership was doomed. "I was still convinced of the profound, and, as I believed, quenchless antagonism between Russia and Germany," he wrote, "and I clung to the hope that the Soviets would be drawn to our side by the force of events." Churchill reiterated his view in a radio broadcast, in words that became famous: "I cannot forecast to you the action of Russia. It is a riddle wrapped in a mystery inside an enigma. But perhaps there is a key. That key is Russian national interest." Not even Churchill anticipated how quickly and explosively the pact between Hitler and Stalin would end.

Soon after the treaty was signed, Germany invaded Poland. As Hitler expected, Britain and France quickly declared war on Germany. Stalin moved quickly to seize eastern Poland and occupy the Baltic states, which he thought would serve as buffers against an eventual German attack.

Stalin was stunned in June 1940 when the Germans conquered France

---

* The partnership between the Nazis and the Soviets would extend beyond the dividing up of other nations' land and the delivery of Soviet raw materials to the Germans. Soviet ships would provide weather forecasts to German bombers terrorizing Britain. The Soviet NKVD and its Nazi counterpart, the Gestapo, would collaborate on new technologies for terror, including a mobile poison-gas wagon that the Nazis later would use to speed up the mass murders of Jews.

in only six weeks and drove the British Army off the continent at Dunkirk. News reports of the Allied defeats left Stalin "cursing like a cab driver." Suddenly the German Army was free to seek new conquests. By the middle of June 1941, German forces were massing on the Soviet border. Stalin discounted warnings that a German invasion was imminent. He did not think Hitler was foolish enough to invade the Soviet Union only a few months before winter—as Napoleon had done in 1812 with disastrous results. In the hours just before the German invasion, Stalin was presented with two final chances to act. First, a young German officer crossed the border and handed Soviet sentries the plans for the invasion, to warn them. Stalin ordered him shot as a provocateur. Then, two of Stalin's most trusted generals finally persuaded the dictator to warn Soviet troops on the frontier of a possible attack. By then it was too late, however: Nazi saboteurs had severed the lines of communication.

One hour before dawn on Sunday, June 22, 1941, Hitler sent 3 million German troops roaring across the Soviet border from the Arctic tundra to the steppes of the Caucasus. The invasion, code-named Operation Barbarossa, was the largest in history. The new battlefront—the eastern front—extended for more than 1,500 miles, which is roughly the distance from New York City to New Orleans. Predawn German bombing raids destroyed 1,200 Soviet planes, virtually wiping out Stalin's air force and leaving his ground forces at the mercy of the German planes. All along the battlefront, the Red Army staggered backward or fled. Tens of thousands of Soviet soldiers deserted, and hundreds of thousands surrendered. The first German bombs fell on Moscow on July 21, 1941—less than a month after the start of the invasion. Stalin ordered the embalmed corpse of Lenin removed from its tomb and placed in a refrigerated railway car for quick evacuation. The Bolshoi Theater and Moscow Puppet Theater were wired to explode. Stalin made plans to evacuate the capital, though he never did. Outside Moscow, the Nazis occupied the estate of Leo Tolstoy and buried their dead near the great author's remains; a German motorcycle patrol used the home of the composer Pyotr Tchaikovsky as a garage. Soon the German armies were within sight of Moscow and Leningrad. Hitler ordered his troops not to capture those cities but to reduce them to rubble.

As soon as Churchill learned of the invasion on June 22, he wrote Stalin offering Britain's help. It was an awkward position for Churchill, who had likened Communism to "foul baboonery" and the bubonic plague after advocating for a military campaign against the Bolsheviks in 1919. Now, however, Churchill saw that an alliance with the Soviet Union could help save Britain and defeat Hitler. "No one has been a more consistent opponent of Communism than I have for the last twenty-five years," Churchill told a radio audience after the Germans had launched Operation Barbarossa. "I will unsay no word that I have spoken about it. But all this fades away before the spectacle that is now unfolding." He said Britain should do everything in its power to help the Soviet Union. Churchill was applying a Sanskrit proverb from the fourth century B.C.: The enemy of my enemy is my friend.

Stalin asked Churchill to launch an amphibious invasion of France, creating a "second front" in Western Europe that would compel Hitler to divide his forces. Churchill considered that impossible. The British Army still had not recovered from being driven *out* of France, and it had abandoned most of its heavy weaponry on the retreat to Dunkirk. The Nazis were fortifying the French coast with bunkers, pillboxes, mines, machine-gun nests, barbed wire, and underwater obstacles. Churchill wrote back to Stalin that the British could not invade France without suffering "a bloody repulse."

Stalin's troops, of course, suffered bloody repulses every day. Stalin never truly seemed to understand why Western leaders shrank from the prospect of heavy losses. Stalin had no compunctions about spilling the Red Army's blood. He ordered suicidal counterattacks and blamed his generals for the resulting disasters. He demanded his troops hold hopelessly exposed positions, causing hundreds of thousands to be killed or captured. At Kiev alone 452,700 Soviet soldiers were captured because

Stalin refused to allow them to retreat. Stalin did not have to defend his decisions to anyone.

Stalin and Churchill kept their first exchange of letters cordial. Neither brought up the odious fact that Stalin had been Hitler's ally just a few weeks before. But they eventually would exchange bitter words over the "second front" and convoy PQ-17.

The relationship between Stalin and Churchill grew even more complicated as President Roosevelt entered the picture. Roosevelt had long been intrigued by the Soviet Union. In 1933, flush with success from his New Deal legislation, Roosevelt formally recognized the Soviet Union for the first time, reversing the policies of the four previous presidential administrations. The scope of the horrors Stalin had visited upon the Soviet people was largely hidden from the West. American news organizations including *The New York Times* and *Life* magazine painted deceptively rosy pictures of Soviet life. As late as 1943, an article in *Life* would describe the murderous NKVD as a national police agency "similar to the FBI." Many Americans still clung to the hope that Stalin's regime would evolve into a more democratic government than those of the tyrannical czars. Roosevelt was among the optimists.

Despite America's official neutrality, Roosevelt had found ways to help Britain against Germany, including the shipping of war supplies to Britain by convoys under the Lend-Lease Act of 1941. The act authorized the president to send arms and other defense supplies to "the government of any country whose defense the President deems vital to the defense of the United States." The supplies were officially loans. Roosevelt famously compared Lend-Lease to lending a hose to a neighbor whose house was on fire, expecting to get it back but not worried about that detail for now. Roosevelt was prepared to extend Lend-Lease to the Soviet Union. First, however, he wanted to make sure he was not simply throwing away supplies if the Soviets no longer had a chance. In July 1941, about a month after the invasion, Roosevelt sent his trusted aide Harry Hopkins to Moscow to assess Stalin and the Soviet Union's prospects of survival. Roosevelt gave Hopkins a letter to Stalin praising the Red Army's "magnificent resistance to the treacherous aggression of Hitlerite Germany" and offering America's help. It was the first of more than three hundred letters Roosevelt and Stalin would exchange.

Stalin exuded such confidence that Hopkins decided the Soviets were still valuable allies. The Soviet Union's size alone made it formidable: It was vast enough to swallow invading forces, as it had swallowed Napoleon's, and populous enough to raise an army of 12 million soldiers. Roosevelt was so encouraged by Hopkins's report on the Soviets' continued viability as a fighting force that he scaled back his plans to mobilize American troops, from calling up 215 U.S. Army divisions to calling up 90.

Yet the Soviets kept creating uncertainty. Roosevelt and Churchill learned from intelligence sources that Stalin was secretly exploring a new peace agreement with Hitler through Bulgarian diplomats. In late August 1941, Roosevelt and Churchill drafted a joint letter promising Stalin they would ship an immense quantity of war supplies via convoys to the North Russia ports of Murmansk and Archangel. They were eager to show Stalin that they, not Hitler, were his best options as allies.

Even as America was entering World War II, Roosevelt already was looking ahead to a postwar world in which America and the Soviet Union would be the superpowers. He was eager to forge a personal relationship with Stalin to reduce conflict in the vacuum left by the defeat of Nazi Germany. Roosevelt's great personal charm was one of his gifts. He thought he could woo Stalin more effectively without the blunt, anti-Communist Churchill stirring the pot. The president wrote Churchill, "I know you will not mind my being brutally frank when I tell you that I think I can personally handle Stalin better than either your Foreign Office or my State Department. Stalin hates the guts of all your top people. He thinks he likes me better, and I hope he will continue to do so." Roosevelt believed the first step to winning Stalin's trust was to provide him with all the war supplies he wanted, with no strings attached. The Arctic convoys were Roosevelt's olive branch.

Not all Americans shared Roosevelt's eagerness to embrace Stalin. The conservative *Chicago Tribune* referred to Stalin as "Bloody Joe." Former president Herbert Hoover declared, "Now we find ourselves promising aid to Stalin and his militant conspiracy against the democratic ideals of the world. . . . If we go further and join the war, and we win, then we have won for Stalin the grip of Communism on Russia, and more opportunity for it to extend in the world."

Roosevelt tried to soften the American public's view of the Soviet state. The president took pains to characterize the Soviet citizens as freedom fighters. The president suggested in a speech that Soviet citizens enjoyed freedom of religion, when, in fact, the Communists had outlawed religion, killed and imprisoned priests, and turned thousands of churches into barns, warehouses, pigsties, and ruins.* "Bloody Joe" became avuncular "Uncle Joe." Soviet propagandists did their part. The official Communist Party newspaper, *Pravda,* changed the slogan on its masthead from "Proletarians of the World, Unite!" to "Death to the German Invaders!"

Churchill dubbed the partnership between America, Britain, and the Soviet Union "the Grand Alliance," but it was less grand than coldly practical. It was a devil's bargain virtually doomed to collapse when the Nazis were defeated. The question was whether it could last even that long.

On September 29, 1941, Roosevelt wrote Stalin another letter, this time addressing the ruthless dictator as "My Dear Mr. Stalin." The president again praised the Red Army and assured Stalin that "ways will be found to provide the material and supplies necessary to fight [Hitler] on all fronts, including your own." Two weeks later, Roosevelt sent Stalin a long list of supplies being sent to Russia in convoys, including 167 tanks, 100 bombers, 100 new fighter planes, 5,500 trucks, and large quantities of barbed wire. "All other military supplies we promised . . . are being

---

* Hollywood would join the campaign to rehabilitate the Soviet Union's image in the United States, producing films such as *Days of Glory,* which starred Gregory Peck as a Soviet "freedom fighter" holding out against the Nazis with a beautiful Russian woman fighting at his side.

swiftly assembled to be placed on ships," the president added. "Three ships left the United States yesterday for Russian ports. Every effort being made to rush other supplies." After finishing his letter to Stalin, Roosevelt fired off a scorching memo to the government administrator handling shipments of war cargo to Russia:

> [N]early six weeks have elapsed since the Russian War began and . . . we have done practically nothing to get any of the material they asked for on their actual way to delivery. . . . Frankly, if I were a Russian I would feel that I had been given the run-around in the United States. Please get out the list and please, with my full authority, use a heavy hand—act as a burr under the saddle and get things moving. . . . Step on it!—F.D.R.

Stalin responded to Roosevelt's letter with a letter expressing his thanks but stressing that Roosevelt must hurry. Hitler was throwing everything he had at the Red Army to try to destroy it before the winter cold and snow forced a pause in the fighting. Stalin added that the Soviet people were making "heavy sacrifices." He seemed to imply "unlike the American people."

By December 1941, when the Japanese attacked Pearl Harbor, the Red Army was the only force on the European continent opposing Hitler. By any measure the Soviets were losing. More than 2.6 million Red Army soldiers had already been killed in action—twenty times the German losses—and 3 million others had been taken prisoner, to be shot or worked to death in slave labor camps. Hitler's armies had overrun one third of the Soviet Union.

In frigid Leningrad, where fuel and food were both scarce, people were dying at a rate of four to five thousand a day. "The mortuary itself is full," a Leningrad woman wrote in her journal on December 26, 1941. "Not only are there too few trucks to go to the cemetery, but, more important, not enough gasoline to put in the trucks, and the main thing is—there is not enough strength left in the living to bury the dead."

Another entire year would pass before American troops would challenge Germans troops on the battlefield. Until then, the front lines of America's war against Nazi Germany would be Arctic convoys such as PQ-17, full of rust-bucket ships like the *Troubadour*, sailed by men who fought among themselves when the Germans were not available.

CHAPTER TWO

HELLISH GREEN

The *Troubadour* was not the only ship at Hvalfjord with a restive crew. On the night of May 18, 1942, Lieutenant William A. Carter, the Navy Armed Guard commander on the American freighter *Ironclad*, set out on his nightly inspection of the ship. He waited at the gangplank for two of his men who were on sentry duty. They were late, but Carter saw no reason for concern. He lit a cigarette and let his gaze wander. There was just enough darkness at 11:00 p.m. that a floodlight above the gangplank formed a pool of light on the water alongside the ship's hull. Carter noticed an object bobbing past. It was an empty crate of light-colored wood bearing the image of a horse. Carter immediately recognized it.

Two months earlier, while the *Ironclad* was still chugging up the East Coast toward Iceland, representatives of the U.S. consulate in Halifax, Nova Scotia, had come aboard lugging several cases of White Horse Scotch whisky, intended for the U.S. embassy in Moscow. The whisky was placed on the *Ironclad* with a level of secrecy normally reserved for battle plans. Only the *Ironclad*'s captain, first officer, and Carter knew it was there. Everyone else on the ship was herded to the stern on a pretext while it was sneaked aboard. The cases were tucked into the forward right corner of the No. 1 cargo hold. The first officer held the only key. The precautions had proven sufficient until a sequence of events beginning April 20.

On that day, the *Ironclad* had set sail from Hvalfjord for Russia as one of twenty-five merchant ships in convoy PQ-14, only to become lost in a dense fog and collide with a jagged shard of floating ice. The ship had been forced to return to Hvalfjord with a four-foot gash in its hull just below the waterline—outside the cargo hold where the whisky was hidden. Several of the *Ironclad*'s crew were organized into a work detail to move cargo out of the welders' way so they could seal up the hull. Apparently, the men on the work detail had discovered the whisky and alerted the rest of the crew.

Carter hurried into the cargo hold and quickly confirmed his suspicions. Whoever had snatched the whisky had not bothered to close up the entrance to the hold. "Loud noises of drunken revelry" issued from the crew's mess and recreation area. Carter was not surprised. Like his counterpart Howard Carraway on the *Troubadour,* Carter regarded the merchant seamen on his ship as unreliable and even traitorous.

Carter was twenty-four years old—the same age as the *Ironclad.* He was bright, ambitious, and brimming with self-confidence. He had grown up on the rural Eastern Shore of Maryland, the son of a railroad worker, and had graduated with honors from St. John's College, a small, private liberal arts school in Annapolis, not far from the U.S. Naval Academy. Carter had envisioned a career in business and was hoping to be accepted into Harvard Business School in early 1941, when the war news out of Europe told him he might as well enlist. Like Jim North, Carter had wanted to become a pilot, but he failed the eye test and entered Naval Reserve officer training instead. One of his instructors at the Naval Academy pointed out that the Armed Guard would immediately offer him an independent command—albeit the command of a small, inexperienced gun crew defending a merchant ship. Carter liked the idea of being on a fast track and seized the opportunity. On a temporary assignment to New London, Connecticut, he went on a blind date and met a college student named Ann Whitmore. Carter soon proposed to her and she accepted, but they agreed not to marry until after he returned from the war. Everything seemed to be falling into place for Carter until the day he stepped aboard the *Ironclad*.

Like the *Troubadour*, the 8,675-ton *Ironclad* was a relic from World War I that had seen hard use since then. A succession of owners had called her the *Mystic, Mummystic,* and *Iberville*, and employed her as a tramp steamer, carrying whatever cargo its agents could book to wherever the customers wanted it taken. The ship had hauled ammonia, gasoline, chrome ore, railcar couplers, and goat hair. It had sailed to Egypt, Australia, Portuguese East Africa, and the Philippines. About the only place it had not been was Russia. But was it still seaworthy enough to get there and back? Men who had sailed on the *Ironclad* called it a rust bucket. "We had joked about the Germans not wasting expensive torpedoes on it," wrote former crew member S. J. Flaherty. "Don't think, however, that this ship was not liked—you can't help liking something that you feel sorry for."

The *Ironclad*'s age had not stopped the War Shipping Administration from cramming the ship full of cargo for Stalin. In addition to the White Horse whisky, the vessel carried ammunition, aluminum, steel, fuel, copper wire, asbestos, and chemicals such as phosphorus and zinc, as well as food, lard, salt, coats, shoes, canvas, and leather. Fastened to the ship's main deck with steel cables were fifteen American-built fighter planes, several U.S. Army tanks, and a small fleet of trucks. The *Ironclad* alone carried enough cargo to launch a small Red Army offensive. But the ship was even more lightly armed than the *Troubadour*, with a single 3-inch, 50-caliber cannon; two .50-caliber machine guns; and two .30-caliber machine guns. Carter dismissed the latter as "more deadly than a BB gun, but not much more." Carter spent much of his time in Hvalfjord begging for ammunition and other vital supplies for his gun crew. He was beginning to conclude that the U.S. Navy, which he had joined with lofty expectations, was "as fouled up as Hogan's Goat."

The *Ironclad* had a veteran captain, Phillip Moore of Weldon, North Carolina, and experienced officers. Moore had managed to hire some capable mariners for the voyage, thanks to the bonuses offered by the U.S. and Soviet governments, but he had to fill out the crew with various idlers and troublemakers—"the sweepings of the Baltimore union halls," as Carter put it. At every port where the *Ironclad* stopped on its way to Hvalfjord, a few men jumped ship and were replaced by the best men the captain could find on short notice. Among the most incorrigible was a hard-drinking ex-prizefighter whom everyone called "the Kid."

Carter assumed the Kid was in the middle of the White Horse whisky caper. Before confronting the drunken mariners, Carter decided to track down the two missing Armed Guard sentries who, like him, were armed with Colt .45 pistols. He was chagrined to find both of them in their bunks, too drunk to speak intelligibly. He informed the captain, who angrily declared the incident a mutiny. It was hardly storybook stuff, but it technically met the definition of "a revolt against discipline or a superior officer." The captain sent Carter and the *Ironclad*'s burly first officer to break up the party. By the time they arrived, the whisky was long gone and the carousers "appeared to be severely the worse for wear and ready to call it a night," Carter observed. The first officer called the men traitors, declared them under arrest, and ordered them to return to their quarters and await justice. All of them meekly complied except the Kid. He seized onto a steel cable and refused to be dragged into his quarters. A cold rain started to fall. Carter handcuffed the Kid to the cable and left him there. The mutiny was over. A contingent of U.S. Marines from the nearby battleship USS *Washington* arrived and took the thirty hungover mutineers into custody. Four of them—but not the Kid—were identified as ringleaders and kicked off the ship. They were replaced by four Icelandic mariners. The two drunken Navy sentries were demoted, and Carter replaced one of them. The other stayed on the ship, mainly because Carter could not find a replacement for him.

As angry as Carter was at the *Ironclad*'s "mutineers," he felt a twinge of sympathy for them. The weeks of waiting in Iceland felt endless. The civilian mariners had worn out their welcome with the Icelandic authorities after a long series of misdeeds, including raiding the nests of eider ducks and throwing the eggs at one another. They were no longer allowed to go ashore. Stuck on their ships in the gloomy anchorage, they had long since played all the cards and Monopoly they could stand. Some had resorted to playing hide-and-seek on their vessels. With no meaningful work to do, they were assigned to chip rust and perform other make-work tasks. At least the Navy men could go ashore at night in nearby Reykjavik, where they could dine and drink and woo the Icelandic girls. But even those activities soon lost their appeal. Most of the Americans were heartily sick of Iceland, which the Allies had occupied in 1940 to prevent it from falling into German hands. Worse than the cold and the boredom was the knowledge—always festering in the back of the mind—that the Murmansk Run was waiting for them.

THE MURMANSK RUN WAS only one of three possible supply routes to Russia. Each presented formidable challenges. The shortest route was across the Pacific, from Alaska to Vladivostok, but any American or British ship in those waters would be attacked by the Japanese. A second route led south through the South Atlantic, around the Cape of Good Hope, north through the Indian Ocean, and then across the Persian Gulf to the Iraqi port of Basra. But that was a 15,000-mile round trip that took four months. Mariners hated the Persian Gulf, where the air temperature soared above 100 degrees Fahrenheit and the bathtub-warm water was infested with black-and-yellow sea snakes that had to be plucked in wriggling clusters from the anchor chains. Sandstorms blew up on the horizon like thunderclouds and broke over the ships with sibilant roars, dumping so much sand that the crews had to shovel it off the decks. On the docks at Basra, British soldiers in khaki uniforms kicked wretched Iraqi laborers in rags. Any cargo arriving at Basra had to be hauled by train for another thousand miles across the Iraqi desert and the Soviet steppes to the battle-front. Stalin far preferred to receive supplies via the Arctic route to the ports of Murmansk and Archangel. For danger and discomfort, however, that route was in a class all its own.

Convoys sailing to North Russia departed from Hvalfjord or from Loch Ewe on the coast of Scotland. From Hvalfjord, the distance to Murmansk was roughly 1,725 miles, which under optimal conditions took eight days. The distance to Archangel was 2,150 miles, which took ten days. The convoy route from Hvalfjord led first north and then east through the Denmark Strait, a turbulent stretch of water dividing Iceland and Greenland. Once the convoy cleared the strait, it steamed east through the Norwegian Sea and hugged the edge of the polar ice field for 600 miles before passing Jan Mayen Island, a lonely wedge of snow-capped basalt, notable mainly as the home of the world's northernmost active volcano. From Jan Mayen, the convoy would continue east for another 600 miles to Bear Island, an even more remote chunk of wave-battered rock. Bear Island marked the beginning of the most hazardous part of the voyage: Once the convoys passed east of it, they were within range of German bombers for all the rest of the voyage to Russia.

From the island, the convoy route led east and then south 400 miles through the Barents Sea to the Murman coast of Russia, which opens into a long fjord named the Kola Inlet. Six miles up the fjord lay Murmansk. Ships bound for Archangel bypassed the Kola Inlet and steamed for more than 400 additional miles farther east and south through the vast, landlocked White Sea. Archangel sat on the wide, muddy delta of the North Dvina River.

The Barents Sea remained open to ship traffic year-round because the tail of the warm Gulf Stream ended there. But with the warmth came some of the roughest seas on earth. Over the Barents Sea, warm air carried up by the Gulf Stream collided constantly with cold air from the North Pole, and then was spun by the earth's rotation into large depressions, which in turn produced gales. The storms built huge, steep waves. Ships climbed up the faces of those waves, hung precariously on the crests with their propellers spinning in midair, and then plunged down the backs of the waves into deep troughs, as the next waves loomed up ahead. A passenger on a merchant ship described the progression of an Arctic storm:

> At first it was just grey pavements of water that came slapping against us, but within the hour it was as though whole roadways were turning over upon themselves and falling upon us. The convoy dispersed. It was not ordered to do so: it just blew apart. The tumbling walls of water cut down our vision to no more than 100 yards and the boiling scum that blew off the tops of the waves filled the air with moisture as though sleet were falling.

A mariner on his first voyage through the Barents Sea said the wind sounded "like a woman screaming in terror while being raped or murdered"—for hours on end. Ship's officers had to shout orders into men's ears or use hand gestures. The average air temperature hovered around zero degrees Fahrenheit but could plunge quickly to 40 below. At that temperature even breathing hurt, and facial hair became weaponized. Beards froze into smothering masks of ice. Eyelashes fell off. Nose hairs froze into needles sharp enough to draw blood. Touching metal with bare skin would burn the skin and maybe even leave a patch of it behind.

Sea spray froze almost on contact with the ships, lending them the appearance of ice sculptures. Guns and portholes froze shut. Ice accumulated on ships' upper decks so fast that mariners had to chip it off constantly with axes and hammers to prevent the vessels from becoming dangerously top-heavy. A U.S. merchant crew claimed to have chipped off 150 tons of ice during a voyage. A British escort vessel capsized after becoming unstable from an accumulation of ice and sank without a trace or any survivors.

In the brief Arctic summer, storms were infrequent, though always possible. More often, the sea lay as placid as a duck pond, beneath brilliant sunshine. The Arctic seemed like an entirely different place, but for men in the convoys it was not necessarily a safer place. Even in midsummer, the water temperature stayed around 40 degrees Fahrenheit, which was cold enough to incapacitate a man in ten minutes and kill him in twenty or thirty. The convoys sailed near the edge of the polar ice field, which was wildly unstable. Some floes broke apart with thunderous cracks; others slammed together with crushing force. Newly calved icebergs from Greenland glaciers drifted through the convoy routes. Unlike the pack ice, the bergs were freshwater, the products of deep snow hardened under pressure. A large berg could weigh 10 million tons and tower 500 feet out of the water, with most of its bulk hidden below the surface. Just as treacherous if less spectacular were smaller chunks of ice called growlers, which rode lower in the water and thus were harder for ships' lookouts to spot. Growlers as big as grand pianos clunked and scraped along the ships' hulls, reminding mariners that in Arctic waters they were never truly out of danger.

The Mariner's Handbook warned: "When operating in ice, a vessel not specifically designed for such work runs the risk of damage in the following ways: strained or broken propeller shafts, broken blades or loss of propellers, strained or broken rudder-head or rudder, damage to steering gear, damage to stern and plating, crushing of the hull and breaking of frames due to ice pressure, buckling of plating and tearing out of rivets." To prepare the *Troubadour* and some other vessels for the Arctic run, the Allies fortified the ships' bows with concrete and replaced their bronze propellers with steel ones that would not break so easily.

The Arctic tricked mariners in ways that shrank their already narrow margin for error. The mingling of the cold meltwater from the ice field and warm water from the Gulf Stream created thermal layers in the water column that confused sonar, making it difficult to detect submerged U-boats. The mixing of cold and warm water also generated banks of dense, billowing fog that could persist for days. The fog hid the convoys from the Germans, but it also hid icebergs and other hazards from the ships' lookouts and hid the sun from navigators trying to fix their vessels' positions. The navigators could expect no help from their magnetic compasses. The Arctic also produced elaborate mirages. Sunlight slanting down on ice created sharp differences in air temperature near the water's surface, bending light rays and producing strange effects. Objects on the horizon looked impossibly large, distorted, or even upside down. A long, low headland sloping into the sea, for example, might be inverted to look like a rocky cliff jutting out *over* the sea. The Arctic mirages were especially cruel to half-frozen lifeboat survivors scanning the horizon for land.

The Arctic's most disorienting feature was its distortion of night and day. The tilt of the earth on its axis points the northern latitudes toward the sun in spring and summer, lengthening the days, and away from the sun in winter, extending the nights. The boundaries of the Arctic Circle do not necessarily reflect conditions on the ground. Some places within the Arctic Circle are relatively temperate, owing to more localized factors, and other places below it are bitterly cold. In much of the territory north of the Arctic Circle—the imaginary line at latitude 66°33′44″ N—the sun does not set in midsummer or rise in midwinter. A British merchant captain summarized the changing balance between light and dark in the Barents Sea:

> From February onwards it is lighting up quickly. At the end of January there are four hours of daylight. End of February eight hours, end of April 20 hours, and July and August virtually twenty-four hours daylight, with sun all the time, which works along the horizon.

Some Americans never got used to how the light fell in the Arctic. "The sunlight was a hellish green," declared Donald Murphy, an American seaman. "That's the way everybody described it, a hellish-green light. It was the strangest thing you ever saw, just like you were in another world. It's hard on you. Say you want to get up and get a cup of coffee. You get up at three in the morning. Christ, you don't know if it's nine o'clock in the morning or at night."

For all the Arctic's dangers and tricks, the Germans posed a far greater menace.

After invading Norway in 1940, Germany had transformed the Norwegian coast into a fearsome stronghold for its air and sea forces—"an Arctic Gibraltar," as one journalist put it. Norway has one of the world's longest coastlines, extending more than 1,600 miles as the crow flies but encompassing over 16,000 miles if one includes the shores of the fjords serrating Norway's rugged, rocky coast and its thousands of offshore islands. The Germans moved their powerful warships and dozens of U-boats there, where the vessels could protect shipments of Swedish iron ore, on which the German war industries depended, and dart out into the ocean to attack Allied convoys. Hitler kept beefing up his forces on the Norwegian coast in the mistaken belief that the British, who had belatedly tried to stop the Germans from seizing Norway, would return and try to drive them out. Hitler insisted Norway was "a zone of destiny" in the war.

The Germans' most devastating weapon in Norway was the giant battleship *Tirpitz*—the most powerful warship on earth. The *Tirpitz* was the sister ship of the more famous *Bismarck,* which the British had sunk at enormous cost in 1941. Like the *Bismarck,* the *Tirpitz* was a floating fortress, 822 feet long and displacing 53,000 tons, with a crew of more than 1,900 men. The great ship bristled with weapons, including its eight imposing 15-inch guns. The *Tirpitz* could slash through the ocean at a speed of 30 knots, which was three times the speed of many merchant vessels. The battleship was so intimidating that it did not even need to leave its anchorage near the Norwegian port of Trondheim to dominate the sea war. The British were so afraid of the destruction the *Tirpitz* might cause if it ever got loose among convoys in the North Atlantic or Arctic that they kept a fleet of warships on standby just to prevent that from happening. Churchill groused in January 1942 that the *Tirpitz* was "holding four times the number of British capital ships paralyzed."

In addition to the *Tirpitz* and various German cruisers, destroyers, and U-boats, Hitler fortified Norway with aircraft. The Nazis built six air bases along the Norwegian coast and filled them with long-range reconnaissance aircraft, bombers, and dive-bombers. Five of the air bases were near the North Cape of Norway, a massive rock headland rising out of the sea in a 1,000-foot cliff at the northernmost tip of the European continent. The North Cape, which Norwegians call *Nordkapp,* is a daunting sight. Indigenous peoples once offered sacrifices to their gods on a jagged horn of rock that protrudes from the rock face. The Nazis used the North Cape as the focal point of their attacks on the Arctic convoys.

From their bases near the North Cape, German bombers could strike at any point within a radius of 350 miles, which included the entire Arctic convoy route east of Bear Island, as well as Murmansk and Archangel. "It might not be so bad if [the ships] could sweep still farther north in a wider arc to get out of reach of the shore-based attackers," the American journalist Negley Farson observed. "But the polar ice stops them. It hems them in, edges them ever closer to the fire and explosion of bomb and shell and torpedo." One of the German bases lay just 35 miles from Murmansk, and the Germans bombed the city relentlessly, blowing apart sections of docks and setting fires in the mostly wooden buildings. Archangel was 400 miles farther away, and at the start of the war the Germans did not bother to bomb it.

The Germans did not attack the Arctic convoys either when the

British first began sending them to Russia in the summer of 1941. At the time, Hitler believed the Soviets' defeat was imminent, and that the convoys were irrelevant. The first Arctic convoy, which bore the code name of Dervish, sailed out of Hvalfjord on August 21, 1941, with only seven merchant ships, six of them British and one Dutch. They were protected by an escort force including British destroyers. A British aircraft carrier and two cruisers stood by at long range in case German warships attacked in force. Dervish, however, steamed into Archangel unharmed.

The next convoy to Russia was code-named PQ-1. P and Q were the first two initials of Philip Quellyn Roberts, a Royal Navy staff officer who helped plan the convoys; the number "1" in PQ-1 reflected the fact that the convoy was the first in a planned series. Subsequent convoys would be named PQ-2, PQ-3, and so forth. Convoys returning to Iceland bore the designation QP, with Roberts's initials reversed.

After ignoring the first five PQ convoys, Hitler changed his mind. The Russian winter and the Red Army had halted the German advance. The Soviets would not be defeated quickly or easily, and the Arctic convoys suddenly no longer seemed irrelevant. They were a valuable supply line to the Soviets from the United States, which had just entered the war. Convoy PQ-6 sailed from Iceland on December 8—one day after Pearl Harbor. Four German destroyers burst from the fjords near the North Cape to intercept the convoy. They damaged a British escort ship but could not reach the merchant ships. A few weeks later, a freighter from the next convoy, PQ-7A, became stranded on the edge of the ice field and was attacked by German bombers and then sunk by a U-boat. The Arctic convoys were targets now.

Convoy PQ-8 showed just how lethal the combination of the Nazis and the Arctic could be. As the seven-ship convoy approached Murmansk on the afternoon of January 17, 1942—in the frosty darkness of the polar night—a U-boat torpedoed one of the merchant ships. The British destroyer HMS *Matabele* went hunting for the U-boat and was torpedoed by a second U-boat. The destroyer's magazine exploded and the *Matabele* vanished in a fiery flash. Rescue ships picked their way through swirling fog to the spot where the destroyer had blown up, but they found only an oil slick full of dead men floating upright in their life jackets. Of the two hundred British sailors on the *Matabele,* only two survived.

Four convoys later, in March 1942, the Germans raised the stakes by sending the *Tirpitz* and two destroyers to attack convoy PQ-12. The *Tirpitz*'s job was to lay waste to the British warships protecting the convoy and then help the German destroyers mop up whatever merchant ships remained. Stormy seas slowed the German warships, however. Fog and snow squalls blinded both sides. At one point the *Tirpitz* passed within 60 miles of the convoy without either knowing it. After two days, the *Tirpitz* gave up looking and turned back for its anchorage in Norway. It almost never made it. The skies cleared unexpectedly and torpedo bombers from a British carrier spotted the battleship. The *Tirpitz* shot down two of the planes but had to dodge torpedoes before regaining the safety of the fjords. The battleship had succeeded only in burning huge quantities of scarce fuel oil. Its narrow escape unnerved Hitler and set the stage for the role the *Tirpitz* would play four months later in convoy PQ-17.

After convoy PQ-12, Hitler became determined to stop the Arctic convoys. He declared they were "sustaining Russian ability to hold out" and "should henceforth be impeded." His subordinates took his orders to heart. Convoy PQ-13 was passing Bear Island in late March when it ran into a ferocious gale with 60-foot waves and bitter cold. When the weather cleared, bombers sank two merchant ships. German destroyers sank a third. The British cruiser HMS *Trinidad* was crippled by its own malfunctioning torpedo. A U-boat sank a fourth freighter, and the survivors climbed into a lifeboat, where they died one by one of exposure. One man's body froze to the bottom of the boat and could not be removed. The drinking water container also froze and men resorted to licking ice. Of the lifeboat's original thirty-four occupants, only seventeen were still alive by the time a Russian ship picked them up. Nine of those seventeen died on the way to a clinic in Archangel. Russian doctors scrambled to save the others. The clinic was woefully short of supplies. One mariner's frozen, gangrenous legs had to be amputated without anesthesia in order to save his life. He recalled: "Someone said, in hesitant English, 'We're going to cut your legs off,' and they went ahead and did it. As soon as the knife hit me, I passed out, and I was delirious for three days."

The next convoy, PQ-14, was engulfed by a fog so dense that twenty-five of the thirty-three ships (including the *Ironclad*) turned around and went back to Iceland. The remaining eight were attacked by bombers and U-boats. After one freighter was torpedoed, the U-boat surfaced near a lifeboat and the German captain asked the castaways whether they were Bolsheviks. They said no. "Then what the hell are you going to Russia for?" the U-boat captain asked. It was the same question some of the mariners in Hvalfjord were asking themselves.

By mid-April of 1942, thanks to Roosevelt's determined efforts, more than one hundred fully loaded freighters and tankers crowded the anchorage at Hvalfjord, waiting their turn to set out on the Murmansk Run. Most of those ships flew the U.S. flag or, like the *Troubadour,* had been loaded and dispatched by U.S. authorities under other flags. Roosevelt constantly urged his aides to load even more ships for Russia.

But the growing losses in the Arctic convoys worried the British Admiralty, which was responsible for organizing and protecting the merchant ships. The lengthening Arctic days provided the German bombers with more and more daylight in which to attack, and the ships with less and less darkness in which to hide. The Germans had amassed more than 250 bombers and reconnaissance planes in Norway and could send them out over the North Cape in waves. In addition, the German heavy cruiser *Admiral Hipper* had slipped into the Norwegian fjords from Germany to add its firepower to that of the *Tirpitz*. If the Germans ever decided to concentrate all their air and sea forces against a single Arctic convoy, they could obliterate it.

British Rear Admiral Sir Stuart Bonham-Carter, who had seen the danger firsthand while sailing with convoy PQ-14, advised his superiors:

> Until enemy aerodromes in north Norway are neutralized I consider convoys to North Russia should be suspended during the months of continuous light unless the very high percentage of losses can be accepted or sufficient air protection can be provided. . . . If [the Arctic convoys] must continue for political reasons, very serious and heavy losses must be expected. The force of the German attacks will increase, not diminish. We in the Navy are paid to do this sort of job, but it is beginning to ask too much of the merchant navy. We may be able to avoid bombs and torpedoes with our speed; a six- or eight-knot ship has not this advantage.

Few in the Royal Navy disagreed with him. Admiral Sir John Tovey, who commanded the British Home Fleet and provided distant cover for the Arctic convoys, suggested they at least be reduced in size to limit the potential scope of a disaster. The First Sea Lord of the Admiralty, Sir Dudley Pound—the operational head of the Royal Navy—warned that losses on the Murmansk Run were growing too steep for the Royal Navy to bear while fulfilling its wider responsibilities, including the defense of the British Isles. "These Arctic convoys are becoming a regular millstone around our necks," Pound wrote to his American counterpart, Admiral Ernest J. King. "The whole thing is a most unsound operation, with the dice loaded against us in every direction."

Churchill shared Pound's apprehension. Churchill had served as political leader of the Royal Navy during World War I and was intensely proud of his naval background; he signed all of his messages to Roosevelt as simply "Former Naval Person." On April 24, Churchill cabled Harry Hopkins to suggest reducing the shipments of supplies to Russia until autumn, when true darkness would return to the northern latitudes.

Churchill may have been trying to enlist Hopkins to make a similar case to Roosevelt. If so, his effort backfired. Three days after writing to Hopkins, Churchill received a stinging reply straight from Roosevelt:

> About the shipments to Russia, I am greatly disturbed by your cable to Harry, because I fear not only the political repercussions in Russia, but even more the fact that our supplies will not reach them promptly. We have made such a tremendous effort to get our supplies going that to have them blocked except for most compelling reasons seems to me a serious mistake. I realize . . . that the matter is extremely difficult. I do hope particularly that you can review again the size of the immediate convoys so that the stuff now banked up in Iceland can get through. . . . I very much prefer that we do not seek at this time any new understanding with Russia about the amount of our supplies in view of the impending assault on their armies. It seems to me that any word reaching Stalin at this time that our supplies were stopping for any reason would have a most unfortunate effect.

The day before Roosevelt's message, convoy PQ-15 had sailed from Hvalfjord. Unlike previous Arctic convoys, it comprised mostly American merchant ships, and included American warships in its escort force— four destroyers, the cruisers USS *Wichita* and USS *Tuscaloosa,* and the battleship USS *Washington.* The voyage began ominously when a British destroyer sank after colliding with a British battleship in the fog off Iceland. Foul weather concealed the convoy for part of its voyage, but the Germans managed to sink two merchant ships, including the British freighter *Cape Corso,* which exploded, killing all but nine of its crew.

On April 30, Roosevelt again wrote Churchill to stress "the urgent necessity of getting off one more convoy in May in order to break the log jam of ships already loaded or being loaded for Russia." Again, the president opposed delaying the convoys "because I believe it would leave an impossible and very disquieting impression in Russia. Our problem is to move 107 ships now loaded or being loaded in the United Kingdom and the United States prior to June 1."

Churchill replied two days later. He pointed out that the Royal Navy had recently lost two cruisers, HMS *Trinidad* and HMS *Edinburgh*,* protecting the Arctic convoys. Britain had lost a dozen bombers trying to destroy the *Tirpitz*. "With very great respect," Churchill wrote Roosevelt, "what you suggest is beyond our power to fulfil. . . . I beg you not to press us beyond our judgment in this operation. . . . I can assure you, Mr. President, we are absolutely extended, and I could not press the Admiralty any further. . . . Three convoys every two months, with either thirty-five or twenty-five ships in each convoy, according to experience, represent the extreme limit of what we can handle."

Churchill sounded like a junior partner beseeching his boss to be reasonable. In many respects, Roosevelt *was* Churchill's boss. Churchill candidly acknowledged that America was the key to Britain's survival and ultimate victory over the Nazis. Before America's entry into the war, Churchill had courted and cajoled Roosevelt to provide Britain with arms, ships, food, and other essentials. "No lover ever studied every whim of his mistress as I did those of President Roosevelt," Churchill later wrote. He also wrote that Hitler's fate was decided on the day the Japanese attacked Pearl Harbor.

Roosevelt made it clear he was not satisfied with Churchill's position. "It is now essential for us to acquiesce in your views regarding Russian convoys," he wrote back to Churchill, "but I continue to hope that you will be able to keep convoys at strength of thirty-five ships." Roosevelt

---

* The HMS *Edinburgh* had gone to the bottom of the Barents Sea carrying 5 tons of Russian gold bullion that had been secretly carried aboard in ammunition boxes. It was meant for the U.S. Treasury as the first installment of payment for Lend-Lease supplies. Decades after the war, salvagers would recover $80 million of the sunken gold, which would be divided among the salvagers and the governments of Britain and the Soviet Union.

added that he would ask Stalin to scale back his requests "to absolute essentials" and would tell Stalin that America and Britain needed to save their vessels for the opening of the "second front." Roosevelt still wanted to launch an amphibious invasion of France in 1942—a prospect Churchill viewed as impossible.

While Roosevelt and Churchill discussed how to deal with Stalin, the Soviet dictator learned from his agents about the backlog of ships in Hvalfjord. He wrote Churchill on May 6:

> I have a request for you. Some ninety steamers loaded with various important war materials for the U.S.S.R. are bottled up at present in Iceland or in the approaches from America to Iceland. I understand there is a danger that the sailing of these ships may be delayed for a long time because of the difficulty to organize convoy[s] escorted by the British naval forces. I am fully aware of the difficulties involved and of the sacrifices made by Great Britain in this matter. I feel however [that it is] incumbent upon me to approach you with the request to take all possible measures in order to ensure the arrival of all the above-mentioned materials in the U.S.S.R. in the course of May, as this is extremely important for our front.

Stalin was not exaggerating the seriousness of the situation on the eastern front, although his poor leadership had exacerbated it. In February and March, he had foolishly ordered counterattacks at Leningrad and in Ukraine that left more than 440,000 Red Army troops dead—almost nine times the German casualties. While the immediate threat to Moscow had abated, Leningrad remained under siege and the Soviet Union's position farther south looked precarious. In May, the Germans retook Kharkov in northeastern Ukraine and then attacked Rostov, which was the gateway to the Volga River citadel of Stalingrad and the oil fields of the Caucasus.

Churchill might have to tolerate being bossed around by Roosevelt—

America was Britain's lifeline—but not by the Communist dictator. Churchill wrote back to Stalin on May 9 challenging the Soviets to provide more protection for the convoys at their end. "I know you will not mind my being frank and emphasizing the need of increasing the assistance given by the U.S.S.R. naval and air forces in helping to get these convoys through safely."

Stalin replied: "We quite understand the difficulties which Great Britain is overcoming, and those heavy sea losses which you are suffering while you accomplish this big task." But "our naval forces are very limited, and . . . our air forces in their vast majority are engaged at the battlefront." Stalin was not exaggerating about that, either. The Soviet Northern Fleet consisted of only eight destroyers, seven frigates, fifteen subs, fifteen patrol boats, and a small collection of torpedo boats and minesweepers. The Soviets had so few fighter planes that Russian pilots defended Murmansk with mostly British aircraft.

Churchill felt caught between Roosevelt and Stalin. In the Royal Navy's official history of the sea war, Captain S. W. Roskill wrote that the Soviets

> seemed not to have cared whether recent convoys had suffered terrible losses or had survived the most menacing dangers. . . . [S]uch considerations as the perpetual daylight of the summer months seemed to trouble them not a whit. Their stubborn pressure for convoys to be run, cost what they might, continued relentlessly and monotonously. Most of this pressure fell, as was natural, on Mr. Churchill; for the American President was able to take a more detached view of the problems involved and the risks entailed.

On May 17, Churchill wrote to his chief of staff, Major Gen. Hastings Ismay:

Not only Premier Stalin but President Roosevelt will object very much to our desisting from running the convoys now. The Russians are in heavy action, and will expect us to run the risk and pay the price entailed by our contribution. The United States ships are queueing up. My own feeling, mingled with much anxiety, is that the [next] convoy ought to sail on the 18th. The operation is justified if a half gets through.

Churchill added: "Failure on our part to make the attempt would weaken our influence with both our major Allies. There are always the uncertainties of weather and luck, which may aid us. I share your misgivings, but I feel it is a matter of duty."

That duty would fall mainly to the men on the ships at Hvalfjord.

ON THE *TROUBADOUR*, Carraway spent the long days reading, dividing his time between literary tomes such as Thomas Wolfe's novel *Look Homeward, Angel* and *Arctic Harpooner*, the diary of a nineteenth-century whale hunt. The weather was so cold and damp that even Carraway's beloved pipe tasted sour. The *Troubadour*'s crew settled down after a rugged, one-eyed Estonian seaman vowed to beat the hell out of the next man who caused trouble. Jim North still took every opportunity to get off the ship. One night, he and two shipmates stole a small boat from the *Troubadour* and sailed it to shore three miles away. North stayed with the boat while his companions hiked to a hut where beer was sold. They returned two hours later, very drunk, and passed out in the boat. North tried to sail it back to the *Troubadour*, but his rudimentary seamanship was no match for the wind. The little boat careened wildly around the anchorage, passing so close to a Navy warship that an officer with a bullhorn warned the boat to keep its distance or be fired upon. In desperation, North seized the hand of one of the sleeping men and bent back one of his fingers until he awoke with a shriek of pain. He helped North sail the boat back to the *Troubadour* before passing out again. The man remembered nothing the next day but complained of a mysterious pain in his finger. By then, North had learned to keep his wiseass remarks to himself.

The official fallout from the White Horse whisky mutiny kept the *Ironclad* from departing with the next Arctic convoy, PQ-16. Carter watched the convoy sail out of Hvalfjord on May 21. It was the largest Arctic convoy yet, reflecting Roosevelt's demand that the convoys be increased in size. Twenty of its thirty-six merchant ships flew the U.S. flag, and several of Carter's friends from Armed Guard training school were aboard them. Carter feared for his friends but wished he was going with them. He tried to be positive. His turn would come. After all, what difference could it possibly make if the *Ironclad* sailed now or waited for the next convoy?

CHAPTER THREE

KNIGHT'S MOVE

May turned to June, and rumors flew around Hvalfjord that convoy PQ-17 would sail in a week. Or a month. Or maybe not at all. On the *Troubadour,* Howard Carraway wrote in his diary that "as far as I can tell, nobody knows a damned thing more than I do. Nothing. A month more it may be, and if so, I think I can take it without breaking down. Which is more than I can say for a few men on the ship. There is fear. Rank, undiluted and disturbing. One poor fellow, a native of Uruguay, paces the deck hour after hour, smoking like a coal-burner, staring rather wildly and refusing to work. . . . I expect him to try to swim ashore, or just go nuts and start hitting people at any time. That has happened on other ships here." Carraway had heard a story—apparently unfounded—that a cook on another ship had gone berserk and murdered a shipmate.

The most obvious sign that convoy PQ-17's departure was actually imminent was that more escort ships were arriving in Iceland. The big warships, such as cruisers and destroyers, stayed outside the harbor, their silhouettes occasionally visible in the gloom. But numerous smaller escorts—including British corvettes, minesweepers, and frigates—dropped anchor among the merchant ships. Those escorts drew only cursory attention from the Americans. Not a man on the *Troubadour* or *Ironclad* would have looked twice at the British antisubmarine trawler HMT *Ayrshire*—HMT stood for Her Majesty's Trawler—or guessed the role it was about to play in their lives.

The *Ayrshire* was one of scores of fishing trawlers the British had requisitioned from their owners and converted into antisubmarine vessels. The *Ayrshire* was only four years old and built sturdily enough to fish the wintry Arctic seas. For its new wartime role, it was equipped with sonar, depth charges, a 4-inch gun on the forecastle, and smaller guns on either side. The *Ayrshire* also had been fitted with an elaborate contraption that used a pressurized steam pipe to hurl hand grenades into the air at planes. The crew avoided using it because they feared it would malfunction and blow up the ship. The *Ayrshire*'s crew included rugged fishermen who had volunteered to hunt for U-boats instead of cod. What they lacked in combat experience they made up for in toughness and seamanship. The *Ayrshire* was 175 feet long—considerably smaller than the smallest merchant ship—and it still looked like a fishing trawler. The sight of it steaming along the edge of a convoy would not inspire great confidence in a merchant crew or great fear in the Germans. Some of the *Ayrshire*'s crew worried that if the trawler ever dropped its depth charges, it might not be fast enough to get clear before they exploded. In the eyes of most sailors, armed trawlers ranked at the bottom of the hierarchy of convoy escort vessels.

What set the *Ayrshire* apart was its commanding officer, Lieutenant Leo J. Gradwell of the Royal Navy Volunteer Reserve. The son of a prosperous Liverpool solicitor, Gradwell had grown up on the banks of the Mersey River, where he taught himself to sail. As a boy he had piloted his 25-foot sailboat across the Irish Sea to Ireland. He had left boarding school at age seventeen to enlist in the Royal Navy, served on a destroyer during World War I, and then studied law and classical literature at

Oxford. In his free time at Oxford, he sailed a yacht belonging to the poet Hilaire Belloc, the father of a classmate. The poet would not let his son take the yacht to sea unless Gradwell was aboard. Soon Gradwell was crewing racing yachts in elite offshore races such as Fastnet and La Rochelle.

Gradwell graduated from college near the top of his class and became a barrister, defending clients in the Liverpool courts. He represented people who had been hurt by errors, or malfeasance, by the government or organizations. Gradwell became skeptical of officialdom. "He was brought up in an intellectual way to think for himself," his daughter, Mary, recalled. "He had a great moral compass." He abandoned his law practice when World War II began, and joined the Royal Navy Volunteer Reserve at the age of thirty-nine, knowing he would be sent back to sea. On the basis of his modest official credentials—a Certificate of Competency as Master of a Pleasure Yacht—he was placed in command of a converted whaling ship, and then of the *Ayrshire*. Gradwell did not complain. His father had taught him always to do his duty, and if that duty was to chase U-boats in a fishing trawler, then so be it.

Gradwell cut a distinctly British figure: tall and slender, with dark, closely trimmed hair, an upper-class English accent, a straight bearing, and an intelligent gaze. At sea, as in court, he was direct and incisive. He treated the rough fishermen in the crew no differently than he had treated the toffs in his classes at Oxford. But Gradwell had no patience with those he considered fools, even when they were fellow officers in the Royal Navy. After a supply officer shorted his men on their regular allotment of one fresh egg a week, Gradwell personally delivered an unappetizing mass of powdered eggs to him and dared him to eat it. On another occasion, when the *Ayrshire*'s supplies had not arrived in time for the trawler to put to sea, Gradwell ordered the crew to fire a round from the 4-inch gun into a hillside directly above the supply depot. The supplies quickly arrived.

Before being sent to Iceland, the *Ayrshire* had escorted convoys in the

Western Approaches to the British Isles. The trawler had weathered two violent gales and rescued survivors of another trawler that had been torpedoed by a U-boat. Gradwell had been at sea when his wife, Jean, gave birth to their son Christopher. He received the happy news in a coded signal: "Red and white buoy adrift from mooring." By the time the *Ayrshire* was assigned to convoy PQ-17 in June 1942, Gradwell and his crew had seen a good deal of the sea war. But even for them, sailing across the Arctic to Russia was a leap into the unknown.

The mariners at Hvalfjord were starving for news of how the previous Arctic convoy, PQ-16, had fared during *its* leap into the unknown. They made frequent stops in their ships' radio rooms and interrogated shipmates returning from shore visits. The crushing boredom of daily life in the anchorage just intensified their curiosity. The only clue they had been able to glean about the fate of convoy PQ-16 was ominous: They had watched one ship from the convoy, the American freighter *Carlton,* being towed back into Hvalfjord after being disabled by German bombers early in the voyage. The *Carlton*'s aborted trip with convoy PQ-16 had been the ship's second failed attempt to reach Russia. She had previously set out with convoy PQ-14 but had turned back after hitting ice. The superstitious mariners at Hvalfjord—and mariners as a group were very superstitious—suspected the *Carlton* was a "Jonah," a bringer of bad luck. The U.S. government did not believe in Jonahs, however, and hurried to repair the *Carlton* in time for a third try at the Murmansk Run with convoy PQ-17.

On June 2, the men in Hvalfjord were alarmed by a radio newscast out of Boston claiming that eighteen of the thirty-six ships in convoy PQ-16 had been sunk. The British Admiralty immediately countered that "only" six or seven ships had been lost. No details were forthcoming, and Carraway wondered whether any of his friends from Armed Guard school had been killed. Over the next few days, some details filtered in. The convoy, in fact, had lost seven ships, along with their 50,000 tons of tanks, planes, trucks, guns, ammunition, food, medical supplies, and other cargo. Carraway's friend Robert Gibson was aboard one of the sunken ships. A friend of Captain Salvesen's was aboard another. Whether either man had survived was unclear. The convoy had been attacked for five days straight by bombers in the Barents Sea before Soviet planes and warships emerged from Murmansk to chase the Germans off. The Liberty ship *Richard Henry Lee* had come under such relentless air attacks that the Armed Guard crew ran out of ammunition and had to break into the ship's cargo for more. After one member of the ship's crew was killed by a plane's machine-gun fire, his shipmates had only enough time to throw a blanket over his body before the next air raid. A few hours later, his funeral was interrupted by yet another air raid that sent the mourners racing for their guns. The news about convoy PQ-16 lifted no one's spirits in Hvalfjord.

A few days later, however, Captain Salvesen returned from a shore visit with much better news—albeit news with no clear impact on the Atlantic war. The U.S. Pacific Fleet had sunk four Japanese aircraft carriers in a huge sea battle near Midway Island, effectively shifting the balance of naval power in the Pacific. The news was electrifying: Midway was America's first major victory in the war. Carraway spent the next day camped out in the *Troubadour*'s radio room, listening for new details about the Battle of Midway with some of his Armed Guard gunners and the radioman, a fellow South Carolinian. "[W]e're all grinning like so many Cheshire cats, just as if it were our own feat," Carraway wrote to Avis. "Well, we are helping."

In fact, convoy PQ-17's time had finally come.

THE BRITISH ADMIRALTY and the U.S. War Shipping Administration chose thirty-five merchant ships to sail in convoy PQ-17, based on the vessels' cargo and their readiness for the Murmansk Run. Together, the vessels carried roughly three quarters of a billion dollars' worth of war supplies—more than $11.2 billion in today's dollars. Only about 20

CONVOY PQ-17 IN FORMATION
July 1–2, 1942

La Malouine
CORVETTE

Ayrshire
ARMED TRAWLER

William Hooper
LIBERTY SHIP

Ironclad
FREIGHTER

Hoosier
FREIGHTER

Palomares
ANTIAIRCRAFT SHIP

Troubadour
FREIGHTER

Bolton Castle
FREIGHTER

El Capitan
FREIGHTER

Olopana
FREIGHTER

Pan Kraft
FREIGHTER

Halcyon
MINESWEEPER

Donbass
TANKER

Rathlin
RESCUE SHIP

Silver Sword
FREIGHTER

Bellingham
FREIGHTER

Navarino
FREIGHTER

Britomart
MINESWEEPER

Dianella
CORVETTE

Alcoa Ranger
FREIGHTER

Gray Ranger*
FLEET OILER

Winston-Salem
FREIGHTER

Salamander
MINESWEEPER

Azerbaijan
TANKER

Empire Tide
FREIGHTER

Earlston
FREIGHTER

Aldersdale
FLEET OILER

Ocean Freedom
FREIGHTER

Benjamin Harrison
LIBERTY SHIP

Zaafaran
RESCUE SHIP

John Witherspoon
LIBERTY SHIP

Honomu
FREIGHTER

Fairfield City
FREIGHTER

Pozarica
ANTIAIRCRAFT SHIP

Zamalek
RESCUE SHIP

Daniel Morgan
LIBERTY SHIP

Carlton
FREIGHTER

P614
SUBMARINE

Northern Gem
ARMED TRAWLER

* *Gray Ranger* left the convoy on July 2 after sustaining ice damage.

P615
SUBMARINE

Lord Middleton
ARMED TRAWLER

Fury
DESTROYER

Lotus
CORVETTE

Paulus Potter
FREIGHTER

Washington
FREIGHTER

Wilton
DESTROYER

Hartlebury
FREIGHTER

Pan Atlantic
FREIGHTER

Direction of convoy advance

River Afton
FREIGHTER

Keppel
DESTROYER

Peter Kerr
FREIGHTER

Empire Byron
FREIGHTER

Leamington
DESTROYER

Christopher Newport
LIBERTY SHIP

Poppy
CORVETTE

Key	
	BRITISH VESSELS (8 merchant ships, 25 escorts)
	AMERICAN SHIPS (20)
	PANAMANIAN SHIPS (2)
	DUTCH SHIP (1)
	SOVIET SHIPS (2)

Samuel Chase
LIBERTY SHIP

Offa
DESTROYER

Lord Auston
ARMED TRAWLER

© 2019 Jeffrey L. Ward

percent of the cargo was arms and ammunition. The rest included raw materials and chemicals for Soviet factories, electronic gear, clothing, medical supplies, and food, including canned meat, salted fish, dehydrated vegetables and fruit, powdered eggs,* pasta, sugar, and coffee. One ship alone carried ten thousand packages of dried beans.

Twenty of the thirty-five ships were American—twenty-two if one counted the *Troubadour* and the freighter *El Capitan*, which were essentially American vessels. The American-flagged ships included the old freighters *Ironclad, Silver Sword, Hoosier, Alcoa Ranger, Bellingham, Honomu, Olopana, Pan Kraft, Pan Atlantic, Peter Kerr, Washington, Winston-Salem,* and the Jonah, *Carlton;* and the newly built Liberty ships *Benjamin Harrison, William Hooper, Daniel Morgan, John Witherspoon, Samuel Chase,* and *Christopher Newport.*

The British had the second-largest number of ships in the convoy, with eight. These included the freighter *Empire Tide,* which carried a single British fighter plane in a catapult near its bow. In an emergency, the plane could be catapulted into the air to fight German aircraft or hunt for U-boats. But when the plane's fuel ran out, there was no room on the *Empire Tide* for the pilot to land. He would have to ditch his plane in the freezing water, or bounce it to a stop on the surface and scramble out before it sank, and then hope to be rescued before he froze to death. The *Empire Tide* was one of dozens of British merchant ships rigged with catapults and planes, in an effort to provide convoys with some air cover until the Allies built miniature aircraft carriers with room for planes to take off *and* land.

Completing the roster of convoy PQ-17's merchant ships were the Dutch freighter *Paulus Potter,* which had been at sea when the Nazis seized Holland, and two big Soviet oil tankers, the *Donbass* and *Azerbaijan.* The *Azerbaijan* would go on to play a memorable role in convoy

---

* The Soviets nicknamed powdered eggs "Roosevelt's eggs," a crude joke based on the fact that the Russian word for them, *yaitsa,* could also mean "testicles."

PQ-17, but even in Hvalfjord it fascinated the Western mariners. The *Azerbaijan*'s crew included about a dozen women, including the ship's bosun—the senior unlicensed member of the deck crew. The mariners took turns gazing at the bosun through binoculars and trying to get her attention. "She's a blonde but she won't wave back," wrote Godfrey Winn, a famous British war correspondent who would sail with PQ-17. "Strict orders from Uncle Joe, I suppose." Carraway and his *Troubadour* shipmates were astonished to see the *Azerbaijan*'s female crew working right alongside the men, which was unthinkable on an Allied ship. The *Azerbaijan*'s cargo tanks contained not fuel for tanks and planes, but linseed oil, whose wartime uses included protecting wooden rifle stocks. The *Azerbaijan*'s crew would be fortunate the ship was not hauling something more volatile.

Having failed to stop Roosevelt and Churchill from sending convoy PQ-17, the leaders of the British Admiralty reluctantly assembled an escort force to try to protect it—essentially an expanded version of the forces that had accompanied previous Arctic convoys. It was divided into three layers, each with a different role.

The innermost layer—the core escort force—was to accompany the convoy all the way to Russia. It consisted of six British destroyers and fifteen smaller vessels, including four corvettes, two antiaircraft ships, two submarines, three rescue vessels, and four armed trawlers, including the *Ayrshire*. The destroyers were the muscle. Fast and heavily armed, they would dart along the edges of the convoy, slashing in as needed to strike at bombers and U-boats. The trawlers and the other small escort vessels would maintain a floating protective screen around the merchant ships as they plodded across the Arctic.

The second, intermediate layer of the convoy's escort force would be four heavy cruisers, including the American USS *Tuscaloosa* and USS *Wichita*, and a separate group of destroyers, including the American USS *Wainwright* and USS *Rowan*. The American vessels were under the Admiralty's command for the voyage. The cruiser force was more formidable than the core escort force, but the cruisers would not stay close to convoy PQ-17. They would shadow the convoy at a distance of 20 to 50 miles unless they were needed to fight off a major attack. And the cruisers would not accompany the convoy all the way to Russia. They would turn back after the convoy passed east of Bear Island and came within range of the German bombers in Norway. The Admiralty did not want to risk losing any more cruisers.

The third and outermost layer of the convoy's protection would be the distant covering force, which was the most powerful of the three but also the least likely to become involved in the action. It included the British aircraft carrier *Victorious,* the British battleship HMS *King George V,* the American battleship USS *Washington,* and a dozen destroyers. These ships would stay hundreds of miles west of convoy PQ-17, well out of range of the German bombers, unless the *Tirpitz* attacked. Even then, they would probably stay out of the battle unless the *Tirpitz* carelessly strayed far enough from Norway that the German bombers could no longer protect it. If that happened, the distant escort force would pounce on the *Tirpitz.* Admiral Tovey, who commanded the distant escort force, was spoiling for a showdown with the *Tirpitz,* but not in waters controlled by the Luftwaffe. Tovey had suggested convoy PQ-17 sail only far enough from Iceland to entice the *Tirpitz* into coming after it, and then turn back to Hvalfjord. Tovey's boss, Admiral Pound, had rejected his idea, which amounted to dangling convoy PQ-17 in front of the *Tirpitz* as bait.

For all its complexity, the British plan to protect convoy PQ-17 became simple after the convoy passed Bear Island and entered the most precarious phase of the voyage. All the big Allied warships in the two outer layers would drop out, leaving only the core escort—the six destroyers and the various smaller escort vessels—to guard the merchant ships on the last leg of the voyage, running across the Barents Sea to Russia.

Admiral Pound was far from confident that the three-tiered escort plan would protect convoy PQ-17 from disaster. He expected a rough time. "Our primary object is to get as much of the convoy through as possible," Pound wrote to the commanders of the escort forces, "and the best way to do this is to keep it moving to the eastwards even though it is suffering damage." He told his commanders in the Arctic he would direct convoy PQ-17's movements personally from London, where he would have access to the latest intelligence about the *Tirpitz's* movements and the weather. Pound promised he would keep his commanders in the field well informed. He added ominously that "circumstances may arise" that would force him to break up the convoy, leaving each of the merchant ships to make its way to Russia alone.

Breaking up a convoy in the face of an overwhelming enemy force was a desperation strategy to ensure that at least some ships got through. The British had scattered a convoy in 1941 in the North Atlantic, with good results: All the merchant ships had escaped while a British escort ship held off the German attack. But Admiral Tovey, the commander of convoy PQ-17's distant escort force, was alarmed that Pound would consider scattering a convoy in the Barents Sea. The merchant ships would have little room in which to scatter. They would be hemmed in by the polar ice field to the north and by the Germans in Norway to the south. Nor would they have anywhere to hide in the perpetual daylight. Tovey thought scattering convoy PQ-17 in the Barents Sea would be "sheer bloody murder." He hoped the Germans would not put Pound in a position where he might actually do it.

The Germans, however, were devising an all-out plan to destroy convoy PQ-17 and its escort of warships. The German naval staff codenamed the plan Operation Knight's Gambit, or Knight's Move—a chess term describing an aggressive opening strategy. The plan was elaborate enough to require Hitler's personal approval. On June 15, 1942, Grand Admiral Erich Raeder, the head of the German Navy, set out along the serpentine road to the Berghof, Hitler's lavish mountaintop chalet in the Bavarian Alps, to pitch Knight's Move to the Führer. Raeder, a sixty-six-year-old tactician, had given Hitler plenty of good advice. Raeder had been the first to suggest invading Norway, and later had warned Hitler against invading the Soviet Union. But Raeder did not enjoy a personal relationship with Hitler, who always called him by his title, "Admiral," while addressing other close advisors by their first names. Nor was Raeder any good at the palace intrigue that pervaded the upper echelons of the Third Reich. He was constantly being outmaneuvered for money and resources by rivals such as Field Marshal Hermann Goering, the chief of the Luftwaffe, whom Raeder despised. As a result, the German Navy did not have a single aircraft carrier. By 1942, the *Tirpitz* and other German surface warships were all but confined to port by a lack of fuel oil. They were allowed to put to sea only in response to enemy action. The Allies were unaware of the severity of the German fuel shortage.

Knight's Move offered the German surface fleet, which had accomplished little in the war to that point, a chance to shine—and perhaps to improve its standing with Hitler. Raeder laid out the plan for the Führer using maps to show how it would unfold: The Germans would find out when the convoy left Iceland, either from intelligence sources or from sightings by U-boats or spotter planes. The U-boats and planes would shadow convoy PQ-17, attacking it as the opportunities arose, until it passed Bear Island. Then they would summon the German bombers. The bombers would strike PQ-17 relentlessly, taking full advantage of the twenty-four-hour daylight.

Meanwhile, the *Tirpitz,* the cruisers *Lutzow, Admiral Hipper,* and *Admiral Scheer,* and several destroyers would slip quietly out of their bases at Trondheim and Narvik. They would creep northeast along the Norwegian coast, concealing their movements by avoiding the open sea and picking their way through the Inner Leads, a maze of narrow channels between the Norwegian mainland and the coastal islands. These German warships would assemble in Altenfjord, a remote fjord near the North Cape. When convoy PQ-17 reached a point 300 miles north of the North Cape, the *Tirpitz* and the cruisers and destroyers would burst out of Altenfjord and devastate the merchant ships and their escorts. If the Allied escort force was strong enough to threaten the *Tirpitz,* the battleship would strike a quick, furious blow and then retreat quickly to Altenfjord, leaving the cruisers, destroyers, U-boats, and bombers to pick the bones of the convoy.

Raeder might have expected Hitler to jump at such a bold plan. In June 1942, Nazi Germany was at the height of its power. German armies controlled Western Europe and had resumed the offensive on the eastern front. Britain was still reeling and America had yet to send troops into combat except in the Pacific, where the Japanese had left the United States no choice. But Hitler, who was boldness personified in land warfare, disliked taking risks at sea. He once had told Raeder, "On land I am a hero, but at sea I am a coward." Hitler was especially protective of the *Tirpitz* after the loss of the *Bismarck,* which had been a propaganda disaster on top of a military one. The *Bismarck* had been sunk after a lucky hit by an aerial torpedo disabled its rudder and left the huge German battleship steaming in circles, a sitting duck. Hitler was determined not to lose the *Tirpitz* in such a way. He told Raeder he approved Knight's Move under two conditions:

First, any Allied aircraft carriers within range of the convoy had to be located and "put out of action." And second, even if no Allied carriers were in position to threaten the *Tirpitz,* Hitler wanted to be consulted one last time before the battleship was turned loose. He wanted a final chance to veto the operation. "The Führer considers aircraft carriers a great threat to the large vessels," Raeder wrote in a summary of the meeting. "The aircraft carriers must be located *prior to* the attack, and they must be rendered harmless . . . before the attack gets under way." He probably walked out of the Berghof into the mountain air muttering under his breath. Under Hitler's conditions, Raeder would have to launch Knight's Move without knowing whether its main component, the *Tirpitz,* would take part. Finding and disabling Allied aircraft carriers would be an enormous challenge. But Raeder had done the best he could. He went back to his headquarters and wrote instructions to his subordinates for executing Knight's Move:

Main task: Rapid destruction of enemy merchant ships. If necessary these should only be crippled and the sinking left to the U-boats and Air Force. The escort force should only be attacked if this is indispensable for accomplishing the main task. In such an event it is primarily the task of the *Tirpitz* and *Hipper* to fight the escort forces, while the *Lutzow* and *Scheer* dispose of the convoy during that time. An engagement with superior enemy forces is to be avoided.

Raeder emphasized that the attack on the convoy would have to be executed quickly enough that the *Tirpitz* could retreat into the fjords before it could be attacked by Allied planes. He added:

The weather is especially favorable in June. The period of spring storms is over. Heavy summer fogs do not occur until July. The ice situation likewise is especially favorable in June. The ice has receded very little to the north. As a matter of fact, beginning about 150 nautical miles West of Bear Island, the enemy convoy has to sail East within 200 to 250 nautical miles off the Norwegian coast. This area is completely dominated by our Air Forces.

WHILE THE BRITISH and the Germans made their respective plans for convoy PQ-17, Stalin dispatched his foreign minister, Vyacheslav Molotov, to London and Washington, D.C., to negotiate the particulars of the Grand Alliance. Stalin wanted a firm commitment from Britain and the United States to establish a second front in France in 1942. He also wanted formal approval from his new allies for the Soviet Union's occupation of the Baltic states and eastern Poland.

Molotov was arguably the second most powerful man in the Soviet Union. *The New York Times* described him as "a prim, schoolmasterish figure," but Molotov's surname was a pseudonym derived from the Russian word *molot,* which meant "hammer," much as Stalin's name was derived from "steel." Molotov was a crafty intriguer who had enthusiastically supported Stalin's purges during the Great Terror. Stalin had installed him as foreign minister in 1940 to replace Maksim Litvinov, a Jew, for negotiations with the Jew-hating Hitler. After the Germans invaded the Soviet Union, it was Molotov whom Stalin had tasked with delivering the news to the Soviet people over the radio. In a masterpiece of Soviet obfuscation, Molotov announced that the Nazi invasion had killed "more than two hundred."

Churchill loathed Molotov and "his smile of Siberian winter." He wrote of the Soviet minister: "His cannon-ball head, black moustache, and comprehending eyes, his slab face, his verbal adroitness and imperturbable demeanor, were appropriate manifestations of his qualities and skill. . . . I have never seen a human being who more perfectly represented the modern conception of a robot." Molotov in turn showed a profound distrust of Churchill. Arriving in London on May 20, he accepted an invitation to stay at Churchill's country house, Chequers, but demanded that his bodyguards be given the keys to every bedroom so they could check for assassins. At night, Molotov slept with a revolver at his bedside and arranged the sheets so he could spring from the middle of the bed if attacked.

The talks reflected the wary atmosphere. Churchill, at Roosevelt's insistence, declared that any discussion of the fate of Poland and the Baltic states must wait until after the Nazis were defeated. Churchill agreed only to a twenty-year treaty with the Soviet Union, with no mention of postwar borders. The issue of the second front divided Roosevelt and Churchill. Roosevelt was eager to invade France in 1942 even if it resulted in heavy loss of life. Churchill insisted such an invasion would meet disaster unless the Allies first gained control of the skies over coastal France and built more landing craft to ferry troops across the English Channel.

In the end, Roosevelt and Churchill offered Molotov only a tepid statement that the invasion might be possible in August or September of 1942. For the foreseeable future, the Arctic convoys would remain the only help Stalin would get from his partners in the Grand Alliance.

On June 17, 1942, two days after Raeder's meeting with Hitler at the Berghof, Churchill arrived in the United States for his second war conference with Roosevelt. Churchill flew to Washington, D.C.—where he cautioned the pilot to be careful not to hit the Washington Monument—and from there to the president's home in Hyde Park, New York. Churchill cut an unusual figure, attired mostly in coveralls and wreathed in cigar smoke. He smoked eight big Havana cigars a day, constantly relighting them and puffing at them.

Churchill pressed Roosevelt to abandon the idea of invading France within the next few months. Roosevelt reluctantly agreed the invasion would have to wait until 1943. The two men put off deciding how to break that news to Stalin. They had weightier issues to discuss at their meeting. They agreed to pool their nations' resources to try to build an atomic bomb. The commitment in money and brainpower would be enormous, but they really had no choice. Hitler was known to be working on an atomic weapon, and they could not let him win that race. "We both felt painfully the dangers of doing nothing," Churchill wrote. He and Roosevelt agreed the project should be based in the United States, where it would be safer from the enemy.

From Hyde Park, Churchill and Roosevelt took a train back to Washington, arriving late on the night of June 20. They had just settled into the president's study when an aide handed Roosevelt a telegram. Roosevelt read it and gave it to Churchill without a word. The telegram said the British fortress of Tobruk in the Libyan desert had surrendered to the Germans. Churchill sat stunned. The surrender came as a complete shock. Churchill wished he were not experiencing this "bitter moment" while sitting across a desk from Roosevelt. The president said nothing but

"What can we do to help?" Churchill thought for a moment and then asked Roosevelt to ship all the newly built Sherman tanks he could spare to British forces in the desert. Roosevelt immediately arranged for three hundred tanks to be loaded onto ships and sent in a convoy to the Middle East.

Before leaving the United States, Churchill and his chief of staff General Ismay accepted an invitation to tour a U.S. Army training camp in South Carolina. They were impressed by the marching drills, and by a new gadget called a walkie-talkie. But Ismay was underwhelmed by the Americans' live-fire exercises. "To put these troops against [German] troops would be murder," he told Churchill. Churchill replied diplomatically that the American soldiers were "wonderful material and will learn very quickly." Churchill believed it took two years to train an army. He was newly relieved that Roosevelt had agreed to postpone an invasion of France until 1943. When Churchill got back to Washington, Roosevelt sent two young Army brigadier generals, Mark Clark and Dwight D. Eisenhower, to discuss preliminary plans for invading France in 1943. Churchill was impressed with both men and felt certain they were meant to play key roles in the invasion. Eisenhower would, in fact, end up leading the invasion, not in 1943 but on June 6, 1944.

Churchill apparently came close to being assassinated as he prepared to board a plane in Baltimore for London. A plainclothes officer noticed a man on the airport gangway gripping a pistol and muttering he would "do him in." The man was arrested and was found to be mentally unbalanced. Churchill got on the plane. He was less worried about the gunman than about a looming showdown in the British Parliament, where his political foes had scheduled a vote of censure against him for his management of the war. The debacle at Tobruk was the latest in a series of defeats in far corners of Britain's global empire. The fall of Singapore had been particularly galling; tens of thousands of its defenders had surrendered to the Japanese.

———

AS THE BRITISH MADE final preparations to send convoy PQ-17, they received a warning that their worst fears about the convoy might come true. The British naval attaché in Sweden presented them with a purloined copy of the German Navy's plan for Operation Knight's Move, obtained from Swedish intelligence sources. The British were not surprised such a plan existed—they would have been more surprised if the Germans had not been thinking about such a strike—but they did not assume the Germans intended to execute it. The plan might be a draft, a feint, a rejected proposal, or even misinformation. One British officer said its discovery felt like "a rumble of distant thunder rather than a shock." In any event, the die was cast. Roosevelt remained adamant that the convoys keep moving, and Churchill supported him. Nothing was going to stop convoy PQ-17 from sailing. Its destination was to be Murmansk, a harbor as dangerous as any leg of the convoy route.

Murmansk was a war zone, under constant threat of invasion by German troops only 35 miles to the west and under daily attack by German bombers, which kept the city of one hundred thousand courageous souls in a state of near ruin. Murmansk was a onetime fishing village that had been transformed into a shipping hub during World War I and had been expanded even further for the Great Patriotic War. Most of the city's inhabitants toiled on or near the docks, moving cargo from newly arrived ships onto rail lines leading to Moscow and Leningrad. They kept constant watch for approaching German Junkers 87 Stuka dive-bombers, which looked and even sounded like giant birds of prey. The Stukas' flared wings were fitted with flutelike devices that emitted bloodcurdling screams as the planes dove. The bombers targeted the docks and the Allied ships moored at them, and ignited firestorms in the city, which was almost entirely built of wood. Soviet antiaircraft batteries thundered from the low hills overlooking Murmansk and from sandbagged bunkers in bombed-out buildings, which by the summer of 1942 outnumbered the intact buildings in the city.

"The antiaircraft barrage was a mighty affair," recalled one British officer stationed in Murmansk. The Soviet gunners "did not believe in just firing at odd bombers. They waited . . . and then let go with a hundred guns. This shook the whole earth for miles around, and my first experience in these salvoes staggered me. . . . We saw planes come plummeting down, some into the wooded hills which they had set on fire, others splashing into the river. One plane crashed not far from us and set the adjacent wharf on fire. Bits and pieces of other planes came hurtling down, including an engine which smashed through the quay a few yards from us." Whenever a bomb smashed into the docks or blew apart a rail line, laborers scurried out of bomb shelters to make repairs, using steel delivered by the convoys and wood delivered by the trains from inland Russia. Soviet salvage teams roamed the harbor, blowing up wrecked vessels to make way for new arrivals. Through constant, Herculean efforts, the Soviets managed to keep the port of Murmansk open and functioning.

The Americans in convoy PQ-17 had heard horror stories about Murmansk but did not quite believe them. Most of the mariners were so sick of Hvalfjord that they were ready to sail anywhere. The *Troubadour*'s crew was causing trouble again. On the night of June 20—the same night the telegram about the fall of Tobruk arrived at the White House—a dozen members of the *Troubadour*'s crew, including Jim North, announced a work stoppage. They declared they had chipped so much rust that their eyes had become infected. They refused to chip any more until they were examined by an eye doctor and issued goggles. The captain was furious, fed up. He told Carraway to arrest the complainers for mutiny. Because the *Troubadour* had no brig, North and the others were confined to the ship's forepeak—the dark, foul-smelling section of the lower deck at the point of the bow. Carraway thought the dispute was overblown: "Such a minor event as refusal to work has long since failed to get a rise out of me," he wrote Avis. But neither side would budge. If the standoff continued, the *Troubadour* would be scratched from convoy PQ-17. After four days, the captain agreed to require less chipping of rust. The crew declared victory and went back to work.

No sooner was the mutiny resolved than a more alarming problem erupted. The Uruguayan seaman whose strange behavior had worried Carraway seemed to be growing more agitated. He threatened to kill some of his shipmates. Men were afraid to turn their backs on him. Carraway and the captain escorted him in a small boat to a Navy supply ship, where a doctor examined him. The doctor readily agreed the man was unfit for duty and promised to send a boat for him before the *Troubadour* sailed for Russia. The captain felt relieved, but Carraway did not expect the doctor to follow through. While the Uruguayan seaman was being examined, Carraway had been pleading with a supply officer for more tracer bullets. He had gotten nowhere. As he guided the little boat back to the *Troubadour*—keeping one eye on the Uruguayan seaman— Carraway felt discouraged. "We still had the crazy man," he grumbled, "and we still had no tracer bullets."

The departure of convoy PQ-17 was scheduled for late afternoon on Saturday, June 27, 1942. Early that morning, all the merchant captains were summoned to a conference aboard the British freighter *River Afton* by the convoy's commodore. Commodores were the convoys' civilian commanders, the links between the merchant captains and their military escorts. Convoy PQ-17's commodore, Jack Dowding, enjoyed a sterling reputation. He had helped evacuate British soldiers from Dunkirk with the Germans closing in. He had led convoys through the North Atlantic. Dowding described to the merchant captains the course convoy PQ-17 would follow. He reminded them not to let their vessels straggle behind, because U-boats feasted on stragglers.

A few hours later, the merchant captains were called to the main convoy conference in a smoke-filled YMCA hall in Hvalfjord. The British officers in command of the escort force took turns speaking. They reminded the captains to stay off the radio to avoid revealing their position to the Germans. They skipped the usual reminders about keeping ships blacked out in the darkness, since convoy PQ-17 would not encounter any darkness. Commander Jack E. Broome introduced himself as the leader of convoy PQ-17's core escort force, which was to stay with the convoy all the way to Russia. Broome was a veteran of the North Atlantic convoys. He could see that the merchant captains were nervous about this voyage. They typically dozed through such conferences, but they were sitting up and asking questions. Some "asked about the *Tirpitz*, the Big Bad Wolf." Broome told them he did not think the Germans would risk sending the giant battleship after the convoy. He predicted the convoy would reach Russia "practically intact."

The next speaker, Admiral L. H. K. Hamilton, the commander of the cruiser force, said bombers probably posed the greatest threat to the convoy. He said it was possible convoy PQ-17 would provoke "a fleet action," a major naval battle. That prospect surely thrilled some of the young naval officers in the room, but it did not thrill Lieutenant Gradwell. "For myself, I don't think much about fleet actions," he told a fellow officer. "I just want to get this convoy through."

The convoy conference broke up, and the merchant captains returned to their ships in a sudden downpour. A few hours later the signal was flashed throughout the anchorage for the ships assigned to convoy PQ-17 to weigh anchor. The author Theodore Taylor described the scene: "Soon there are whistles bleating all across the roadstead, some hoarse, some mournful. The serenade is a fitting farewell to bleak Hvalfjord. . . . Men with hoses . . . wash mud from the clanking anchor chains. The ship's captains, now heavily clothed for long, cold hours on the bridge, stare toward the foredecks as the chief mates supervise the heaving in of the anchors." From the bridge of the battleship USS *Washington,* Admiral Robert Giffen signaled, "The best of luck, and remember science and skill cannot but prevail over ignorance and superstition." A seaman on the antiaircraft ship HMS *Pozarica* heard a man call out from the shore, "Good luck, you'll need it!"

Jim North had been waiting for this moment but ended up missing it. He was sent below deck to stow the *Troubadour*'s huge, grimy anchor chain as it rumbled up from the bottom. Howard Carraway, however, drank in the experience as the *Troubadour* chugged toward the mouth of Hvalfjord. For a few minutes, all Carraway's frustrations with the ship, the crew, and the U.S. Navy fell away. Convoy PQ-17's departure was "something of a holy moment," he wrote Avis. "We are under way to Russia! We have weighed our anchor in the Hvalfjord and passed the boom through the great submarine net! We are out of Reykjavik harbor, in the deep water, steam up, dander up, and thumbs up! Yes, it is true. The gallant warrior, the Joan d'Arc of the Battle of the Atlantic, the stepchild of misfortune and Father Time, our dearly beloved and frequently accursed old tub, the *Troubadour,* is on her way again. Headed for what? I wonder. For a great adventure, thrilling and exciting? For a humdrum voyage? Or for disaster? I wonder."

Hundreds of miles to the east, off Jan Mayen Island, ten U-boats in the "Ice Devils" group, bearing the images of polar bears on their conning towers, spread out in a line like a huge drift net to snag a first glimpse of convoy PQ-17. Commanders of the German air bases in Norway canceled all leaves. The *Tirpitz* prepared to thread its way through the Inner Leads toward the North Cape and the point of attack.

CHAPTER FOUR

FIRST BLOOD

A convoy is simply a collection of defenseless or lightly defended vessels protected by warships. The concept dates back to antiquity. Julius Caesar mentioned using convoys in his account of the Roman invasion of Britain in 55 B.C. The basic concept had changed little since Caesar's day, though it had been refined considerably to incorporate twentieth-century tools of war such as sonar, radar, depth charges, submarines, and long-range bombers. The attackers of convoys, of course, had developed new tools as well. Both sides would employ all the latest technological advancements in the fight over convoy PQ-17.

As the merchant ships of the convoy chugged toward the mouth of the harbor at Hvalfjord, the clouds parted and the sun shone on them. The air was so clear that the mariners could see every ridge on craggy Botnsulur. Even the air was warm. Suddenly, the dreary anchorage looked like a picture postcard. The old freighters and tankers were a less impressive sight. "So many dirty ducks waddling out to sea," wrote Douglas Fairbanks Jr., a Hollywood actor serving as a U.S. Navy lieutenant on the cruiser USS *Wichita*. "I dare say all who watched the motley tubs offered some half-thought prayers." A British seaman on one of the departing ships imagined people on shore thinking, "Thank God we're not going with that lot, poor bastards"—which was exactly what *he* had been thinking when he had watched the previous convoy depart.

It took several hours for all thirty-five merchant ships of the convoy to pass single file through the submarine nets at the mouth of the fjord. The moment they reached the open sea, a heavy swell caught them and the air turned bitter cold. They had entered the Denmark Strait, the rough, ice-clogged channel between Iceland and the remote southeast coast of Greenland. The ships rode the swells and waited outside the harbor mouth until all the vessels had emerged. Then the order was passed by signal flags for the ships to move into their assigned positions in the convoy. Convoy PQ-17 was divided into nine columns, with four ships in each column. Convoys were always much more wide than deep. A ship presented its biggest target from the side. If too many ships sailed in a row, one behind the other, a U-boat could simply fire a torpedo at the side of the convoy from a distance and have a good chance of hitting something.

From the air, convoy PQ-17 looked like a floating rectangle roughly five miles wide and less than a mile long. Within the convoy, each ship was supposed to maintain a distance of 1,000 yards from the ships on either side, and a distance of 600 yards from the ships ahead and behind. The crews had to keep close watch to maintain those distances, especially in the fog. Ships often collided within convoys due to missed signals for course changes.

All along the convoy's perimeter, the trawler *Ayrshire* and the other small escorts used sonar devices on retractable domes on their hulls to probe the water for U-boats. Sonar beamed sound waves through the water to detect submerged objects. Different objects produced different sonar profiles. If an object fit the profile of a U-boat, the escorts would race to a spot directly above the object and drop depth charges—cylinders of explosives that could be preset to blow up at various depths. A single depth charge could destroy a U-boat if it exploded within 35 feet of it or cause serious damage if it exploded within 100 feet. But hunting down and destroying a U-boat usually took time, and the escorts had little time to spare. Their chief duty was to maintain a constant defensive screen around convoy PQ-17. If they left their positions in the screen for too long to pursue a U-boat, another U-boat might squeeze through the gap they had left and wreak havoc on the convoy. Some German U-boat "aces" had become household names in Germany by staging just such attacks. The convoy escorts usually had to be satisfied with harassing the U-boats with depth charges and then hurrying back into their positions in the screen.

The wind slackened and convoy PQ-17 passed through curtains of rain and fog. Fog is a visible mass of water droplets or ice crystals that forms when warm air and cold water meet, winds are calm, and the air temperature is warmer than the water temperature by 1.8 to 3.6 degrees Fahrenheit. The Arctic summer provided all those elements, as well as ice floes and a constant mixing of warm and cold currents. Veteran mariners who considered themselves connoisseurs of foul weather rated the Arctic variety of fog particularly disagreeable. "A slimy fog," grumbled one of Lieutenant Leo Gradwell's men on the *Ayrshire*, "ship feels sticky." Jack Broome, the commander of the convoy's core escort force, called the fog a "solid white chunk of oblivion" produced by "hot sun on cold ice, exclusive to those regions." Soon the lookouts had to strain to see the vessels around them. All the ships deployed their fog buoys—small objects towed astern that sent up rooster tails of spray to warn off ships approaching from behind. Even with the fog buoys and other precautions, near misses kept occurring. Ships passed much too closely, their crews staring wide-eyed at one another through the gloom. Floating ice appeared in the water, first small floes and then growlers. One of the trawlers warned of a suspicious vessel ahead of the convoy, only to discover it was an iceberg. The sea was the color of lead.

The *Ayrshire* steamed along the left side of the convoy toward the rear, closest to the Liberty ship *William Hooper,* which occupied the left rear corner of convoy PQ-17. The corners of convoys were nicknamed "coffin corners" because they were the most exposed positions. The *Ironclad* was directly in front of the *William Hooper,* occupying the third position in the leftmost column. The *Troubadour* was just to the *Hooper's* right, the last ship in the second column. Their captains would have preferred spots in the middle of the convoy, where ships were shielded from U-boats by the other merchant ships around them. At least the *Troubadour* and *Ironclad* had avoided the coffin corner.

From their vantage points near the rear of the convoy, the men on the *Troubadour* and *Ironclad* could see the three rescue ships, which had been converted into floating first-aid stations from their original purposes— hauling cattle, passengers, and mail. Each was equipped with sick bays and operating tables and was staffed by a surgeon and medics. The rescue ships would trail behind the convoy and pick up survivors of bombed and torpedoed vessels. The presence of three such ships in convoy PQ-17 reassured the mariners, but also seemed to suggest the convoy expected serious trouble. In fact, however, the British Admiralty had decided to send the three rescue ships with convoy PQ-17 so that they could bring home some of the more than 1,200 Allied mariners who were already stranded in North Russia after their ships were sunk in previous convoys. The rescue ships had been added to the convoy late in the planning process. One of them, the *Zamalek,* had sailed for Hvalfjord with shipyard workers still installing gun tubs on the vessel.

On the *Troubadour,* Howard Carraway stewed. As he had expected, no one from the Navy had come to remove the troubled Uruguayan seaman from the ship. Carraway also thought the *Troubadour's* defenses were alarmingly feeble. He got the idea of prying open the three General Lee tanks that were bolted to the ship's main deck and engaging their 37mm turret guns against the Germans. Breaking into a ship's cargo is illegal—the nautical term is barratry—but Captain Salvesen enthusiastically supported the idea. Carraway discovered that the turret guns were in excellent working order and could be elevated sufficiently to shoot at planes. Each tank also contained three Thompson submachine guns for use by the tank crews. Carraway thought the Tommy guns might come in handy too. His initiative impressed Salvesen, who bragged to others on the ship that if Carraway ran out of bullets he would hurl "sticks, stones and tomato cans" at the Germans. For his part, Carraway noticed the captain was calm and confident guiding the old *Troubadour* through the fog and drifting ice.

William Carter, the *Ironclad*'s Armed Guard commander, decided his ship's only truly useful weapon was the 3-inch, 50-caliber gun on the stern. Carter moved his mattress and blankets into the gun turret, a small, armored room adjacent to the gun platform, and resolved to live there for the duration of the voyage. Carter taught his men a simple approach to defending the *Ironclad* against air attack: Fire at the closest plane. He told them not to try to swing the guns to follow the fast-moving planes, but to choose a point in the air between the planes and the ship and then pour out enough antiaircraft rounds to create a fiery wall of shrapnel. Each round burst into a ball of hot shrapnel 15 feet in diameter. Not every pilot would fly through such a wall to press an attack.

Just after midnight on June 28 the convoy encountered thicker ice. Growlers bounced off the ships' hulls with audible clangs. Curious mariners climbed out of their bunks for a look. "To most of us [the ice] was a beautiful sight as it bumped and scraped against the ship's sides in the weird light of that hour and place," wrote one young crewman on the *Ayrshire*. "Most of the ship's company hung over the gunnels gazing at it, debating whether it would be possible for us to get through or not." Some men waxed poetic. Godfrey Winn, the British war correspondent, saw in the ice "batik designs . . . crisscrossed with patterns of mauve, indigo and emerald green." But at 2:30 a.m. on June 29, the ice, not the Germans, drew first blood from PQ-17.

A sharp floe tore a hole in the hull of the Liberty ship *Richard Bland*, the newest ship in the convoy. The vessel had been christened only weeks earlier at a Baltimore shipyard. Its cargo included 300 tons of TNT. The ice damage was severe enough that the *Bland* had to turn around. The ship was halfway back to Hvalfjord when it ran aground and had to be towed the rest of the way. The *Bland* nonetheless would go on to play a significant role in the story of convoy PQ-17, and particularly in the life of the *Ironclad*'s Carter.

No sooner had the *Bland* turned around when the ice claimed a second American freighter. The venerable *Exford*—one of the oldest ships in the convoy—impaled itself on a sheet of ice 100 feet wide and 15 feet thick. The ice gouged a hole in the hull and crumpled the bow. The *Exford* was in no immediate danger of sinking, but it would never make it to Russia. It too turned back. Then the British oiler *Gray Ranger* struck ice. The *Gray Ranger* had been assigned to stay with convoy PQ-17 all the way to Russia. Now it was instructed to turn back at Bear Island. The convoy had lost two and a half ships before encountering the Nazis or even getting out of sight of Iceland.

The British tried to distract the Germans from convoy PQ-17 by dispatching a dummy convoy from Scotland on June 29. The decoy, code-named Force X, consisted of four empty colliers and fourteen small escort vessels. Force X steamed north as if heading for Russia, but soon plunged into fog. Since the decoy could not possibly divert the Germans unless they saw it, the ships turned south and then east to try to get out of the fog. They finally gave up and Force X returned to Scotland without the Germans ever noticing it. Commodore Jack Dowding observed wryly that the decoy convoy had "failed to tempt the enemy." The Germans' attention remained fixed on the waters east of Hvalfjord.

Convoy PQ-17 continued to move through fog and rain. The ocean around it lay flat as a lake. The air remained cold, and the mariners piled on layers of clothing, topped with specially issued sheepskin coats and hats. Still they shivered. They broke into a cheer when the six British destroyers in the core escort force joined the convoy, along with the two antiaircraft ships. All of those warships had sailed separately from their base at Seydisfjordur on Iceland's east coast. The destroyers looked huge, formidable, slicing through the murk. They took positions at the front of the convoy, arranging themselves in the shape of an arrowhead, with Commander Jack Broome's destroyer, the HMS *Keppel,* at the tip, leading the way. The antiaircraft ships, HMS *Pozarica* and HMS *Palomares,* took their positions at the convoy's rear, one on either side. They had been banana boats until the British government requisitioned them from their owners and packed the afterdecks with guns, including Swedish-built Bofors 40mm antiaircraft guns that could pump out 120 rounds a minute. The antiaircraft ships also had high-powered sound systems. They serenaded the American mariners with "Deep in the Heart of Texas" and "Pistol Packin' Mama" as convoy PQ-17 plodded eastward, waiting for the Germans to make a move.

THE GERMANS, IN FACT, had already made a move. Their bombers were pummeling Murmansk. The city was accustomed to being bombed, but this bombing went on for three days with little letup. A Communist Party official in Murmansk wrote in his diary:

> Looking down at the city from above, all one sees is a continuous sea of fire. The wooden houses are burning like waxed candles. The smoke has drifted some kilometers over the city. . . . Firebombs are strewn on the ground, having been put out by the inhabitants. The sidewalks and wooden fences are catching fire. People are tearing off planks that are burning. They use planks to extinguish the firebombs.

The party official asked his bosses in Moscow to send Murmansk more firefighting gear. He noted that the Germans were using a new type of firebomb that burned for a short time and then exploded in a lethal shower of shrapnel. He added that the citizens of Murmansk were "behaving stoically and heroically." They kept their valuables stored in boxes and suitcases. When their homes caught fire, they moved in with relatives, friends, or neighbors whose homes were still intact. When they ran out of homes to move into, they fled into the hills above the city, where they slept under scrubby bushes and ate at makeshift tables, on which they placed vases of wildflowers. "Clever people here in Murmansk," the party official observed. "It is impossible not to be victorious with a people like this."

Immediately after the intensive bombing, the senior British naval officer in North Russia warned Allied authorities to divert convoy PQ-17 from Murmansk. "Inasmuch as the Germans are breaking through the Soviet defenses and bombing quite at will, it is merely a question of time until the docks are rendered useless." He recommended the convoy bypass Murmansk and head for Archangel. It was not really a recommendation so much as an observation: With Murmansk in flames, the convoy had nowhere else to go. Its destination was shifted to Archangel.

The Germans found convoy PQ-17 just before 1:00 p.m. on July 1, just southeast of Jan Mayen Island. The ships were passing through fog banks interspersed with short intervals of bright sunshine when the mariners heard the drone of a plane engine. The drone intensified into a roar. "A plane flew over the convoy about 200 feet high over the *Ironclad*," wrote Francis Brummer, one of Carter's Armed Guard gunners. "I was watching through a pair of glasses. . . . Some ships opened fire on the other side of the convoy." Brummer recognized the aircraft from a photo in a training manual as a Blohm & Voss 138 flying boat. The Blohm & Voss was a long-range reconnaissance aircraft, a convoy hunter. It could stay aloft for eighteen hours without refueling. Once it located a convoy, it would radio its position to the German bases in Norway. Then it would continue to circle the convoy, staying just out of range of its guns, and guide U-boats and bombers to the target. Search planes such as the Blohm & Voss and the similar Focke-Wulf 200 Condor inspired visceral contempt in some of the mariners. Winn wrote of the Blohm & Voss's "clumsy, bat-like wings" and the way its nose "tipped slightly toward the water, as though she were smelling out her prey." Mariners called the reconnaissance planes by a rich variety of nicknames, many of them crude. The printable ones included Charlie, Smokey Joe, the Vulture, the Stool Pigeon, and the Shad.

The Shad's appearance over convoy PQ-17 changed the mood on the ships, even though the mariners had been expecting it. The German pilot immediately radioed the convoy's position to his commander, who forwarded the information to Admiral Raeder and the various German commands in Norway. The U-boats found the convoy at about the same time as the Shad. Two of the Ice Devils reported a convoy southeast of Jan Mayen Island with destroyers as escorts. Both U-boats were forced to crash-dive immediately after they completed their radio transmissions and ended up fleeing from depth-charge attacks by the destroyers. Unlike the German bombers, the U-boats did not thrive in twenty-four-hour daylight and calm seas, which made concealment difficult. Even the wakes of the U-boats' periscopes were easy to spot on the still surface of the water. Four U-boats were assigned to shadow the convoy while six others spread out across its path.

With an attack by the Germans looking imminent, Carraway test-fired one of the turret guns on the *Troubadour*'s tanks. It worked perfectly, and Carraway resolved to use it at the first opportunity. He trained his Armed Guard men to fire it and also trained several volunteers from the merchant crew, including Jim North. Later that afternoon, one of the Armed Guard men glimpsed a U-boat on the surface near the convoy but got so flustered he forgot to sound the alarm. The sub quickly submerged. A couple of the small escorts raced out and dropped depth charges, to no apparent effect, and then hurried back to their positions in the screen. Another U-boat positioned itself directly in front of the convoy and submerged. The U-boat commander tried to keep the sub underwater just long enough for the six destroyers to pass overhead, and then to surface in time to spray torpedoes at the first row of merchant ships. Twice he

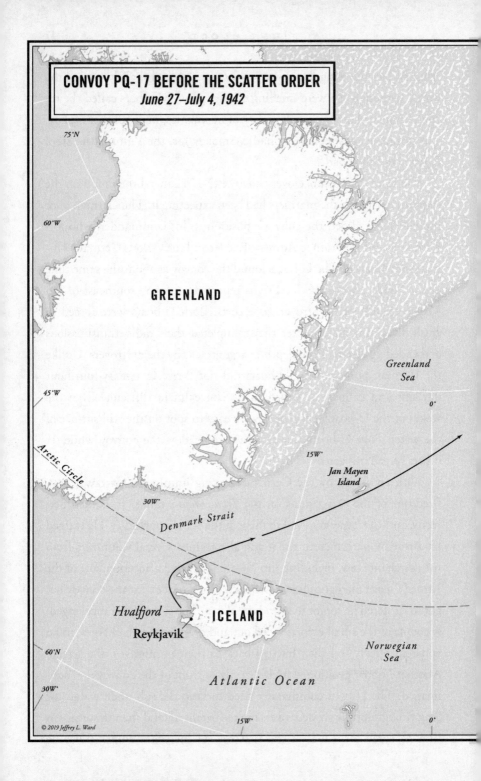

CONVOY PQ-17 BEFORE THE SCATTER ORDER
June 27–July 4, 1942

75°N

60°W

GREENLAND

Greenland
Sea

45°W

0°

Arctic Circle

15W°

30W°

Jan Mayen
Island

Denmark Strait

Hvalfjord

ICELAND

Reykjavik

60°N

Norwegian
Sea

30W°

Atlantic Ocean

15W°

0°

© 2019 Jeffrey L. Ward

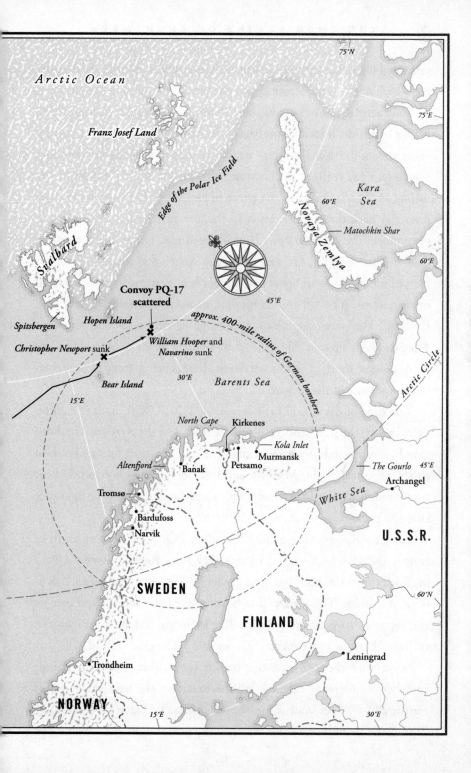

Arctic Ocean

Franz Josef Land

Edge of the Polar Ice Field

*Kara
Sea*

— Matochkin Shar

Novaya Zemlya

75°N

75°E

60°E

60°E

45°E

**Convoy PQ-17
scattered**

Svalbard

Spitsbergen

Hopen Island

approx. 400-mile radius of German bombers

✕ William Hooper and
Navarino sunk

Christopher Newport sunk ✕

Bear Island

30°E   *Barents Sea*

15°E

Arctic Circle

North Cape   Kirkenes

• *Kola Inlet*
Petsamo Murmansk

• *The Gourlo*
Archangel

45°E

Altenfjord • Banak

Tromsø •

White Sea

U.S.S.R.

• Bardufoss
Narvik

SWEDEN

60°N

FINLAND

• Leningrad

• Trondheim

NORWAY

15°E   30°E

mistimed his attack and the U-boat surfaced right in front of the destroyers, which nearly sank it with depth charges.

Soon after the Shad's arrival, the *Troubadour*'s air-raid alarm sounded
for the first time. It meant bombers—the Armed Guard's chief reason for
being aboard the ship. Carraway scrambled onto the platform of the ship's
4-inch gun and realized to his dismay that he was afraid. "My heart was
racing, my hands unsteady," he wrote in his diary. No planes came. Carraway lay back down in his bunk in the gun turret. "I'm too excited to
sleep much," he wrote to Avis. "But I'll need rest, I'm afraid, before this
time tomorrow night. So, sleep well, my Angel, and keep your fingers
crossed for us. We're in hot water, icy but hot. Remember that you're all
my life to me. That all I do is for you, one way or another. I love you,
Darling." The convoy kept passing through patches of fog and sunshine.
The Shad kept circling. The snarl of its engine was the only sound except
for occasional muffled thumps of depth charges being dropped by escorts
in distant parts of the convoy.

The time of day meant little to convoy PQ-17. With no interruption
by darkness, the days tended to run together. On the *Ayrshire,* Gradwell
gave his crew standing orders to man the trawler's guns for one hour on
either side of midnight, when the sun was closest to the horizon. U-boat
commanders were trained to watch for momentary tricks of the light that
could help them approach targets unnoticed.

Early on the morning of July 2, convoy PQ-17 passed just south of
convoy QP-13, which was on its way back from Russia. Convoy QP-13
included thirty-six ships, fourteen of them American and eight each British and Russian. The Ice Devil U-boats spotted the homebound convoy
and reported its position. Admiral Raeder instructed them to ignore it
entirely. "Let this convoy pass," Raeder said. "The goal is PQ-17."

Soon after the two convoys passed each other, a British cruiser
launched a floatplane called a Walrus to survey the ice field ahead of
convoy PQ-17. The Walrus, unlike the disposable plane on the *Empire
Tide,* could be retrieved from the sea with a crane after each flight. The

Walrus's latest ice report was encouraging. The polar ice field had re-treated 80 miles north of Bear Island, which would enable the convoy to pass north of the island rather than south of it—the first time an Arctic convoy had been able to do so. Passing north of Bear Island would keep convoy PQ-17 outside the range of the German bombers for another half a day. Still, the ships would need to proceed cautiously. The Walrus pilot reported icebergs and floes in the strait north of the island, including two huge bergs he originally mistook for ships. The pilot also observed three life rafts drifting along the ice edge with no one inside them—"floating tombstones," Douglas Fairbanks Jr. called them. Toward the end of the Walrus's flight, the pilot spotted a long, dark object on the water's surface and dropped a depth charge squarely on top of it. It turned out to be a whale. "Just passed small whale without tail," the destroyer *Wainwright* reported. Whales looked so much like U-boats from a distance that scores of whales were killed by Allied escort ships and planes during the sea war.

Early on the afternoon of July 2, the warships hoisted for the first time the square black pennant meaning "air attack." Seven German planes ap-proached convoy PQ-17 from the port side, flying in a loose formation. They split into two groups, with three planes going after the ships at the front of the leftmost column and four going after the ships at the rear of that column, where the *Troubadour, Ironclad,* and *Ayrshire* were. The *Iron-clad*'s guns were the first to open fire, quickly followed by guns from nearby ships. The sky erupted in black and gray puffs of exploding antiair-craft rounds. The men on the ships saw the planes were not bombers but Heinkel 115 seaplanes—"big, growling bastards," Carter called them—equipped with machine guns and aerial torpedoes. The Heinkel 115s were among Hitler's most recent additions to the Norwegian air bases.

The wall of antiaircraft fire seemed to daunt the German pilots, who dropped their torpedoes short of the convoy and veered off in the direc-tion from which they had come. One seaplane took heavy fire from the gunners on the rescue ship *Rathlin*. The aircraft caught fire and splashed into the sea within sight of the convoy. The mariners watched through binoculars as the three-man crew got out of the sinking plane. They inflated a rubber raft and got into it. Another German seaplane landed on the smooth water nearby. The mariners suddenly realized a rescue attempt was under way. A British destroyer raced toward the second plane, firing shells that produced spouts of water around the plane. The Germans in the raft paddled over to the plane and were helped aboard. The pilot revved the engines and took off. The mariners were impressed. Winn wrote that "you couldn't help admiring the maneuver, even [while] regretting it meant another pilot who was safe to bomb us again."

The halfhearted attack by the seaplanes did not leave convoy PQ-17 unscathed. Two men on the *Rathlin* had been injured by machine-gun fire, and a third had lost an eye when a round shattered the glass in the ship's wheelhouse. Two torpedoes had passed close to the rear of the convoy. Carraway was encouraged, however. "We have had our baptism of fire, and it's not so bad," he wrote in his diary. He had overcome his initial jitters. The men in his Armed Guard unit had performed well, though they were exhausted from manning their guns for long hours. With the danger past, they were "sleeping like children anywhere, everywhere—on the deck, at their guns, in bunks, chairs, all over. One is snoring on the mess room table, his head on his .45."

Carraway noted sourly that only three of the ship's merchant mariners had turned out to help man the guns and carry ammunition, including Jim North. Friction between Navy Armed Guard men and civilian merchant mariners was common on merchant ships, where the Navy men took their orders from their commanders and the merchant mariners from the ships' captains. Navy men and volunteer mariners came from vastly different cultures. The Navy men tended to regard the civilian mariners as slackers, and the mariners tended to view the Navy men as landlubbers obsessed with pointless spit and polish.*

---

* Pay was an underlying cause of animosity between U.S. Navy men and civilian mariners. The Navy men resented the fact that the mariners were paid significantly better once their

There was no such divide aboard the *Ayrshire,* where the entire crew answered to Gradwell. But there were other sources of conflict. After the air attack, a twenty-eight-year-old British sailor named Walter John Baker asked himself why he was putting his life in jeopardy for Stalin and the Soviet Union. Baker had left a job as a bookkeeper to enlist in the Royal Navy even though he could not swim. He was proud to serve England, but he could not see how hauling precious war supplies to the Soviet Union was accomplishing that purpose. "I felt pretty sore about the necessity of risking my skin to take supplies to the Russians when I felt that with their system of gangster government they were no better than the Germans," Baker wrote. "In fact, I'm sure their methods were worse and my opinion was that we should have left the two of them to fight it out." He argued frequently with a Scottish shipmate who insisted that "Joe Stalin was a good guy and the Russians could do no wrong." Baker and the Scotsman had tapped into the conflict at the heart of the Grand Alliance.

BUT AS CONVOY PQ-17 approached Bear Island, the leaders of the Grand Alliance were occupied by other matters. Churchill stood before Parliament on July 2 to defend himself against a vote of censure arranged by his political rivals. In two days of acrimonious debate, his accusers recounted a series of British defeats from the Pacific to the Mediterranean to Tobruk. (The British had not been part of the U.S. Pacific Fleet's victory at Midway.) Churchill's rivals argued he was mismanaging the war and should give up some of his authority to conduct it. Churchill knew going into the debate that his foes lacked the votes to censure him. He

---

various bonuses were included. But the mariners were paid only when they were actually sailing; their pay stopped the moment a voyage ended, even if it ended with a torpedo strike in midocean. Unlike Navy men, merchant mariners had to pay income tax and received no government benefits. Postwar studies have shown that when all the various factors were considered, the merchant mariners and the Armed Guard men were paid roughly the same.

employed his gifts as an orator to accuse them of playing political games while he conducted vital talks with Roosevelt in Washington. "Our American friends are not fair-weather friends," Churchill declared. "They never expected that this war would be short or easy, or that its course would not be checkered by lamentable misfortunes." The no-confidence vote failed by a lopsided 475–25. Roosevelt cabled a message to Churchill saying simply, "Good for you."

For Roosevelt and the United States, the war was widening rapidly. The president had just committed American bombers to start flying day-time missions over Germany from England—an extremely hazardous operation that surely would cost American lives. Along the U.S. coast, U-boats were sinking merchant ships every day while the U.S. Navy daw-dled over organizing convoys to protect them. Four merchant ships would be torpedoed in U.S. waters on July 2 alone. One U-boat laid a string of mines across the mouth of Chesapeake Bay and blew holes in two American tankers—a symbolic slap at the U.S. Navy, whose main base on the East Coast was only a short distance away in Norfolk, Virginia. In the Pacific, Japanese troops invaded the remote Solomon Islands with the intention of building an airfield on Guadalcanal Island, from which they could threaten the sea routes to Australia.

Roosevelt made plans to spend the Fourth of July weekend at his new presidential retreat in the Catoctin Mountains of western Maryland, which he had named Shangri-La (President Eisenhower would rename the retreat Camp David after his grandson, David Eisenhower). For Roosevelt, the trip to Shangri-La would be a working vacation. As reading material, he brought a copy of *Jane's Fighting Ships,* a reference book of all the world's warships. While the president was thumbing through the book, some of the ships featured in its pages would play roles in a drama Roosevelt had set in motion in the Barents Sea.

Stalin sent no congratulatory message to Churchill. The Soviet dicta-tor was preoccupied by a looming crisis in the south. The Germans had broken through Soviet defenses in the Crimea and captured the Black Sea resort city of Sevastopol. Their obvious next step would be to attack the Volga River citadel of Stalingrad. German and Soviet armies already were converging on Stalingrad for one of the pivotal battles—arguably *the* pivotal battle—of World War II. For the time being, at least, the leaders of the Grand Alliance had little time to think about the fate of the latest Arctic convoy.

THE GERMANS, however, were not distracted. Around 8:00 p.m. on July 2, the *Tirpitz* and the German cruisers and destroyers began steaming up the Norwegian coast to get in position for Knight's Move. The *Tirpitz* relied on tugboats to guide it through the harbor at Trondheim but set out through the Inner Leads under its own power. The 600-foot battleship glided through deep, narrow fjords of gin-clear water, between sheer rock walls still dusted with snow—the world's most powerful warship passing through some of the world's most breathtaking scenery. The *Tirpitz* was a racehorse, with a top speed of nearly 30 knots, but it had to creep through the tight channels, and sometimes it shut down its boilers for short periods to conserve fuel. The boilers were refired when the battleship passed inlets leading to the open sea, where enemy attack was more likely.

From the *Tirpitz*'s bridge, General Admiral Otto Schniewind commanded all the naval components of Operation Knight's Move. Schniewind was Admiral Raeder's former chief of staff. He was a gaunt, balding man whose subordinates called him "the Undertaker" behind his back. Schiewind had a knack for planning complex operations, and he was decisive and aggressive—so much so that he had started the *Tirpitz* through the Inner Leads before receiving the official order. It seemed increasingly clear, however, that Hitler's conditions for the *Tirpitz* participating in the attack would be hard to satisfy. Fog and clouds inhibited German reconnaissance pilots' search for Allied carriers. Even in fair weather, flying in the Arctic was hazardous; pilots often had to take off and land on cement or wooden runways, and to squeeze their planes through narrow valleys buffeted by crosswinds. And if the Luftwaffe found a carrier close enough to pose a threat to the *Tirpitz,* then "neutralizing" that carrier, as Hitler had demanded, would pose an even bigger challenge. But if the German air force could do its part, Schniewind would make sure the *Tirpitz* was ready.

Not all the German warships assigned to Knight's Move managed to navigate the tricky Inner Leads. The cruiser *Lutzow* and three destroyers hit submerged rocks and were forced to drop out of the action and return to port. The cruisers *Hipper* and *Scheer* reached Altenfjord intact, however, as did twelve other destroyers. Knight's Move would not lack naval firepower. And while the warships worked their way to Altenfjord, German bombers would execute the next phase of the attack on convoy PQ-17. The Heinkel 115s that had attacked earlier in the day were perhaps the least formidable of them.

The mainstays of the German bomber force in Norway were big, fast Junkers 88s, which could carry large payloads and absorb heavy punishment; Heinkel 111 bombers with glassed-in noses, capable of skimming the wavetops at 220 miles per hour; and the flare-winged, screaming Stuka dive-bombers. The Germans mixed various types of bombers in their attacks to confuse and overwhelm the ships' gunners. German pilots worried more about antiaircraft fire from the warships than from the merchant ships, whose gun crews, they knew, tended to lack experience and firepower. From the air bases nearest to the North Cape, the German bombers could reach the convoy routes in just two hours. They could bomb the convoy, return to Norway for more bombs and fuel, and bomb the convoy again before it had traveled 100 miles.

IN THE EARLY HOURS of July 3, convoy PQ-17 encountered small icebergs. "They are beautifully colored," Carraway wrote. "Blue, green and white striations blended to perfection. They start out in the calm, cold water like perfect peaches. They are rounded smooth by waves and wind, unbelievably perfect." The beauty of the Arctic was so striking that mariners marveled at it even when it threatened them. Soon the ships were picking their way through bergs larger than they were. "We began to pass majestic icebergs and saw polar bears basking themselves upon ice floes which sailed silently by like giant water lilies," recalled an officer on a British escort vessel. The bergs gave way to a vast field of pancake ice— small, rounded blobs of melting ice.

Beyond the pancake ice the convoy passed through a mass of drifting wreckage—"spars, furniture, timbers and debris of all kinds from ships lost in other convoys." The wreckage included a large bomber encased in a mass of drifting ice. The sight was so disturbing that no one spoke about it. Later, a gap in the swirling fog revealed a U-boat and a German seaplane sitting together on the calm surface, as if having a picnic. The fog closed back in before anyone could sound an alarm. Some of the mariners listened to the daily radio broadcast of the Nazi propagandist Lord Haw-Haw, who taunted the Allies in his nasal, upper-crust British accent. They were surprised to hear Lord Haw-Haw addressing them, boasting that on the following day—the Fourth of July—the Germans would treat convoy PQ-17 to "a real display of fireworks."

Carraway had begun to wonder where all the big warships in the convoy's escort had gone. Other men on the *Troubadour* had seen the cruisers on the horizon through the fog once or twice, but he had not. The only escort he saw regularly was the *Ayrshire*, steaming along near the coffin corner. Carraway regarded the trawler as "a relic" but felt enough of a connection to it to refer to it in his diary as a companion. "He wasn't much protection," Carraway wrote of the *Ayrshire*, but "he made us feel good." Carraway found the fog even more comforting. "Thank God for the beautiful, murky, pasty, thick, pea-soupy, lonely, impenetrable fog!" he wrote. He felt so secure in the fog's clammy embrace that he allowed himself to bathe for the first time in days and put on a clean uniform. Then he crawled into his bunk and slept soundly for six hours.

At 2:30 p.m. on July 3, the pilot of a British Spitfire fighter flying over

Trondheim, Norway, peered down at the *Tirpitz's* anchorage and saw the battleship was gone. His radioed report set the Admiralty astir. Soon afterward, British code breakers at Bletchley Park decrypted a German message that the heavy cruiser *Admiral Hipper,* which normally anchored at Trondheim, had arrived at Altenfjord. Taken together, these two scraps of information suggested the German warships were on the move to intercept convoy PQ-17. But no further information was forthcoming, and the decrypted message was hours old.

The Germans sent their secret messages through the Enigma coding system, in which typewriterlike encrypting machines scrambled the messages at the transmission end and then unscrambled them at the receiving end. The British had broken the Enigma code, but the Germans stubbornly remained convinced it was invincible. The Germans did take the precaution of changing the code settings of the Enigma machines at noon every day. Each time the settings were changed, the British had to rebreak the code, which took as long as nine hours. The resulting lag time between intercepting Enigma messages and being able to decrypt them was problematic at times for the Allies. It would be devastating for convoy PQ-17.

In the waning hours of July 3, Salvesen informed his crew on the *Troubadour* that the convoy was passing Bear Island. Carraway and some of his shipmates threw on their heaviest clothing and stood on deck in the chill fog hoping to catch a glimpse of it. By all accounts, Bear Island was a gloomy chunk of rock, girdled by steep cliffs and pounded by surf. The island had been named by the sixteenth-century explorer Willem Barents after a tense encounter with a polar bear there. For convoy PQ-17, Bear Island marked the frontier, the dividing line between neutral waters and enemy waters. Bear Island was the last land the mariners were likely to see until Russia. It might be the last land they would ever see. Some of the men claimed to have glimpsed the island's dark silhouette, but Carraway, staring hard into the murk, saw nothing at all.

CHAPTER FIVE

FIREWORKS

ndependence Day 1942 found convoy PQ-17 seven days out of Hval-fjord and eight days from Archangel, steaming in and out of fog banks. The thermometer said 3 degrees Fahrenheit, but it felt colder. The fog muffled all sounds except the grumbling of the ships' bilge pumps and the clacking of their steam pipes—sounds the crew had stopped hearing long ago. None of the mariners could sleep or even relax. With Bear Island behind them, they knew they could be attacked at any moment. S. J. Flaherty described the mood on the Liberty ship *John Witherspoon:* "Everybody goes about his job watching and waiting; there is not much to be said. This is tension—the same type that quiets a cornered animal before an attack." Any man who tried to sleep did so fully clothed, wearing a bulky jacket, sea boots, an inflatable Mae West life vest, and a thick cork life belt. A willingness to accept discomfort, one sailor wrote, "could mean just that difference between living and dying."

At two o'clock in the morning, a German torpedo bomber materialized like an apparition out of the fog and flew low over the *Troubadour.* The pilot might have been as surprised as the men on the ship. The plane veered off. Carraway and his men stood at their guns, staring into the gray void, wondering if the plane would circle back from a different direction. But an hour dragged by, then two, and then three. On the opposite side of convoy PQ-17, a hole opened in the fog and a Heinkel 115 seaplane dropped through it. The pilot had turned off his engines so he could approach the convoy in silence. The plane glided down along the rightmost column of ships, flying mast high, and released two torpedoes. The Heinkel 115's engines growled back into life and the plane rose and swooped off.

The torpedoes were easy to spot, churning through the glassy water. Aerial torpedoes were smaller and less powerful than torpedoes fired by U-boats, but they could still sink ships. They often skipped like flat rocks when they first landed, then bit into the water and accelerated under the power of their own small motors. The Heinkel 115's torpedoes headed straight for one of the antiaircraft ships, which dodged them. The torpedoes kept going, right at the freighter *Carlton,* the Jonah on its third attempt to reach Russia. The lookouts on the *Carlton* saw the torpedoes and shouted for the helmsman to turn the ship and dodge them. The old freighter narrowly succeeded. One of the torpedoes passed harmlessly out to sea. The other cut through the convoy diagonally and headed straight for the starboard side of the Liberty ship *Christopher Newport,* the lead ship in the eighth column.

Men on the *Christopher Newport* saw the torpedo coming. A member of the ship's Navy Armed Guard, Hugh Patrick Wright, poured a stream of .30-caliber machine-gun fire into the torpedo. The rounds seemed to hit the target but deflect off the water or the torpedo. The torpedo kept coming. The men carrying ammunition for Wright's gun turned and fled, yelling at Wright to flee too. Every man on that part of the ship ran except for Wright. "He continued firing and changing [clips] as fast as he emptied them," his commander wrote. "Realizing the complete uselessness of his .30-caliber, Wright kept firing until the torpedo passed out of sight under the starboard lifeboats. . . . Wright's fire was very accurate and his coolness was evidenced by the fact that he kept up a running stream of oaths directed at his 'son-of-a-bitching gun.'"

After the torpedo disappeared beneath the ship, all was quiet for a moment. Then a tremendous explosion shook the *Christopher Newport*. Wright was hurled from the machine gun onto a deck two levels below, where he lay motionless. Another Armed Guard gunner, Paul Webb, was blown "like a rag doll" into the ship's smokestack. Webb had stayed at his gun trying to clear it after it jammed. The crippled *Christopher Newport* veered sharply to starboard, forcing the ships behind it to swerve to avoid colliding with it.

The torpedo had found the *Christopher Newport*'s engine room, blowing a hole in the hull, cracking steam pipes, and stopping the ship dead. Freezing seawater poured in through the hole and swirled over the blazing-hot boilers. The boilers exploded, killing all three men on watch in the engine room. Sudden death in the engine room was common in the U-boat war. Men toiling down there were blind and deaf to all that happened outside. They had no idea the ship was under attack until a torpedo burst into their workplace. If they survived the explosion, they had to scramble up ladders through steam and inrushing seawater just to reach the main deck.

The torpedo that hit the *Christopher Newport* started a fire in the cargo holds, which contained 200 tons of TNT. The captain ordered the crew to abandon ship. The rest of convoy PQ-17 left the *Christopher Newport* behind, as convoys always did when a ship was sinking, disabled, or straggling. Any ship that stopped to help risked becoming the next victim. Men on vessels near the stricken *Christopher Newport* stood in the cold for a final look. Most of them had never seen a ship sink before. From the *Troubadour,* on the opposite side of the convoy, Carraway mistook the sinking vessel for a different Liberty ship, the *Benjamin Harrison,* on which another of his friends from the Armed Guard served. Now Carraway had two friends to wonder about.

The evacuation of the *Christopher Newport* went smoothly. Someone revived Wright, the determined machine gunner, and helped him into a lifeboat. He suffered from a headache and a badly sprained ankle. The rescue ship *Zamalek* swooped in and collected him and forty-six other survivors from the lifeboats. Wright immediately offered to help man the *Zamalek*'s antiaircraft guns. Most of the survivors did not even get their feet wet. The only dead were the three unlucky souls in the engine room—the first casualties of convoy PQ-17. The *Christopher Newport*'s captain took a revolver aboard the rescue ship. He declared he needed it to control the black members of his crew. His rescuers on the *Zamalek* insisted he turn over the gun to them. The *Christopher Newport* stayed afloat in the convoy's wake, its main deck crowded with U.S.-built tanks, trucks, and crated-up planes. The fire apparently had died short of the cargo of TNT.

The trawler *Ayrshire* had fallen behind the convoy and was hurrying to catch up when it came alongside the deserted, listing *Christopher Newport*. Lieutenant Leo Gradwell talked about boarding the ship to salvage some of its more valuable cargo. His men were relieved when he kept the trawler on course to return to the convoy. The *Ayrshire* already was tempting fate by straggling. The trawler passed two British submarines that had been sent back from the convoy to try to sink the *Christopher Newport* so it would not be a hazard to future convoys. On other escort ships in convoy PQ-17, young officers pulled out charts displaying the structure of the convoy and marked the box representing the *Christopher Newport* with an X.

The mariners could hear German planes flying overhead, but the fog was thick enough to conceal the planes from the ships and the ships from the planes. Some of the German pilots dropped bombs blindly through the gloom, hoping for a lucky hit. They had been unlucky, but the random bombing unnerved the mariners. Bombs suddenly materialized out of the billowing gray fog and splashed into the sea, like thunderbolts hurled from the clouds by angry gods. One bomb narrowly missed a British corvette; two others straddled the freighter *Washington* but did no damage. On the *Ironclad*, Lieutenant William Carter reassured himself that the odds were against any ship being hit: "Mathematically, there is a lot more open water surface within the overall boundaries of a convoy than there is ship surface area to be bombed." Still, "For my own part, this 'bombs through the fog syndrome' was the scariest thing I had yet encountered. It must have been the fact that it had such an eerie aspect to it that made it so frightening."

Like Howard Carraway, Carter had wondered since joining the Navy how he would react the first time he found himself in real danger. Now he knew. "I was relieved to find that I had no awareness of fear during the action itself," he wrote. "I was too busy. My mind took over and went into its problem-solving mode at breakneck speed, pushing everything else out of the way in the process." After the danger passed, he replayed the action in his head, "sort of like going to a movie and watching all that scary stuff happen to someone else." Then, after thanking God for keeping him alive, Carter turned analytical, "thinking about what was likely to happen next, and whether there was anything more that could be done to prepare for its coming."

Not all men on the *Ironclad* could channel their fear into constructive action. Carter's shipmates encouraged him to check on a mariner whom they agreed "had gone nuts." The first air attack had left the man so shaken that he had stopped standing his watches and performing his other duties. All he did was sit in a chair outside the galley. Carter could not persuade him to return to work and had no idea what to do about him. Everyone on the *Ironclad* was edgy. The chief engineer stopped by Carter's quarters to say the captain was tired of Carter sounding the ship's General Quarters alarm and summoning the crew to lifeboat stations at every hint of an attack. Carter replied as diplomatically as he could that he had the authority to sound the alarm whenever he saw fit.

After an hour or so, the bombs stopped falling through the fog and the sound of the planes' engines died away. Only the Shad remained, circling. It had in effect become part of the convoy. At one point, according to several mariners' accounts, men on one ship signaled the German pilot that they were getting dizzy watching the Shad's endless circles. They asked the pilot to fly in the opposite direction for a while. He signaled back, "Glad to oblige," and the Shad flew in the opposite direction. On another occasion, the Shad fired a burst from its machine guns into the sea near the *Ayrshire* when the trawler started lagging behind the convoy again. The pilot did not seem to be trying to hit the *Ayrshire,* only to nudge it closer to the convoy so the Shad would not have to fly such wide circles. The interactions with the pilot did not lessen Carraway's enmity for the "accursed" Shad. He kept hoping the pilot would get careless and stray within range of the ships' guns.

At 8:00 a.m. on the Fourth of July, the American ships in convoy PQ-17 began taking down their U.S. flags in unison. Some of the British sailors thought the Yanks were striking their colors, surrendering. "The yellow muckers!" shouted a British seaman on one of the antiaircraft ships. But the Americans were not giving up. They were replacing their oily, wind-torn American flags with brand-new ones to celebrate Independence Day, 800 miles from the North Pole while hauling arms to Soviet Russia. Although the Panamanian-flagged *Troubadour* did not raise a new U.S. flag, the Norwegian captain Salvesen invited Carraway to his stateroom to toast the Fourth of July with "a wee drop" of Scotch. The Americans' show of patriotism impressed the British. "It was a splendidly defiant gesture in the face of the enemy," wrote Paul Lund and Harry Ludlam. "Loud music came from some of the American ships and their crews could be seen dancing around on deck." Godfrey Winn tried to imagine what convoy PQ-17 was like for the Americans: "They are much farther from home than we are; their ships don't possess any real armament like ours; for many of them it will be their first voyage through hostile waters, and anyway they've been at sea weeks longer than we have, with all the time the tension increasing."

Out of sight of the convoy, the big British and American warships in the cruiser force and the distant covering force exchanged holiday greetings. The captain of the British cruiser HMS *Norfolk* pointed out, "The United States is the only country with a known birthday." The captain of the American destroyer USS *Rowan* joked that England, as America's mother country, could celebrate July 4 as Mother's Day. He added that Americans liked to enjoy fireworks on the Fourth of July and "I trust you will not disappoint us." Admiral L. H. K. Hamilton, commander of the cruiser force, added his good wishes to the Americans: "It is a privilege for us all to have you with us and I wish you all the best of hunting."

Beyond this shipboard holiday bonhomie, however, confusion and stress were setting in among the men responsible for protecting convoy PQ-17. In London, Admiralty officials had learned nothing of the *Tirpitz*'s whereabouts since the battleship's berth at Trondheim was discovered empty the previous afternoon. Clouds and fog hampered aerial reconnaissance. Admiral Sir Dudley Pound—who as First Sea Lord outranked everyone else in the British Admiralty—sent a message to Admiral Hamilton giving him permission to keep the cruisers near the convoy for a while longer if he thought it wise, rather than turn them around near Bear Island for their own protection, as originally planned.

Every minute the cruisers stayed near the convoy increased the chance of them being sunk by the *Tirpitz,* or even by the bombers and U-boats already swarming around convoy PQ-17. By allowing Hamilton to keep the cruisers in harm's way, Pound was taking a risk. He also was bypassing Admiral Tovey, who was Hamilton's immediate boss. Tovey bristled when he saw Pound's message to Hamilton; he wanted the cruisers to get away from the convoy immediately. Tovey quickly sent Hamilton a message ordering him to withdraw the cruisers from convoy PQ-17 as soon as the ships reached a point 150 miles east of Bear Island, unless it was crystal clear by then that the *Tirpitz* was not going to attack.

The messages to Hamilton from Pound and Tovey did not exactly conflict, but they showed indecision at the highest ranks of the British Admiralty over whether to protect the convoy or its escorts from the Big

Bad Wolf. Hamilton found himself in an awkward position. He informed Pound and Tovey he was going to refuel his cruisers from the British fleet oiler *Aldersdale,* which was sailing in the midst of convoy PQ-17. Hamilton may have thought the refueling would buy time for the British to locate the *Tirpitz,* and for his two bosses to agree on what he should do.

The Germans were only slightly less confused. They at least knew where the *Tirpitz* was—safely anchored at Altenfjord, the jumping-off point for its planned strike at convoy PQ-17. The *Tirpitz* could reach the convoy from Altenfjord in about ten hours. But German reconnaissance pilots had provided conflicting reports about the presence of an Allied aircraft carrier in the convoy's escort force. One pilot's report had left the Germans wondering if *two* Allied carriers were in the area. Until those conflicts were resolved, the *Tirpitz* was going nowhere. Admiral Raeder tried to contact Hitler with an update on the situation but was told the Führer was "not available." That was hardly an encouraging sign for Knight's Move.

The German bomber squadrons in Norway did not need to wait, however. They had battered previous Arctic convoys with no help from the *Tirpitz.* Luftwaffe chief Hermann Goering was happy to upstage Admiral Raeder and the German Navy. So far, the Luftwaffe had merely probed convoy PQ-17. Now it would mount a serious attack. A little before 1:00 p.m., a squadron of Junkers 88 bombers took off from the air base at Bardufoss near the North Cape. Next went the Heinkel 111 bombers, whose glassed-in noses were all too familiar to survivors of the London Blitz. The planes had been converted into torpedo bombers for Arctic convoy duty. They roared over the Norwegian tundra and out over the North Cape and the Barents Sea, with nothing between them and the North Pole except convoy PQ-17.

The Junkers 88s reached the convoy first. Their mission was largely diversionary: to fly over the convoy at high altitude and distract the ships' gun crews. Men on the ships saw the Junkers 88s approaching on the horizon, but by the time the planes reached the convoy the clouds obscured them. The rumble of their engines filled the air. The ships sent up a barrage of antiaircraft fire. The Junkers quickly departed. To the south the sky was clearing. On the horizon the mariners saw a cluster of tiny black dots bobbing up and down, heading at them. "Small, fast bugs skimming just above the water line," one mariner wrote. It looked to Carter as if every German bomber in Norway was heading for the convoy. The sound of the planes' engines grew from a faint bumblebee buzz into a drone. The black dots resolved themselves into Heinkel 111 torpedo bombers. A trawler blinked a signal that eight bombers were approaching, then quickly increased the estimate to ten, and then to twenty. In fact, twenty-three bombers were racing at convoy PQ-17, each of them carrying two torpedoes in its bomb racks. The ships' gunners stood by their weapons and waited. Word came over the escorts' loudspeakers to "Stand by." Commodore Dowding wondered if the convoy should execute a sharp change of course to try to confuse the German pilots. But it was too late for maneuvering.

The Heinkels split into two groups. Ten planes approached convoy PQ-17 from the right front corner; the other thirteen circled around toward the convoy's rear. The planes in the first group could not have chosen a worse moment to attack. They arrived just as one of the warships in the cruiser force, the American destroyer USS *Wainwright,* had finished refueling from the oiler in the convoy. The *Wainwright* otherwise would have been miles away from the merchant ships with the rest of the cruiser force. The *Wainwright* charged at the inbound planes and delivered a thunderous broadside with its 5-inch guns. The destroyer disappeared in a cloud of its own gun smoke. Men on the merchant ships thought for a moment that the *Wainwright* had exploded. The clear sky ahead of the bombers erupted into a storm of shrapnel. Most of the Heinkels dropped their torpedoes early and fled. Only one plane kept coming. It launched its torpedoes just as one of the *Wainwright*'s shells set its fuselage afire. The destroyer dodged the torpedoes and the burning Heinkel plunged into the Barents Sea.

The *Wainwright* turned back to the convoy, passing close alongside the *Troubadour*, whose Armed Guard gunners cheered and waved "like the student section at a high school football game," Carraway wrote. The ship's radioman was practically dancing, "happy as a kid in his first long pants. If this was war, then he liked it!" One of the antiaircraft ships sent the *Wainwright* a message of congratulations, adding, "We have had the fireworks we were talking about." The fireworks display was not over, however. Just as the ships emerged from a fog bank into brilliant sunshine, the other thirteen Heinkel 111s raced at convoy PQ-17 from behind.

The commander of the Heinkel squadron, Lieutenant Konrad Hennemann, was a rising star in the Luftwaffe. He recently had received a personal commendation from Goering for sinking 50,000 tons of Allied shipping. He seemed determined to add to his total regardless of the cost. He flew his bomber straight up the center of the convoy at the height of the ships' masts, strafing the decks of the merchant ships with his machine guns. Dozens of the ships' guns swung toward him, including the turret gun on the *Troubadour*'s tank. The tank gun produced a distinct *BUNG, BUNG, BUNG* sound. Jim North watched the tank fire at the plane. The shots appeared to miss, but North thought he saw the plane wobble slightly—as if the pilot was startled to be attacked by a tank in middle of the ocean.

Just as the Heinkel released its torpedoes, North saw a red glow near the front of the plane. The glow blossomed into a flame. The Heinkel roared over the front of the convoy, with antiaircraft fire still pouring into it, and crashed into the sea. By the time the convoy reached the spot where the plane had gone down, nothing remained but an oil slick with a small flame guttering in the middle. Hennemann had no chance to escape. "A very brave man," Commodore Dowling reflected. "The concentrated fire on him was terrific and he must have been riddled with every kind of projectile." Hennemann would be posthumously awarded the Knight's Cross.

One of Hennemann's torpedoes narrowly missed the American freighter *Bellingham*, the second ship in the fourth column, and sped out to sea. The other torpedo struck the British freighter *Navarino* directly below its bridge. The *Navarino* shuddered and slowed. The *Bellingham*, directly behind it, had to swerve to miss it. Some of the *Navarino*'s crew panicked and launched lifeboats while the ship was still moving. Two of the lifeboats capsized. Other crewmen jumped into the sea as ships surged past them on either side. A man in the water shouted optimistically, "On to Moscow! See you in Russia!" The rescue ships moved in behind the sinking *Navarino*, racing the clock and the icy water. Rescuers pulled one man out of the water but decided he was dead, his body limp, his eyes open and staring. When they lowered him back into the sea, however, he let out a faint groan, and they quickly pulled him aboard again. He would spend the rest of the voyage in the boiler room, the hottest place he could find. Ten other men escaped the *Navarino* on a raft and watched with alarm as the rest of convoy PQ-17 steamed out of sight. "The horizon emptied and we were on a raft in the middle of the Arctic Ocean," one of them recalled, "and we began to fear that the others had reported that we had gone down with the ship." One of the rescue ships finally returned for the raft. The only man killed on the *Navarino* was a young fireman who, like the dead on the *Christopher Newport*, had been standing watch in the engine room.

Other German pilots followed Hennemann's example, flying low into the heart of convoy PQ-17. The mariners were shocked to see the German bombers—54 feet long, with 74-foot wingspans—zooming past them at eye level. They could look down into the cockpits. The noise of the guns was deafening. Some Navy gunners fired through low-flying planes into other ships. One of Carter's men on the *Ironclad* accidentally shot a tanker, although he insisted afterward, "I didn't hurt her much." The *Ironclad* in turn was hit by a stray round from another vessel—possibly the *Troubadour*. Commodore Dowding noted afterward that the American gunners kept firing even after planes had passed, spending precious ammunition to punish empty air. "The U.S. ships have not had much experience of this sort of thing," Dowding added.

Carraway kept up a steady fire with one of the *Troubadour*'s .30-caliber machine guns although, as he had suspected, those guns lacked the fire-power to bring down planes, and his rounds simply bounced off. The scene on the *Troubadour* was chaotic. "All the crew . . . were running around the deck, yelling and screaming in all their forty tongues, looking like demons or wild men in their bundled Arctic clothing, clumsy life jackets, silly shrapnel helmets, gas masks and addled brains," Carraway wrote. But he happened to glance up at the bridge and saw Salvesen standing "calm as an oak in the midst of all the confusion. . . . I was proud of the captain."

A Heinkel 111 flew so close over the *Troubadour* that the mariners could smell its exhaust. Carraway watched in horror as a torpedo skipped across the water straight at the ship's bow. "[M]y knees buckled, my heart crowded my tonsils, my blood turned to water, and fear gripped me," he wrote Avis. He thought of the men he had stationed in the tank. If the ship went down, they might never get out. Carraway ran across the deck to the tank, "faster, I think, in all the heavy clothing and boots, than I had ever run on a cinder track," and shouted at the men inside, "Get out—Torpedo!"

Carraway was not the only one who saw the torpedo coming. Jim North, standing lookout on the *Troubadour*'s bow, shouted and pointed. Salvesen yelled to the helmsman, "Hard left, full stern!" The torpedo vanished under the ship directly below North. Expecting an explosion, North half ran, half fell down a ladder from the bow to a lower deck, his rubber boots slipping on the ladder's rungs. For decades afterward, North's heart would race anytime his feet slipped, even on a polished floor in his home. The torpedo did not explode. It popped out of the water on the opposite side of the *Troubadour*. It zoomed away from the ship for about 100 feet, and then turned around and ran back toward the port side of the *Troubadour,* where North had stopped running. The torpedo seemed to be chasing North around the ship. The Armed Guard fired at it with machine guns to no avail. Mariners shouted at it in Spanish and Portuguese, "Go away!" Just before it reached the *Troubadour* again, the torpedo stopped, turned on one end, and sank. The crew stared at the spot where it had disappeared, half expecting it to resurface and pursue the ship a third time, but it did not. Men flung themselves down on the *Troubadour's* deck and thanked the Almighty. The captain hollered, "Did you see that? Did you see that? Don't tell nobody, they won't believe it." At that moment, North decided God did not intend for him to die in convoy PQ-17. Still, he was shaking so badly that he could not light a cigarette, even with a long kitchen match.

North then heard a muffled roar to his left as a torpedo exploded into the side of the Liberty ship *William Hooper,* which occupied the dreaded coffin corner next to the *Troubadour* and directly behind the *Ironclad.* North watched transfixed as the *William Hooper's* entire engine room seemed to burst out of the ship's smokestack in a fiery mass. Flames engulfed the *Hooper.* Some of its crew jumped overboard before the captain gave the order to abandon ship. The captain had to interpose himself between other crew members and the remaining lifeboats. He shouted at them: If you launch a lifeboat while a ship is still moving, the lifeboat will capsize. The crew retreated. The Armed Guard kept shooting at the bombers and managed to hit one. But that would not save the *William Hooper* or its 8,600 tons of war supplies. The captain ordered the men to abandon ship, which they did in three lifeboats and two rafts. The only three casualties on the *Hooper* were—like the casualties on the *Christopher Newport* and *Navarino*—men on watch in the engine room.

The rescue ships *Zamalek* and *Rathlin* picked up the survivors from the rafts and lifeboats. A young Filipino seaman from the *Hooper* claimed to have been blown so high into the air by the explosion that a Heinkel 111 had flown *under* him. The rescue ships' duty was extremely hazardous. Saving men from sunken ships meant stopping dead in the water in the convoy's wake, where U-boats waited for stragglers. Rescue ships would lower meshed nets for men who still had the strength to climb up them, and motor lifeboats to save men too weak or injured to help themselves. Men in the water often were coated with thick, black bunker oil from their sunken ships. Sometimes their bodies were so slippery they could not be pulled into the boats. Men who had swallowed oil could die from its toxic effects hours, days, or even years after being rescued from the sea. Motor lifeboats had rescue swimmers who swam after helpless men. The *Rathlin*'s rescue swimmer, who was a competitive swimming champion before the war, never entered the water without a knife to protect himself if someone he tried to save became hysterical. The surgeons on the rescue ships performed delicate medical procedures in the middle of air raids. The *Zamalek*'s surgeon had just finished operating on the gunner who had lost an eye in the previous day's attack when the ship wheeled around to pick up survivors of the *William Hooper*.

Men pulled from the freezing sea after less than twenty minutes could usually recover fully, but those who had been longer in the water faced a more uncertain future. The British author Paul Kemp described the emergency treatment for half-frozen, semiconscious mariners in Arctic waters:

> On being brought aboard they were stripped and wrapped in warm blankets. Artificial respiration was started immediately and intramuscular injections of camphor in oil were given. The mouth, nostrils and eyes would be gently cleansed of oil fuel. As soon as breathing became more regular, the patient was not interfered with until a pulse could be felt and the pupils began to contract. A prolonged bout of shivering would follow, after which consciousness would return. The patient would then be moved to a warm bunk and sleep would be induced, by morphine, if necessary.

If a man did not recover within forty-eight hours, he might need long-term treatment for exposure, or worse. Severely frostbitten limbs could turn gangrenous and require amputation. An American seaman in Archangel described visiting a building near the hospital where about twenty mariners "were lying in a small room with a dirt floor. Their ships had been torpedoed, they'd been out in lifeboats in the freezing weather, and had suffered from severe frostbite. One guy had one leg off, the other guy two."

While the rescue ships picked up the *William Hooper* survivors, Gradwell ordered the *Ayrshire* to drop behind the convoy to protect the rescuers. The trawler took aboard six of the survivors. German planes launched torpedoes at the *Ayrshire*. At one point, the trawler's coxswain had to execute a zigzag maneuver to dodge torpedoes approaching from two directions at once. "In spite of his twisting and turning, one (torpedo) ran so close along *Ayrshire*'s port side that I could have read the maker's name without glasses," wrote First Officer Richard Elsden. "It was very nasty for a few moments." Gradwell took it in stride. In the midst of the air attack, the *Ayrshire* passed a British corvette and Gradwell called out flippantly to an officer on the corvette, "Are you happy in the Service?" The officer asked for more time to consider his answer.

A torpedo crashed into the Soviet tanker *Azerbaijan*, whose blond female bosun had obsessed the mariners at Hvalfjord. "[T]he ship trembled violently," the tanker captain Izotov recounted, "a violent explosion was heard, the whole aft part of the ship from the mainmast disappeared behind a mass of oil from the diesel fuel, which soared upwards into a huge column above the mast." The bomb had hit the tanker's reserve fuel tank. Men on nearby ships assumed the *Azerbaijan* had blown up, but the tanker stayed afloat, trailing smoke and flames behind it. It swerved out of formation, nearly colliding with the British freighter *Empire Tide*—which had narrowly escaped being hit the previous day when the *Christopher Newport* was torpedoed and similarly swerved out of formation.

Izotov personally took charge of the firefighting. Eight Russians on the aft end of the tanker leaped into the water to escape the flames. One of the rescue ships picked them up, and then picked up a ninth man who had jumped in after them. The ninth man introduced himself as a commissar, the Communist Party's eyes and ears on the *Azerbaijan*. The commissar demanded that the eight men who had jumped overboard ahead of him be returned immediately to the *Azerbaijan*. The captain of the rescue ship refused: One of the Russian seamen already was in the process of being treated for a serious leg injury. The *Azerbaijan* lowered its lifeboats as a precaution, and four other crew members climbed into one of them and cast off. The captain shouted at them to return, and one of the tanker's officers fired a rifle shot over the lifeboat to get their attention or perhaps to warn them to come back or be shot. They rowed the lifeboat back to the *Azerbaijan*. The Russians slowly brought the fire under control. The intense heat had melted and warped part of the tanker's main deck. The ship's entire cargo of linseed oil had spilled into the Barents Sea. The rescue ships drew close to the tanker, assuming the Soviet captain wanted the crew examined for burns and possible smoke inhalation. "Go away!" Izotov shouted at them in English. "We don't want you!" The would-be rescuers retreated.

The *Azerbaijan*'s third assistant engineer got the ship's engines restarted—he "showed himself a Communist who is loyal to his homeland," Izotov reported. Izotov also commended a machine gunner named Ulyanchenko, who had clung to his machine gun and kept firing despite being "bathed from head to foot with oil and water." The *Azerbaijan*, still smoldering, hurried back to its position in the convoy. The Western mariners could scarcely believe it. "Her crew were singing and smiling," observed Jack Broome, the commander of the core escort. "A couple of lusty dames waved cheerfully from her bridge." The *Azerbaijan*'s phoenixlike resurrection would not be its last.

The air raid abruptly ended. The last of the Heinkel 111s disappeared over the horizon in the direction of the North Cape, leaving only the

Shad to continue its endless circles. The Barents Sea around convoy PQ-17 looked like a battleground. Pieces of wreckage drifted in patches of oil. The rescue ships darted back and forth to make sure they had not missed anyone. The upper decks of the antiaircraft ships were so littered with spent shell casings that men had to wade through them. A British destroyer picked up four German airmen who had escaped their downed Heinkel into a dinghy. The *Navarino* and *William Hooper* drifted forlornly in the convoy's wake, listing badly but refusing to sink. Two British minesweepers were dispatched from the convoy to send them to the bottom. Their gunfire alarmed the men on other ships, who thought for a moment that the Germans were back. The horizon, however, was empty. "The sea was flat calm and seemed to be oil instead of water," recalled Walter Baker on the *Ayrshire*. "Not a bit of mist or fog was there, and looking away into the distance we swore that we could see the curvature of the earth's surface. Perhaps it was that we wanted to be over there beyond the horizon—away from this spot as quickly as possible."

The morning's air attacks had cost the convoy three ships and seven men—three men each from the *Christopher Newport* and the *William Hooper,* and one from the *Navarino*. More than a dozen other men had been injured, some of them by friendly fire. A stray round from an American freighter had shattered the thigh bone of a gunner on the *Empire Tide*. A wild shot from a destroyer had struck a corvette sailor in the buttocks. The Germans had lost four planes.

The mariners were exhausted but full of themselves. The Germans "had thrown all they had at us for three days," Carter wrote. "For a convoy of old rust buckets, with a few new Liberty ships thrown in, we had given a pretty good account of ourselves, and we had also given the famous Luftwaffe about as much as it could handle." One of his young Armed Guard gunners, Francis Brummer, realized he was still chewing some food he had stuffed into his mouth when the air alarm first sounded an hour before. "I'd been too scared to swallow it," he reflected. "It was all dried up, like sawdust." One of the Icelandic seamen who had joined the *Ironclad* at Hvalfjord had taken cover from the planes by hiding in a tank on the ship's deck. Another Icelander had stayed on deck and gotten a piece of shrapnel lodged in his back, apparently from a plane's machine guns. On the *Troubadour,* Jim North observed, "everyone was high as a kite on excitement and fear, laughing and shaking." On the *Ayrshire,* Gradwell gave the order to "splice the main brace"—to give each man an extra tot of rum for the day. The *Ayrshire's* coxswain did the honors, while accepting hearty congratulations for having maneuvered the trawler out of the way of the torpedoes. The cook gave each man a can of corned beef, and the men built enormous sandwiches. "Eagerly we discussed the events we had lived through," Baker wrote. "The words spilled from our mouths in the relief of the moment. We felt unconquerable. We couldn't lose now." Even the seasoned convoy veterans felt optimistic. Broome on the destroyer *Keppel* wrote in his diary: "My impression on seeing the resolution displayed by the convoy and its escort was that, provided the ammunition lasted, PQ-17 could get anywhere."

Few men in convoy PQ-17 realized their fight with the torpedo bombers would be the high point of the voyage. More than 3,200 miles away, a decision at the Admiralty headquarters in London was about to trigger a disastrous chain of events that neither the Allies nor the Germans, in all their planning for convoy PQ-17, had seen coming.

CHAPTER SIX

SCATTERED

First Sea Lord Sir Dudley Pound, Admiral of the Fleet and operational head of the Royal Navy, had complained that the Arctic convoys were "a most unsound operation" and "a regular millstone around our necks." As convoy PQ-17 lumbered through the Barents Sea on the Fourth of July 1942, that millstone hung heavily around the First Sea Lord's neck.

Pound understood the importance of the Arctic convoys, but that did not make him like them any better. The convoys mainly benefited the Soviet Union. In fact, they diverted American war supplies to the Red Army that otherwise would have gone to Britain. To Pound and most of his subordinates in the Admiralty, the convoys to Russia were more of a political necessity than a military one, which made the prospect of sacrificing precious Royal Navy ships and lives in the Arctic even less palatable than losing them in the North Atlantic. At least in the North Atlantic, the Royal Navy was protecting ships and supplies heading for Britain.

The British had lost two cruisers on Arctic convoy duty in only the past few months. Those losses had followed the losses of two Royal Navy battleships in the Pacific and a third, the HMS *Hood,* off Iceland. The *Hood* had been sunk by the *Tirpitz*'s sister ship the *Bismarck* in 1941 with a staggering loss of 1,415 lives. Although the Royal Navy was still the most powerful navy on earth, it had no way of replacing such losses. It was critically short of aircraft carriers and convoy escort vessels, with the war's end nowhere in sight.

Pound could not shake the fear that protecting convoy PQ-17 from the *Tirpitz* would cost the Royal Navy yet more of its dwindling supply of powerful warships. He had received no reports on the *Tirpitz*'s whereabouts since the German battleship's berth at Trondheim had been discovered empty on the afternoon of July 3. Pound knew nothing about the restrictions Hitler had placed on the *Tirpitz*'s movements. For all he knew, the ship had already raced out of the Norwegian fjords near the North Cape and was knifing through the Barents Sea, readying its 15-inch guns to savage convoy PQ-17 and its escorts.

Pound was sixty-four years old and had spent most of his life as a Royal Navy officer. He had risen through the ranks by single-minded dedication and tireless work rather than tactical brilliance or force of personality. He had served as flag captain on a battleship during the Battle of Jutland, the greatest naval engagement of World War I. Some of his superiors thought him ill suited for the post of First Sea Lord because he tended to take on too much responsibility and to dismiss opposing views. But the untimely deaths and illnesses of other contenders for the job had left it to him in 1939—just in time to lead the Royal Navy into the crucible of World War II. Pound had spent the first three years of the war toiling for long hours under incredible stress. He had been diagnosed with a brain tumor that eventually would kill him. An arthritic hip forced him to limp painfully from place to place with a cane. The discomfort also made it hard for Pound to sleep at night, and he was known to nod off in the middle of meetings.

Churchill placed great trust in Pound, though he sometimes

grumbled Pound was too cautious and lacked "the Nelson touch"—the boldness of the British naval icon Admiral Horatio Nelson. Being compared unfavorably to Nelson was no grave insult. But some of Pound's subordinates thought he had a different flaw: He tended to meddle in decisions that properly belonged to commanders in the field.

While convoy PQ-17 was fighting off the Junkers and Heinkels, Pound gathered his senior naval staff at the Admiralty headquarters in Whitehall. He oversaw a series of meetings that occupied much of the afternoon of July 4. No one could offer him any new information about the *Tirpitz* or the Germans' intentions. That evening, Pound left his office and limped to the Citadel, the bombproof underground chamber that served as Britain's nerve center for the sea war. The Citadel's centerpiece was a large table on which the movements of convoys and the reported movements of U-boats were represented by ship models, flags, and other markers. The markers were constantly moved from one place to another as new intelligence arrived from code breakers, reconnaissance pilots, and resistance fighters watching the docks and shorelines. The Citadel also housed the offices of Rodger Winn, who was responsible for tracking U-boats, and his counterpart Norman Denning, who tracked German surface warships, including the *Tirpitz*. It was Denning and Winn that Pound wanted to see.

Pound asked Denning where he thought the *Tirpitz* was. Denning said he was confident the battleship was at Altenfjord. Pound asked if Denning could assure him the *Tirpitz* was not already at sea, rushing at convoy PQ-17. Denning acknowledged he could not. The information in recent batches of decoded German messages was too sparse. Denning pointed out, however, that the absence of information was significant in itself. There had been no flurry of German messages that normally would accompany a major ship movement. Nor had the Germans notified their U-boats in the Barents Sea that the *Tirpitz* was coming, which they surely would have done as a precaution to keep the *Tirpitz* from being torpedoed by mistake. Similarly, the Germans certainly would send destroyers to sea ahead of the *Tirpitz* to make sure the way was clear. But British submarines on patrol near the North Cape had sighted no destroyers.

The fictional British detective Sherlock Holmes solved one of his most famous cases by noticing that a dog had not barked in the night when it logically would have been expected to make a racket. Denning essentially was suggesting to Pound that if the *Tirpitz* had put to sea, some kind of "dog" would have barked. Pound was not satisfied. He said Denning was providing "negative information" when Pound needed positive proof. Denning said he expected newly decoded German messages from Bletchley Park soon and would inform Pound as soon as they arrived. Pound moved on to the U-boat tracking room, where Winn told him a dozen U-boats were in the vicinity of convoy PQ-17. The U-boats obviously posed a threat to any British warship near the convoy. If an Allied cruiser was torpedoed in the Barents Sea, it would be hundreds of miles from a friendly port, at the mercy of German planes and submarines.

Pound returned to the Admiralty headquarters in Whitehall. He gathered half a dozen of his senior staff around an eighteenth-century wooden table in the dark-paneled boardroom, beneath paintings of Admiral Nelson and King William IV. Pound told his staff he was considering withdrawing the escorts from convoy PQ-17 and instructing the merchant ships to scatter. That way, at least some of the merchant ships probably would reach Archangel, and the Royal Navy would avoid a potentially disastrous confrontation with the *Tirpitz*. He went around the table asking his staff officers for their opinions. All but one opposed scattering the convoy. But the Admiralty was not a democracy; the decision belonged solely to the First Sea Lord. The way he reached it was "almost melodramatic," recalled his director of operations, Admiral John Eccles.

The First Sea Lord leaned back in his leather-backed chair and closed his eyes—an invariable attitude of deep meditation when making difficult decisions; his hands gripped the arm of the chair, and his features which had seemed almost ill and strained, became peaceful and composed. After a few moments the youthful Director of Plans . . . whispered irreverently, "Look, Father's fallen asleep." After thirty long seconds, Admiral Pound reached for a Naval pad Message and announced, 'the convoy is to be dispersed.' As he said this, he made a curious but eloquent gesture to the others, indicating that this was his decision, but he was taking it alone.

It was a shocking decision, a bet-the-house gamble based not on any fresh knowledge but on a continuing lack of knowledge. It went against the best intelligence the Admiralty possessed of the *Tirpitz*'s movements. It usurped virtually all decision making from Pound's veteran officers in the field, while leaving them to puzzle over its meaning and deal with its consequences. It would scatter dozens of ill-equipped ships and thousands of frightened men across an utterly unforgiving landscape, with the enemy already upon them. Although Pound was trying to save lives, the scatter order would amount to, as Admiral Tovey had put it, "sheer bloody murder."

Pound wasted no time in communicating his decision to the convoy leaders in the Arctic. At 9:11 p.m. on July 4, he personally wrote a signal to send to Admiral L. H. K. Hamilton, commander of the cruiser force:

> MOST IMMEDIATE: *Cruiser force withdraw to westward at high speed.*

When the message arrived, the cruiser force was within sight of convoy PQ-17, closer, in fact, than at any previous point in the voyage, because the cruisers were refueling from the oiler sailing with the convoy. The "withdraw" signal had included no explanation of why, but the instruction to withdraw "at high speed" suggested urgency. Hamilton concluded the Admiralty's order meant the *Tirpitz* was fast approaching from the west and that the cruisers were being diverted to intercept it. Hamilton could not ask for clarification without breaking radio silence and revealing the cruisers' position to the Germans. One of Hamilton's cruisers had just launched a Walrus spotter plane to survey the ice ahead of convoy PQ-17. The Walrus was still visible in the distance, but the cruiser could not attract the pilot's attention to tell him to come back. The cruisers would have to leave the Walrus pilot to fend for himself.*

Pound's "withdraw" signal went out to all the cruisers and was copied to Jack Broome, the commander of the convoy's core escort force. The Admiralty's signal had not mentioned the core escorts, and Broome did not think it affected them. Unlike Hamilton, Broome did not recognize at first that the "withdraw" signal heralded a dramatic turn of events. After all, the original plan for convoy PQ-17 had been for the cruisers to turn around after the convoy passed Bear Island. Broome assumed the "withdraw" signal was nothing more than Pound's long-anticipated order for the cruisers to do so. Given that the cruisers were in dangerous waters, withdrawing them "at high speed" only made sense. Broome still felt optimistic after the convoy's performance against the torpedo bombers. His sense of humor remained intact as well: After a British submarine commander signaled that he hoped to keep his vessel on the surface for as long as possible if the Germans attacked, Broome—whose vessel was not a sub but a destroyer—replied, "So do I." Broome did not yet suspect what Pound had in mind.

Twelve minutes after the "withdraw" signal, Pound ordered a second signal sent to all the escort warships. This signal bore the less urgent heading of "IMMEDIATE":

> Owing to the threat from surface ships, convoy is to
> disperse and proceed to Russian ports.

Once Broome saw the second signal, he concluded, as Hamilton had, that the *Tirpitz* was hurtling at convoy PQ-17 and that the cruisers were

---

* The Walrus would return from its two-and-a-half-hour ice reconnaissance mission, low on fuel, to find the cruiser long gone, but another Allied ship would take the air crew aboard and the Walrus in tow.

being sent to intercept it. Broome immediately suggested that the freighter *Empire Tide* launch the fighter plane from its catapult to shoot down the Shad, which would make the convoy harder for the *Tirpitz* to find. But the Admiralty's second signal was maddeningly short of vital information. How close was the *Tirpitz*? Why were the merchant ships dispersing to "Russian ports" when the only port available was Archangel? More broadly, what was going on? Pound had promised to keep his commanders in the Arctic fully informed; now he seemed to be withholding information.

While Broome and the other escort commanders puzzled over the second signal, one of Pound's aides reminded him that the proper nautical term for breaking up a convoy was not "disperse" but "scatter." The aide pointed out that the merchant captains might misinterpret "disperse" to mean split into small groups, whereas Pound wanted each ship to sail alone. At 9:36 p.m.—thirteen minutes after the second signal and twenty-five minutes after the first—Pound ordered a third signal sent:

MOST IMMEDIATE: *Convoy is to scatter.*

On the bridge of the destroyer *Keppel*, Broome looked up to see the ship's chief telegraph operator holding out the signal to him. The telegraph operator was out of breath. He had run all the way from the telegraph room to the bridge. Broome stared at the paper in astonishment. The signal, he recalled later, "seemed to explode in my hand." The words were only part of what made the message so jarring. The way in which the three signals had been sent—one quickly following the last, with no context—suggested a crisis unfolding so fast that the Admiralty could not keep up with it or even take time to explain it.

Every sailor on lookout duty began frantically scanning the horizon for the *Tirpitz*. "We were all expecting . . . to see the cruisers open fire, or to see enemy masts on the horizon," Broome wrote. Everyone thought that an enemy attack "was now not only a possibility, it was a certainty, it was on the convoy's doorstep."

Moments after the signal was sent, Pound was informed by one of Denning's colleagues in the Citadel that freshly decrypted Enigma messages supported Denning's view that the *Tirpitz* was still at Altenfjord, ten hours and hundreds of miles from the convoy. The new messages—which were hours old—showed the Germans had been expecting the *Tirpitz* to anchor at Altenfjord. In addition, the U-boats had been assured there were no German surface ships in the "operational area" off the North Cape. To Pound, the new messages were unpersuasive; they were further "negative information" rather than proof. They did not change his mind. "We have decided to scatter the convoy," Pound said, "and that is how it must stand."

The men on the merchant ships of convoy PQ-17 still had no inkling that anything unusual was happening. They had not been privy to the Admiralty's three signals. They had not even been informed that the *Tirpitz* had left Trondheim. They were going about their routine shipboard duties, grateful for a lull in the German attacks. Some were still talking about their successful fight against the torpedo bombers. Others were taking the opportunity to get a little sleep. Not one of them was aware of the catastrophe about to engulf them.

Broome, as commander, had the duty of breaking the news to them. Although he felt certain the Admiralty had compelling reasons for issuing the scatter order, Broome keenly felt the weight of having to implement it. That simple act would instantly transform the calm, orderly convoy into a chaotic scramble for self-preservation. "I was angry at being forced to break up, to disintegrate such a formation, and to tear up the protective fence we had wrapped round it, to order each of these splendid merchantmen to sail on by her naked, defenceless self," Broome wrote later. The moment he relayed the scatter order, he knew, "convoy PQ-17 would cease to exist."

Broome dutifully instructed the signalman on the *Keppel* to hoist the pennant meaning "scatter" onto the destroyer's signal halyards. The scatter pennant was white with a red St. George's cross extending along its

Hvalfjord—"Whale Fjord" in Icelandic—the remote, gloomy staging area for convoy PQ-17 and other Allied convoys preparing to sail for North Russia.

The American freighter *Mary Luckenbach* explodes on the Arctic run after a German bomb ignited its cargo of ammunition. This sinking occurred in convoy PQ-18 in September 1942.

Even in midsummer, mariners on the voyage to North Russia encountered ice in virtually all its forms.

James Baker North III as he looked as a young seaman in World War II, "5-foot-10 and 125 pounds with bad tonsils and a loud mouth," as he put it.

Ensign Howard E. Carraway, U.S. Naval Reserve, at his graduation from Navy Armed Guard school. A South Carolina farm boy, he was assigned to command the Navy gun crew on the freighter SS *Troubadour*.

Lieutenant William Carter of the U.S. Naval Reserve and his fiancée, Ann Whitmore, decided to wait until after convoy PQ-17 returned to marry.

A monstrous storm wave looms before a British escort warship on an Arctic convoy run.

The old freighter SS *Troubadour*, which was sent to the Soviet Union crammed with war supplies and flying the Panamanian flag to avoid U.S. Coast Guard safety requirements.

The freighter SS *Ironclad* in 1929, when she was named the *Mystic*.

In Moscow, Soviet dictator Joseph Stalin (second from right) beams as Soviet foreign minister Vyacheslav Molotov (seated, center) prepares to sign a pact in 1940 allying the Soviet Union with Nazi Germany. German foreign minister Joachim von Ribbentrop stands directly behind Molotov. Stalin originally forged an alliance with Hitler rather than with Britain and the United States.

Adolf Hitler tours a German warship. The Führer never felt comfortable with naval warfare, declaring at one point, "On land I am a hero, but at sea I am a coward." However, he was determined to stop the flow of supplies via convoy to the Soviet Union.

President Franklin D. Roosevelt wanted to use the convoys as a first step in establishing a relationship of trust with Stalin. British prime minister Winston Churchill, shown here fishing with Roosevelt at the presidential retreat Shangri-La (later renamed Camp David) in Maryland in 1941, did not believe Stalin trusted anyone, nor should he be trusted in return.

Churchill did most of the traveling to hold together the Grand Alliance of Britain, the United States, and the Soviet Union. Here he lands in Africa in 1943 to relieve an underperforming general. Churchill was on his way to Moscow for a stormy meeting with Stalin.

The North Cape of Norway, a rock cliff jutting into the Arctic from the northernmost tip of continental Europe. The Germans built a stronghold for air and sea forces near the cape.

The British armed fishing trawler *Ayrshire*, as photographed by Ensign Howard E. Carraway from the deck of the *Troubadour*. In the right foreground is the turret gun of one of the tanks Carraway armed so that it could shoot at planes.

A glass-nosed Heinkel 111 light bomber, one of the planes the Germans used to attack the Arctic convoys.

The German battleship *Tirpitz*—the "Big Bad Wolf"—hidden between the rock walls of a Norwegian fjord.

Dancing girls perform for the crew of the *Tirpitz*. For all its firepower, the battleship was largely kept out of action, and the German Navy felt it was necessary to arrange entertainment for the bored sailors.

Lieutenant Leo J. Gradwell of the Royal Navy Volunteer Reserve, an independently minded Oxford scholar, barrister, and yachtsman, aboard the *Ayrshire*.

Royal Navy seaman Walter John Baker, a crewman on the *Ayrshire*.

Members of the *Ayrshire*'s crew pose for the camera while conducting a gunnery drill.

A member of a U.S. Navy gun crew aboard the destroyer USS *Wainwright* gazes out over convoy PQ-17 near the start of the voyage. The gunners grew nervous as the convoy approached Bear Island, where it would come within range of the German bombers.

Convoy PQ-17 as photographed from a German reconnaissance plane—the "Shad"—early in the convoy's voyage to North Russia.

German bombers close in on the convoy on the morning of the Fourth of July, 1942.

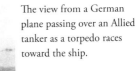

The view from a German plane passing over an Allied tanker as a torpedo races toward the ship.

A mariner's eye view of an attacking bomber. The blurry objects in the foreground are apparently one of the ship's masts and part of the vessel's superstructure.

The Soviet tanker *Azerbaijan* is engulfed by smoke and flames
after a bomb hit its auxiliary fuel bunker.

Sir Dudley Pound, First Sea Lord (center), who gave the order to scatter Convoy PQ-17.

The scatter order.

The freighter *Troubadour* in the process of being painted white to blend in with the ice field.

The *Troubadour* (foreground) and the *Ironclad* (background) approach the mouth of the Matochkin Shar, a narrow strait bisecting the remote Soviet archipelago Novaya Zemlya.

An unidentified Allied freighter in convoy PQ-17 is torpedoed in the Barents Sea after the scatter order. This photo was taken from a U-boat.

A U-boat enters a mass of wreckage from a sunken PQ-17 ship. Some of the survivors are barely visible clinging to wreckage in the middle distance.

The American freighter *Carlton* sinks in the Barents Sea after being torpedoed.

Lifeboats with survivors from the *Carlton* adrift on the Barents Sea. This photo was taken from a U-boat that subsequently took many of the castaways prisoner.

Survivors of the sunken American freighter *Washington* shiver in their lifeboats on the icy Barents Sea.

Some of the shipwrecked *Washington* survivors on the cold, rocky "beach" of Novaya Zemlya. The men huddled around driftwood fires and ate eider ducks they managed to catch.

A U.S. Navy tally sheet, with markings in pencil, illustrates the struggles by Allied leaders to determine what had become of the various merchant ships in convoy PQ-17.

Survivors of sunken Allied ships in convoy PQ-17 arrive at the docks in Archangel after being rescued by Soviet vessels.

A white-camouflaged U-boat, possibly the U-255, returns triumphant to its port in Narvik, Norway, after a devastating attack on the scattered convoy PQ-17. The large flag flown by the sub was taken from an Allied merchant ship it sank.

Hvalfjord, the starting point of convoy PQ-17, is a remote corner of Iceland even now.

The busy, gritty Murmansk waterfront in 2017.

This massive concrete statue of "Alyosha," honoring the defenders of Murmansk and the surrounding territory, towers above the harbor of Murmansk today.

length and breadth. The pennant was included in the merchant ships' Admiralty-issued codebooks, but most of the civilian mariners had never noticed it or given it any thought. No one at the preconvoy conference in Iceland had mentioned the possibility of scattering the convoy. When the pennant was hoisted onto the destroyer's signal halyards, the merchant captains had to thumb through their codebooks to see what it meant. Even when they found it, they were not sure what to make of it under the circumstances.

On the bridge of the British freighter *River Afton*, Commodore Jack Dowding, the convoy's civilian commander, recognized the pennant but assumed it was a mistake. Why would the convoy be scattered? Dowding signaled Broome on the *Keppel* to confirm the message, and waited for a correction. Instead the *Keppel* confirmed the scatter order. Dowding still did not believe it. Broome ordered the *Keppel* to turn around and steam back to the *River Afton* so the two men could speak in person. Broome and Dowding had known each other for years. As the *Keppel* approached, Broome saw Dowding waiting on a wing of the *River Afton*'s bridge, looking calm but puzzled.

Broome described to his old friend the signals he had received from the Admiralty. Dowding kept his thoughts and feelings to himself. Broome imagined him wondering if the leaders of the Admiralty had lost their minds. In any case, there was nothing more for Broome and Dowding to discuss, and no time for them to waste.

Broome wondered what he was supposed to do with the convoy's core escort force, including the six destroyers as well as the corvettes, antiaircraft ships, minesweepers, rescue ships, trawlers, and other small antisubmarine vessels. They had originally been assigned to protect convoy PQ-17 all the way to Russia. But the point of the scatter order was for all the ships in the convoy to get as far apart from one another as possible. How could the core escort protect thirty-three widely scattered ships? On the other hand, Broome thought, the *Keppel* and the other five destroyers in the core escort might help Hamilton's cruisers in a showdown with the

Tirpitz. The destroyers might even tip the scales in such a fight. Broome proposed that the six destroyers leave the convoy and join Hamilton's cruisers in their run westward. Hamilton agreed: He needed all the help he could get against the *Tirpitz.* Gun crews on the cruisers already were replacing antiaircraft shells with armor-piercing shells in expectation of trading salvos with the *Tirpitz.*

The news of the scatter order was just starting to spread to the men on the merchant ships. The mariners watched in puzzlement as the cruisers and destroyers raced past them. At least one of the big warships cut through the still orderly convoy. The effect on the mariners' morale was profound. Their protectors appeared to be running away. "Come back!" shouted a seaman on the American freighter *Honomu.* As the *Keppel* prepared to join the exodus, Broome sent a farewell message to Dowding on the *River Afton.* He might have been speaking to all the men being left behind.

Sorry to leave you like this. Goodbye and good luck.
It looks like a bloody business.

Dowding replied:

Thank you. Goodbye and good hunting.

Some American and British sailors on the departing warships found it painful to look back. "We hate leaving PQ-17 behind," wrote Douglas Fairbanks Jr. on the cruiser USS *Wichita.* "It looks so helpless now since the order to scatter came through. The ships are going around in circles, like so many frightened chicks. Some can hardly move at all." Officers on the *Wichita* did not assume the cruisers and destroyers were racing to fight the *Tirpitz.* "We all feel we have run away," Fairbanks wrote. "We cannot yet analyze the situation. Information is restricted. We are 'high-tailing it' westward. We could have been a great help [to the convoy] against the air and submarine attack. And what if there was a risk? What kind of high command have we that, with such a great force in operation, we cannot fight it out? Have the British become gun-shy? How can wars be won this way? Those are the angry questions heard throughout the ship."

Soon the cruisers and destroyers were swallowed up by a fog bank. The convoy's small escort vessels began steaming away. Broome had concluded they also were supposed to scatter. He ordered them to "proceed independently to Archangel." The only exceptions were the convoy's two British submarines, whose commanders Broome instructed to act on their own, thinking they might get a chance to sink the *Tirpitz*. Broome's order raised practical questions for the commanders of the small surface escort ships—and, arguably, moral questions as well. Most of the small escorts were antisubmarine vessels, equipped with sonar and depth charges to fight off U-boats. They had little or no defense against bombers. The antiaircraft ships, on the other hand, were equipped to defend themselves against planes but not U-boats. The captain of the antiaircraft ship *Palomares*—the highest-ranking officer remaining after Broome's departure—recognized his ship's vulnerability to U-boats and ordered two of the minesweepers to join the *Palomares* and make a dash for the Russian coast. His order infuriated some men on the minesweepers, who thought they should stay and protect the helpless merchant ships regardless of orders. "It seemed wrong that my anti-submarine minesweeper was being used only to escort a heavily armed antiaircraft ship," the commander of one minesweeper wrote.

The commander of the second antiaircraft ship, the *Pozarica*, proposed gathering some of the merchant ships into a small convoy and trying to shepherd them to Russia. But the *Palomares*'s captain rejected that idea as a violation of the scatter order. At that point, the *Pozarica*'s captain followed the *Palomares*'s example and ordered three corvettes to join the *Pozarica* for its own dash to the coast. An officer on one of the corvettes pleaded with his captain to stay with the merchant ships: "My God, we can't just leave these poor devils to their fate and shove off."

Another officer hurled a chair in anger. Other men on the corvettes complained that the commanders of the antiaircraft ships were selectively interpreting the scatter order to save their own lives. The reality was more complicated. Each antiaircraft ship had more than three hundred men aboard, and their captains did not expect to reach land safely. The *Pozarica*'s captain advised each of his men to "make peace with his Maker." He said they might survive a fight with German destroyers but not with the *Tirpitz*. In any case, he vowed, "We will fight these ships to the last shell, and if need be, go down fighting."

The fact remained, however, that the fastest and best-armed of the small escort vessels left the slower, utterly vulnerable merchant ships behind.*

The merchant ships and trawlers in convoy PQ-17 were the last to scatter. Many of their captains were still trying to figure out what to do next. Even the most cynical had never expected to be left in the middle of the Barents Sea. "Now it was every man for himself, and the Devil, in the shape of a U-boat or a dive bomber, take the hindmost," wrote Walter Baker on the *Ayrshire*.

A coxswain on the trawler *Northern Gem* wrote:

> To say that all of us on the *Gem* were stunned would be putting it mildly. I can remember the words that I said at the time. "What are we splitting up for, we're better off as we are, on our own we have no chance at all." The more we thought and talked about it, the more horrified we became. I was only twenty-two, and like many others of my age, was still young

---

* After the war, the Dutch author Jan de Hartog wrote a novel entitled *The Captain,* based loosely on convoy PQ-17. The hero of de Hartog's story, the commander of one of the convoy's escort ships, faces the same choice the captains of the British antiaircraft ships faced, but he chooses to stay with the merchant ships. He explains his decision: "If I was concerned about man's humanity, to leave that convoy . . . to its fate in order to save my own skin would be moral suicide."

enough to want to live and come through this war, but now I felt that my time had come. It was probably only because I had a responsible position that I was able to keep my worst thoughts to myself. More than two-thirds of our crew had never been to sea before. . . . One of them acted up badly, constantly saying to everyone, "We'll never get there. . . ." I literally had to shake him by the shoulders to get him to stop saying what most of us were thinking; by saying it out loud, he was making everyone feel much worse.

Confusion engulfed the *Ironclad*. "Having heard the expression 'All hell broke loose' used many times as a figure of speech, we found ourselves in the middle of the real thing," Lieutenant William Carter wrote. Everyone on the *Ironclad*'s bridge agreed the scatter order meant the *Tirpitz* was coming. The codebook contained a diagram illustrating how to scatter a convoy—in a fan-shaped pattern, with ships veering out of formation at 10-, 20-, and 30-degree angles. Even so, Carter recalled, "Every ship was demanding further information and instructions." Commodore Dowding set an example by moving the *River Afton* out of its position at the head of the middle column and steaming ahead alone. "The rest of us followed her example and the fan began to take shape, becoming increasingly ragged," Carter wrote. Most of the ships were still blinking messages. The Shad continued to circle, but in a closer radius now that the destroyers and their 5-inch guns were gone. Carter imagined the German pilot looking down at the convoy and giddily radioing word to his superiors in Norway that convoy PQ-17 was breaking up.

Carter received a request from Phillip Moore, the *Ironclad*'s captain, to join him in his quarters. Moore appeared calm. He told Carter he had known many Germans and regarded them as "a logical people with a practical approach to problem solving." He felt certain the Germans would expect most of the merchant ships to run for the nearest Russian soil, and a few to turn around and try for Iceland. Moore therefore proposed a maneuver he said was so illogical, it might not occur to the Germans: The *Ironclad* would head north into the polar ice field. "If we can get even a few feet into the ice pack," the captain told Carter, "it will protect us from torpedoes." Moore gave the order to point the *Ironclad* in the direction of the North Pole. Carter liked the idea, although not nearly enough to feel optimistic. Only an hour before, he had imagined Archangel lying just over the horizon. Now Archangel seemed "half a world away . . . but the odds were that we would never see it."

Captain Salvesen and his fellow Norwegian officers on the *Troubadour* greeted the scatter order with a stream of curses. Everyone else on the bridge stood stunned. "Brought into the fire and then told there was no water," Howard Carraway wrote. "Our hearts hit the deck with a dismal thud." No one hurried to relay the news to the ordinary seamen. Jim North emerged from below deck to start his watch as a helmsman and wondered where all the ships were going. He jumped at the hoot of a ship's claxon and watched as one of the British escorts approached the *Troubadour*. A British officer with a megaphone paraphrased the scatter order. North could make out little except "Disperse and good luck!" Shaken but still confused, he made his way up to the bridge to take his turn at the helm.

North heard the captain tell someone that the *Troubadour*'s only chance was to head into the ice field. The captain expressed confidence that his experience on seal-hunting ships would enable him to keep the *Troubadour* afloat. He told North to point the ship north into the ice field. North instinctively glanced at the compass, but the compass needle was spinning around. The *Troubadour*, like most of the merchant ships in convoy PQ-17, was equipped with only a magnetic compass. Only a few of the now departed escort vessels had gyrocompasses that were not affected by their nearness to the Magnetic North Pole.*

---

* A gyrocompass is a nonmagnetic compass with a motorized gyroscope whose rotating axis, mounted in a horizontal plane, stays parallel to the earth's axis of rotation, and thus points to the geographical North Pole rather than the Magnetic North Pole.

On the bridge of the *Ayrshire,* Lieutenant Gradwell turned to his first officer, Richard Elsden, and asked in a calm voice, "Now what the hell are we going to do?" The scattering ships had few options. Some were running southeast in the direction of the Murman coast of Russia, which was 400 miles away. Archangel was 600 miles away. Other ships in the convoy appeared to be fleeing due east, toward a large, crescent-shaped Russian island named Novaya Zemlya. Novaya Zemlya was less than 300 miles away, but on the charts it looked like a frozen wasteland. The trawler *Northern Gem* flashed a signal inviting the *Ayrshire* to follow it eastward. Gradwell declined. He did not think the *Ayrshire* could win a race with the Germans across the Barents Sea.

Gradwell and Elsden agreed the *Ayrshire* should head north into the ice field and lie low until the Germans quit looking for them. Then, with any luck, the *Ayrshire* could pick her way east along the edge of the ice field to Novaya Zemlya, and from there to Archangel. First, however, the *Ayrshire* had a fundamental problem: It was getting low on coal. It might have enough for a straight run to Archangel, but not for the long, round-about voyage Gradwell now envisioned. He would need to beg some coal from one of the old coal-burning freighters, and he would need to do it quickly, before all the merchant ships scattered. At the same time, Gradwell decided to see if any of the merchant ships wanted to accompany the *Ayrshire* into the ice.

To Gradwell, the scatter order resembled the clueless acts by official-dom he was accustomed to fighting in courtrooms. No matter how sensible the order might have seemed to the Admiralty in London, it made no sense in this remote stretch of the Barents Sea. Without a doubt it would get men killed. It was a terrible mistake, and Gradwell had no intention of obeying the order and abandoning the merchant ships. His men on the *Ayrshire* never expected him to. "My father had a very inde-pendent nature," his daughter, Mary Corrigan, recalled. "If he was told to do something he thought was wrong, he would not simply obey just be-cause of authority. He used to say to us children, 'You've got to think for yourself, you mustn't rely on other people to think for you, because they don't always know what they're doing, and they aren't there. You have to think on your feet.'" Gradwell ordered the helmsman to steer the *Ayrshire* toward the ice field, where a couple of the merchant ships were heading. A corvette signaled, "Where are you going?" Gradwell replied, "To hell, and the first one to come back, we hope."

The *Ayrshire* caught up to the *Troubadour* near the edge of the ice barrier around midnight, as July 4 turned to July 5. Gradwell brought the trawler alongside the old freighter. He did not try to assume authority over Salvesen. As far as the merchant captains were concerned, the scatter order had obliterated any chain of command. Gradwell suggested the two vessels could simply help each other. The *Ayrshire* needed coal, which the *Troubadour* possessed in abundance. The *Troubadour* needed protection, and the *Ayrshire* had sonar, depth charges, and deck guns. Salvesen agreed readily to the partnership. The two vessels "sallied forth into the clear midnight sea," Carraway wrote. The midnight sun hung just above the horizon. The fog, for a change, had vanished entirely. The bright sunshine lifted Carraway's spirits, even though it made the ships easier for the Germans to spot. Carraway thought back to warm spring days in the South Carolina lowlands and wondered if he would ever see another one.

Less than an hour later, around 1:00 a.m. on the fifth, lookouts on the *Troubadour* and *Ayrshire* spotted another freighter heading north. It was the *Ironclad*. The *Ayrshire* approached and Gradwell invited the *Ironclad*'s captain to join the flight into the ice field. Moore quickly agreed. Soon the vessels encountered a fourth ship, the American freighter *Silver Sword*, whose cargo included several fully assembled fighter planes cabled to the main deck. The *Silver Sword*'s master, Captain Clyde W. Colbeth Jr. of Maine, agreed his vessel would join them too.

Carraway reflected that the four vessels comprising the new convoy were the dregs of convoy PQ-17—a fishing trawler and three rust-bucket freighters, with a total of four useful deck guns, plus the *Troubadour*'s three tanks. They were perhaps the last ships in the convoy that anyone would expect to survive its disintegration in the Barents Sea. But maybe together they would prove greater than the sum of their parts. Walter Baker on the *Ayrshire* wrote:

> We were only a very small ship with a very small armament, but the faith those American sailors had in us was wonderful to see. . . . The idea of spreading out to make a less concentrated target might have seemed all right on paper but there is still truth in the old saying, "There's safety in numbers." So northward we steamed together making as good a speed as was possible. It was a lovely night here up on the roof of the world, with no darkness to draw a curtain between us and the enemy.

The chill in the air intensified as the four vessels neared the ice barrier. They angled northwest, in the general direction of Spitsbergen, and hunted for an opening in the ice large enough to admit them. The *Ayrshire* stopped to effect minor repairs on its rudder. Gradwell again took the opportunity to "splice the main brace" and the crew again ate corned beef sandwiches. Gradwell wanted to make sure they had full stomachs in case the Germans came quickly. He ordered all the 4-inch shells in the trawler's magazine to be stacked on the gun platform, to avoid even a moment's delay in reloading. He ordered the crew to pile all the *Ayrshire*'s depth charges on the bow, along with several drums of oil. If the *Tirpitz* appeared, Gradwell told the crew, he would try to ram the trawler into the giant battleship.

UNTIL THE SCATTER ORDER, the Germans had experienced mostly frustration in their efforts to wipe out convoy PQ-17. The U-boats had proven ineffective, often losing the convoy in the fog. The Luftwaffe had lost four bombers while sinking three ships—a decent but unexceptional rate of return. German reconnaissance planes, still hampered by clouds and fog, had been unable to pinpoint the locations of Allied carriers near the convoy. There was still no point in even asking Hitler to set the *Tirpitz* loose.

Crew members on the *Tirpitz* spent a restless night wondering if they might finally see action. "There was a film show that evening to relax the nerves a bit," the French author Leonce Peillard wrote, "and then many of the crew came up on deck to admire the midnight sun. They had seen it go slowly down behind the snow-covered peaks, stop just as it was about to disappear, then rise again into the sky, more quickly this time, like a ball of fire. No one felt like turning in, and it took a good deal of admonition from the wiser heads, saying that they needed all the rest they could get before the big day. Even when they were in their hammocks, few got much sleep in their excitement and the lightness of the polar night."

As the men on the *Tirpitz* tossed and turned, the German admirals received a startling message: Convoy PQ-17 was breaking up. It did not occur to the Germans to attribute the breakup to the idle *Tirpitz*. They assumed the Allies had been unnerved by the air attacks. The German High Command's war diary said the convoy "was dispersed as a result of a heavy air raid on the evening of 4 July." But the Germans did not need to understand the reasons why they had been handed such a magnificent gift. All they had to do was seize it.

CHAPTER SEVEN
INTO THE ICE

The first thing Jim North noticed as the *Troubadour* crept into the ice field was a polar bear. Startled by the approaching ship, the bear scrambled away, looking back over its shoulder, and loped out of sight behind a ridge on a large ice floe. The bear was not the first the mariners had seen on the voyage, but the other bears had sat placidly on ice floes and peered at the convoy as it passed. This bear seemed to think its world had been invaded. On other floes North saw seals—the polar bears' chief prey—and enormous clouds of birds. North could spare no more than a glance at any of them. He was steering the *Troubadour* into a dazzling labyrinth of ice.

The polar ice field in the 1940s extended for millions of square miles—roughly two thirds of the area of the Arctic Ocean. Near the North Pole, the ice could reach a thickness of 12 feet and remain stable for years. But on the ice pack's outer edges, where the four ships were picking their way, the ice thinned to only a few feet in places. It was a jumble of floes, hummocks, and bergs, constantly shifting under the influence of the wind and the currents. Floes slammed together with enough force to pile up their ice into mounds and pressure ridges. Other floes broke apart with cracks like cannon shots.

The ice often separated to create long lanes of open water known as leads, wide enough for ships to pass through them. The mariners' guidebook *Arctic Pilot* warned that leads present "tempting opportunities to the mariner watching . . . from the open water, but when a vessel has once entered one of these leads, which are constantly changing and closing, all control is lost and [the ship] runs great risk of being crushed before an escape can be effected." Embedded in the ice were countless icebergs, some of them towering above the freighters' masts. Icebergs were far less stable than their bulk suggested. Large bergs could become hollowed out by the wind and current and suddenly implode, creating deadly waves and whirlpools. Smaller bergs became top-heavy and capsized when their underwater parts melted faster than their above-water parts. Because 90 percent of most icebergs lay beneath the surface, the danger was not always easy to spot. The ocean liner RMS *Titanic,* whose sinking in April 1912 had cost 1,503 lives, had not simply slammed into a massive wall of ice; it had struck the long, submerged "foot" of an iceberg whose visible portion the ship had avoided. Even ice floes too smooth and rounded to poke holes in ships' hulls could disable rudders and propellers. Navigating in ice was complicated by the thick fog that often clung to the edge where the ice met the open water. The *Arctic Pilot* recommended that ships discharge guns or blow steam whistles into fog banks near the ice edge so that the echo would betray any hidden bergs.

Seasoned ice sailors improved their chances of survival by heeding clues that nature provided. A phenomenon called "ice blink," a bright reflection of the sun on the undersides of clouds, suggested a large ice field nearby. Conversely, "water sky," a dark or unreflective area on the otherwise bright bottoms of clouds, signaled a stretch of open water. But the dangers of sailing in ice were so numerous that even the most experienced mariners fell victim. During the fifteen years preceding World War II,

106 Norwegian seal-hunting ships had been lost, along with thousands of lives. In 1940, the biggest seal-hunting ship in Hammerfest, the *Saalen*, was trapped by the ice and crushed, although the veteran crew managed to survive until another ship rescued them.

The captains of the *Ayrshire, Troubadour, Ironclad,* and *Silver Sword* agreed to halt their ships in a patch of open water only a short distance inside the ice field—just far enough for the ice to block any torpedoes that might be launched at them. The ships dropped anchor. Some of the men who had gotten little sleep for two days collapsed into their bunks. Others were still too excited to close their eyes. The captains conferred by blinking messages back and forth. Gradwell's only map was a *Times Handy Atlas,* a tourist publication, but it at least showed the Barents Sea. The ships were not far from a tiny speck of land named Hopen Island. Gradwell thought they might be able to anchor in the lee of the island and hide there until the fury of the German attacks subsided. No one wanted to venture any farther into the ice field than necessary.

The discussion by blinker was still in progress when the sonar operator on the *Ayrshire* detected underwater explosions to the south. Suddenly the ships' radios, which had been silent since the convoy scattered, erupted with SOS calls. Some of the merchant ships that had tried to outrun the Germans across the Barents Sea had already lost the race. Howard Carraway entered the *Troubadour's* radio shack and saw the radioman scribbling frantically, writing down all the messages as they came in. One merchant ship reported a nearby ship being attacked by U-boats. Another vessel was beset by torpedo bombers. One stricken ship gave its location as only 20 miles south of the four ships in the ice field. Gradwell signaled that the time had come to head deeper into the ice. All three merchant captains agreed. The ships weighed anchor. "We were scared stiff," Carraway wrote to Avis. "Planes were within 20 miles, five minutes of us, and the trawler and our few guns were all the protection we had. The skies were clear and bright. . . . We manned our guns and waited. It was pretty awful I assure you. Poor 'Sparks'* got very sick, threw up over the rail, from fear and excitement."

The first SOS call marked the end of the British freighter *Empire Byron*. The U-703 fired four torpedoes at the ship before a fifth torpedo found its engine room. The violence of the explosion hurled trucks in the deck cargo high into the air. The ship sank too fast for the radio operator to send a distress call. The SOS came from a nearby American freighter, the *Peter Kerr*. The sinking of the *Empire Byron* claimed the lives of nineteen men. The dead included a man whose legs were pinned in the wreckage as the water rose over his head. A shipmate struggled in vain to free him. His last words were, "For Christ's sakes, don't leave me. . . . Chop my bastard legs off." Paradoxically, the death toll might have been higher if not for the frigid weather: A British sailor cut his legs badly while clambering into a lifeboat, but his wounds froze over before he could bleed to death.

The U-703 surfaced and approached the lifeboats, which together contained forty-two men. A blond German officer emerged from the main hatch, accompanied by a subordinate with a machine gun. The officer spoke excellent English. He chided the survivors for not rowing their lifeboats more efficiently and asked them if they were Bolsheviks. When they said no, he asked them why they were helping the Russians. He seemed to be taunting them. Another member of the U-boat crew filmed the encounter. The blond German asked the *Empire Byron*'s officers to identify themselves. The mariners knew that the Germans sometimes took ships' officers as prisoners; the *Empire Byron*'s officers had removed the epaulettes from the shoulders of their uniforms to avoid giving away their ranks. The men in the lifeboats lied that all their officers had been killed. The Germans noticed a castaway dressed in a British Army coat. He was an engineer traveling to Russia to instruct the Soviets

---

* On merchant ships, the radioman was always nicknamed Sparks. Along similar lines, a ship's carpenter was always called Chips.

on how to operate some British tanks the convoy was carrying. The crew of the U-703 took him prisoner and then distributed biscuits, sausages, and cans of food to the men in the lifeboats. The men asked how far they were from land and the Germans told them 250 miles, apparently referring to Novaya Zemlya. The U-703's captain, Hans Bielfeld, broke radio silence to report he had sunk a 10,000-ton freighter loaded with tanks and had captured a British officer.

Bielfeld added, "Convoy in rout . . . I am following hard."

The *Empire Byron*'s two lifeboats would drift for six days through the cold and fog before the occupants were picked up by a British corvette that had been dispatched from Archangel to search for survivors. By the time they were rescued, the men in the boats—including two apprentices, ages fifteen and sixteen—were subsisting on rations of two ounces of water and small helpings of biscuits and two malted milk tablets every six hours. Some men had resorted to drinking salt water, which exacerbated their thirst and caused them to hallucinate. All the survivors were exhausted and most were frostbitten. Several ended up losing fingers, toes, or feet to amputation.

The second SOS to crackle over the *Troubadour*'s radio came from the American freighter *Carlton*—the Jonah ship. After the scatter order, the *Carlton* had been sailing alone across the Barents Sea when a torpedo from the U-88 crashed into its starboard side. The explosion ignited the oil in the fuel tanks and flooded the engine room, killing all three men on watch there. The Armed Guard crew manned the guns but could not see anything to shoot at. Flames spread through the old freighter, whose cargo included TNT. The captain gave the order to abandon ship, even though only one of the *Carlton*'s three lifeboats was still intact. Men slid down ropes into the freezing water and tried to scramble into the lifeboat or onto rafts. The U-boat sped off in search of other victims, which were in plentiful supply. German seaplanes soon landed on the water and took twenty-two of the *Carlton* survivors as prisoners. Seventeen other survivors were left to try to row or sail the lifeboat to Russia.

THE SOS CALLS from the sinking merchant ships also came over the radios of the British and American cruisers and destroyers that had left the convoy to race "westward at high speed." As the hours passed, the men on those warships stopped expecting the *Tirpitz* to appear out of the fog to engage them in a ferocious battle. The men were confused. Why had they left the convoy in such haste? Five hours after the scatter order, they received a new message from the Admiralty saying that the German warships were "presumed" to be near the North Cape but "IT IS NOT REPEAT NOT CERTAIN THEY ARE AT SEA." The revelation that the Admiralty had scattered the convoy on flimsy intelligence shocked the men on the warships, including Admiral L. H. K. Hamilton, the commander of the cruiser force, who had assumed the Admiralty knew more about the *Tirpitz*'s whereabouts than he did. Hamilton could imagine how the sailors under his command felt about leaving the convoy, and he sent them a message of encouragement:

> I know you will all be feeling as distressed as I am at having to leave that fine collection of ships to find their own way to harbor. The enemy under cover of shore-based aircraft have succeeded in concentrating a far superior force in this area. We are therefore ordered to withdraw. We are all sorry that the good work of the [cruiser force] could not be completed. I hope we shall all have a chance of settling this score with Hun soon.

No one was more distressed than Commander Broome, who had pulled the six destroyers from convoy PQ-17's core escort because he thought they could better protect the convoy by racing west with the cruisers to intercept the *Tirpitz*. Broome felt betrayed by the Admiralty. He signaled Hamilton that he was ready to turn his destroyers around and go back to the convoy. Hamilton replied it was too late: The Allied warships were already 150 miles from the point where the convoy had scattered. Broome noted ruefully that while the Royal Navy offered detailed instructions for how to scatter a convoy, it offered no guidance for putting one back together.

Broome did not know it, but officers on one of his destroyers, the HMS *Offa,* had discussed faking a mechanical problem and sneaking the *Offa* back to protect the convoy. "We very nearly did this," recalled Vice Admiral W. D. O'Brien, who was a lieutenant on the *Offa* at the time. All his life, O'Brien would regret that he and other officers on the *Offa* did not press their captain to disregard the Admiralty's order and turn their ship around. "Our instinct that we should turn back was right," O'Brien recalled. "[I]t was a moment to disobey; there must always be a sense of shame that we did not do so."

The captain of the American cruiser USS *Wichita* felt it necessary to produce a special edition of the ship's newspaper explaining the events of the previous day and declaring the Allies did not lack courage: "No one can accuse us of ever having a faint heart, nor can anyone say the British lack 'guts'; after all, they have been fighting this war for nearly three years; for one whole year they fought it alone. . . . Anyone who has seen the people of [the bombed cities of] London, of Liverpool, Bristol, Portsmouth, Coventry or Southampton can testify to their worth."

A few hours after the luckless *Carlton* was torpedoed, the American freighter *Peter Kerr*—which had sent the SOS call on behalf of the *Empire Byron*—was attacked by a squadron of Heinkel 115 seaplanes. The Heinkels kept dropping torpedoes and the freighter kept swerving to avoid them. The *Peter Kerr* managed to dodge thirteen torpedoes in a duel that dragged on for nearly two hours. Then four Stuka dive-bombers took over the attack, swooping down on the ship with their signature high-pitched raptor shrieks. The Stukas dropped incendiary bombs in capsules that peeled open in midflight to release dozens of little sticks that would ignite where they landed. The sticklike incendiaries littered the *Peter Kerr* and set fires all over the ship. Flames destroyed the radio room and licked at three U.S.-built planes chained to the main deck. A near-miss bomb disabled the *Peter Kerr*'s steering gear. The ship's officers, crew, and Armed Guard escaped into two lifeboats. The boats reached a safe distance from the ship before the fire ignited volatile cargo in the holds and the *Peter Kerr* exploded. The only casualties were the ship's 6,600 tons of planes, trucks, steel, food, and explosives—and, perhaps, the Russians whose lives that cargo might have saved.

A short distance from the *Peter Kerr,* the American freighter *Honomu* shuddered as a torpedo from the U-456 burst into its engine room. The *Honomu* had been running southeast when a Blohm & Voss 138 spotted it and summoned the U-boats. The U-456's torpedo disabled the *Honomu*'s engines and killed two men in the engine room. The captain gave the order to abandon ship, moments before a second torpedo shook the vessel. Only one lifeboat remained functional, so most of the thirty-seven survivors had to clamber onto rafts, which were little more than wooden pallets nailed to floating drums. The U-boat did not stop to interrogate the survivors.

The carnage was just getting started at 11:00 a.m. on July 5 when the sky west of Bear Island finally cleared enough for a lone German reconnaissance plane to spot the British carrier *Victorious* sailing with convoy PQ-17's distant cover force, nearly 800 miles from the scattered merchant ships. That was the reassuring news Raeder had been waiting for. He managed to reach Hitler quickly and informed the Führer that no Allied carrier was in a position to threaten the *Tirpitz*. Hitler agreed to unleash the *Tirpitz,* along with the cruisers *Admiral Hipper* and *Admiral Scheer* and seven destroyers. By 3:00 p.m. on the fifth, the *Tirpitz* had passed through the submarine nets and other defenses at Altenfjord and out into the Barents Sea. The battleship turned east and raced in the direction of the southern tip of Novaya Zemlya to intercept any fleeing merchant ships before they could enter the White Sea. The German High Command was still skittish, and sent Admiral Schniewind on the *Tirpitz* a final cautionary message:

> A brief operation with partial successes is more important than a total victory involving major expenditure of time. Report at once if overflown by any enemy aircraft. Do not hesitate to break off operation if situation doubtful. On no account grant enemy success against fleet nucleus.

AS THE *AYRSHIRE, TROUBADOUR, IRONCLAD,* and *Silver Sword* crept farther into the ice field, they found it impossible to stay together. They passed in and out of one another's sight behind icebergs and pressure ridges. Jim North on the *Troubadour* could see only the tops of the masts of the other vessels. "Everywhere you looked was ice," Francis Brummer on the *Ironclad* recalled. "We saw icebergs as big as a city block. From the distance, they looked just like mountains. It was like you were in northern Arizona looking from the desert at the mountains." At first, the leads went on for miles. The weather kept changing back and forth from fog to clouds to bright sunshine. "It was calm, quiet, no wind, no seas," Jim North recalled, "a kind of eerie twilight with some patches of fog and low clouds." North and the other helmsmen tried to keep the ships heading toward what they thought was north. But as the *Arctic Pilot* had pointed out, once a ship entered the ice field it lost control of its voyage; it had to go where the leads allowed it to go.

None of the ships had detailed charts of the ice field. The poor visibility and the lack of functioning compasses reduced navigation to guesswork. The captains could not even use dead reckoning—estimating a ship's position by its speed over a given period of time—because the ships constantly had to change speeds while maneuvering through the ice. Soon the leads narrowed. Ice scraped and clunked along the hulls on both sides. "The noise below decks as we ground our way through the ice was frightening," wrote Walter Baker on the *Ayrshire*. "Every moment it sounded as though the bulkhead would burst in under the pressure or be cut cleanly through as by a giant [can] opener." Elsden, the *Ayrshire*'s first officer, scrambled up to the crow's nest to look for a way forward.

Sometimes the leads disappeared entirely and the ships had to force their way through the ice as if they were icebreakers. The *Ayrshire* and *Troubadour* led the way because their bows were reinforced with concrete. North recalled that Captain Salvesen "would ease the bow up against the ice and push slowly until a crack would open up." As the ice grew thicker, the captains would nose the ship's bows up on top of the ice, and the weight of the ship would crack it. If the ice refused to give, the captains would back the ships up and try another spot. "One ship would break through the ice, another would follow it through the crack," recalled Brummer. The twenty-two-year-old *Troubadour* was no longer suited to the rough work of an icebreaker. "Frequently the old ship shakes and rattles from stem to stern as every timber in her creaks," Carraway wrote. Every man on deck scanned the clear sky for little black dots. Any seabird gliding across the southern horizon looked at first like a Heinkel 111. The ships were so deep in the ice field that they had no room to maneuver or even dodge a bomb or aerial torpedo. If they were ever spotted by the Germans, they were sunk, literally. Six days into their voyage, they were still 800 miles from Archangel. And now, they were getting farther away as they crept deeper into the ice field.

A larger-than-normal lead expanded into a pool of open water large enough for the ships to gather in a semicircle. More SOS messages from numerous convoy PQ-17 ships had come over the radios:

TWO SUBS ATTACKING.

BEING DIVE-BOMBED.

HAVE JUST BEEN TORPEDOED.

ATTACK BY SEVEN PLANES.

UNDER HEAVY ATTACK.

UNDER ATTACK BY AIRCRAFT.

Lieutenant Gradwell dispatched First Officer Elsden on a "morale-boosting" tour of the three American ships. Elsden scrambled cautiously over some pressure ridges to the *Troubadour,* which lowered him a rope ladder. As soon as Elsden came aboard, he had an idea: The big, gray freighters stood out plainly in the whiteness of the ice field. If a German plane came anywhere near, the ships would be impossible for the pilot to miss. Elsden asked if the *Troubadour* had any white paint aboard. Salvesen replied that the ship had a whole storage locker full of it. White paint was a key component of the ship's endless fight against rust. The paint was mixed with lampblack to create a battleship-gray sealant for parts of the freighter where rust had been chipped off. Elsden suggested painting the three freighters white, or at least painting their starboard sides, which faced south toward Norway.

Salvesen and the other captains quickly agreed. The ships' stewards rounded up every paintbrush they could find, along with any brooms, mops, and other objects capable of applying paint. Men were summoned from their bunks and card games and handed brushes and two-gallon buckets of paint. They were issued goggles to protect them from snow blindness, a temporary but painful loss of vision from prolonged exposure of the corneas of the eyes to the sun's ultraviolet rays. The men quickly discovered that the goggles steamed up from their breathing, so they set them aside. When they felt snow blindness coming on, they would retreat to the shade of the lower decks for a while. Some mariners painted as if their lives depended on it. On the *Troubadour,* Carraway wrote, "There were thirty and more brushes slapping white paint over our decks, housing, rails, boats, funnels, masts, forecastle, everywhere." Even the tanks were painted white.

While the painters worked, the *Ayrshire* came alongside the *Troubadour* and Gradwell joined Elsden, Salvesen, and Carraway for a "war conference." Carraway found both of the *Ayrshire's* officers "British to the core" in manners and speech. Gradwell suggested it was time for the ships to retreat out of the ice and start working their way east toward Novaya Zemlya. Salvesen thought it was too soon. He suggested the ships keep heading north until they could go no farther, and then lie low for a while longer. Gradwell agreed. Before returning to the *Ayrshire,* Gradwell suggested another source of camouflage: white linens. Soon the freighters' stewards were pulling dirty sheets and tablecloths from laundry hampers and spreading them across the ships' decks, weighting them down with spare fire bricks from the boilers. Some of the sheets were wrapped around the masts and tied in place with string.

Since the *Ayrshire* already was camouflaged with streaks of white paint, Walter Baker and some other men from the trawler rowed a small boat over to the *Silver Sword* to help its crew with the painting. The Brits and Americans traded sea stories and tobacco. Baker rejoiced at acquiring a can of Sir Walter Raleigh pipe tobacco, which he considered far superior to the British brands. He found the Yanks to be generous and sincerely grateful for the Brits' help. He also found them "somewhat naïve about war," and realized for the first time what a new experience it was for most of them.

Carraway painted the *Troubadour* for six hours straight and then flopped into his bunk. When he awoke several hours later, "the ship was a mass of white. I never saw such a transformation!" Not all the mariners were enthusiastic. The messmen grumbled that they ought to be paid overtime for painting the ship. "Everybody was bitching," North recalled. As usual, North had drawn one of the least desirable assignments. He and another mariner were ordered to paint the lower hull of the ship near the waterline while standing on a makeshift scaffold. The scaffold consisted of a 2x12 wooden plank suspended from the main deck by ropes on either end. The work was tedious and North's mind began to wander.

Suddenly he felt the 2x12 shifting under his feet. An ice floe was passing beneath the plank, upending it from below. North and his shipmate grabbed on to the ropes as the plank splashed into the icy water. They scrambled hand over hand up the ropes and sprawled out on the main deck, panting from the exertion. No one else on the ship had even noticed they were in danger, and an officer barked at them to quit lying around and get back to work. North silently cursed the officer, as well as his friend back in the States who had promised North "easy money" in the Merchant Marine. But he had to admit that painting the ships was smart. From the *Ayrshire,* Gradwell signaled the *Troubadour, Ironclad,* and *Silver Sword* that the white paint had rendered the vessels practically invisible in the ice field.

Farther south, however, the Germans were having no trouble locating and destroying the ships on the open water. The departure of the convoy's armed escorts freed the U-boats to travel on the surface without fear of being attacked. As a result, the U-boat commanders were able to stay in close touch by radio with the spotter planes, which directed them from one target to the next. A dense fog had lifted from the North Cape, allowing the Luftwaffe to launch three squadrons of fast Junkers 88 bombers—sixty-nine planes in all. Bombers swarmed over the British rescue ship *Zaafaran* and sank it. One of the ship's firemen dragged himself out of the freezing sea onto a raft and celebrated by bursting into the Al Jolson standard "How Deep Is the Ocean."

The singing fireman used his helmet to help paddle the raft through the floating wreckage and pick up other survivors. All ninety-seven men on the *Zaafaran*—officers and crew, medical personnel, and survivors of previously sunken vessels—were picked up by the rescue ship *Zamalek.*

A short distance to the north, a bomb from a Junkers 88 fell close enough to the British oiler *Aldersdale* to pierce its hull and send cold seawater pouring into the engine room. The ship sank but, for a change, the men on watch in the engine room survived.

On some of the fleeing merchant ships, discipline gave way to fear and apathy. Some mariners had lost interest in risking their lives after the scatter order. The American freighter *Pan Kraft* was maneuvering among ice floes when it was attacked by four Junkers 88 bombers. A near-miss bomb ruptured some of the ship's steam and oil lines, and the captain decided, as he later explained, "It was no use staying on the ship when it was being bombed." The second officer remained to help other crewmen escape into lifeboats, only to be killed, along with a seaman, when a bomber strafed the *Pan Kraft*'s deck with its machine guns.

The captain of the Dutch freighter *Paulus Potter* also ordered his crew to abandon ship after several near-miss bombs damaged the vessel. The bombers departed and the ship stayed afloat. Some men who had abandoned it rowed their lifeboats back to the *Paulus Potter,* went aboard to retrieve warm clothing from their quarters, and then got back in their lifeboats and rowed off. Later, the U-255 happened upon the abandoned *Paulus Potter,* which looked undamaged, and sent a boarding party to see if the freighter could be towed to Norway, where the Germans could use the American planes and tanks in its cargo against the Soviets. The boarding party concluded the ship was too badly damaged for towing, but the Germans were delighted to find secret papers describing the cargo, the composition of convoy PQ-17, and the Allied convoy routes to Russia. After collecting all the documents, the U-255 sank the *Paulus Potter* with torpedoes.

Men on other merchant ships fought hard. The Liberty ship *Daniel Morgan* dodged bombs while its Armed Guard gunners shot two Junkers 88s out of the sky. But the planes kept coming and the gunners grew exhausted after standing at their posts for twenty-eight hours with no rest. Their ammunition was running out. One of the guns overheated from constant firing and jammed. Finally, two bombs exploded close enough to the *Daniel Morgan* to separate the hull plates, and the ship took on water. The crew escaped in lifeboats. A U-boat surfaced and a German officer asked the survivors what cargo they were carrying. "General cargo," the captain lied, "food and leather." The German snapped, "I don't believe that," and ordered the lifeboats to follow his U-boat to Norway. They had traveled only a short distance when the U-boat suddenly sped off and left them.

The lifeboat survivors of the *Daniel Morgan* would be picked up the next day by the Soviet tanker *Donbass,* which had been fighting off air attacks since the breakup of the convoy. Members of the *Daniel Morgan's* Armed Guard unit immediately volunteered to man the *Donbass's* forward 3-inch gun, which was similar to a gun on the *Daniel Morgan.* The Americans helped the Soviet crew fight off attacks by several Junkers 88s and damaged one of the planes. The *Donbass* would reach Archangel safely and the Armed Guard men would be awarded medals by the Soviet government.

Elsewhere on the Barents Sea, the Germans were engaged in a feeding frenzy, with bombers and U-boats rushing from one helpless ship to the next. Bombers sank the American freighter *Fairfield City* and disabled the British freighter *Earlston.* Two other freighters, the *Washington* and the *Bolton Castle,* joined together to flee east toward Novaya Zemlya. But the Germans were expecting that. A Shad found the two ships, and dive bombers attacked them in waves, sinking the *Bolton Castle* and crippling the *Washington.* Both crews abandoned ship and frantically rowed their lifeboats away from their burning vessels and their explosive cargoes.

All over the Barents Sea, lifeboat survivors had to decide in which direction to row toward land. There was no obvious choice. The British captain of the *Bolton Castle* decided to point his lifeboat south toward the Russian mainland. The Dutch captain of the *Paulus Potter* decided to head east toward Novaya Zemlya. The two captains shook hands and wished each other luck.

The prospect of any merchant ship staying afloat looked so hopeless that when the American freighter *Olopana* came alongside the lifeboats from the *Washington* and *Paulus Potter,* the men in the lifeboats refused to be taken aboard the ship. They reasoned that the *Olopana* soon would be sunk as well, and that if they went aboard the ship now, they might not survive the *Olopana*'s sinking. They preferred to take their chances in their lifeboats, where the Germans would not shoot at them, and try to reach Novaya Zemlya. The *Olopana* kept going. The men in the lifeboats would next see the *Olopana* two days later, sinking into the Barents Sea after a U-boat attack killed six men on the ship.

The Germans' final victim on July 5 was Commodore Dowding's flagship, the *River Afton*. A torpedo from the U-703 blew away part of the ship's stern, and the captain gave the order to abandon ship. Dowding decided to stay and try to save the *River Afton,* or at least some of the men still aboard it. A second torpedo tore off the rest of the stern. Dowding ran to the bridge and threw the ship's secret documents overboard. He helped pull a badly injured man up from the flooded engine room by a rope tied around the man's waist. A third torpedo exploded into the *River Afton.* Dowding and a couple of other mariners loaded the injured man onto a raft and carried it across the steeply listing deck to launch it. The ship was breaking up. Dowding had just gotten the raft into the water when the *River Afton* turned turtle. One of its falling masts snagged the raft and capsized it, hurling Dowding, the injured man, and several other mariners into the frigid water. Dowding swam to the raft and righted it, then pulled the injured man aboard. Two cooks climbed on. Dowding secured the raft to two other rafts with men aboard. A short distance away, the captain's lifeboat was towing another raft full of survivors. The U-boat surfaced and a German officer, speaking good English, apologized for sinking their ship and leaving them in such a godforsaken place. He advised them to row for Novaya Zemlya, which was about 200 miles away. But the men on the rafts had nothing to row with.

The SOS calls from the *River Afton* and other recent victims came over the radios of the antiaircraft ship *Pozarica* and the three corvettes that were fleeing as a unit to Novaya Zemlya. They had left the plodding merchant ships far behind. The new distress calls rekindled the anger of some of the men on the corvettes, who had seethed at being ordered to protect the well-armed *Pozarica* rather than staying with the helpless merchant ships. The corvette commanders asked the *Pozarica*'s captain, Edward Lawford, to allow them to go back and try to save the men on the radios. Lawford was torn. He pointed out that if the corvettes went back, they would place themselves in grave danger and might not even find any survivors. He suggested the corvette commanders keep their vessels with the *Pozarica* "unless you feel strongly to the contrary." The commander of the corvette *Lotus*, Lieutenant Henry Hall, immediately turned the *Lotus* around and headed back toward the sinking ships. Watching the *Lotus* steam away, a young sailor on the *Pozarica* marveled at the courage of the corvette's crew but doubted he would ever see any of them again.

The *Lotus*, as it turned out, had no trouble finding and rescuing survivors of sunken ships. The corvette picked up forty-five men from the *Pan Kraft* within an hour after leaving the *Pozarica,* and then picked up thirty-six survivors from the *River Afton,* including Commodore Dowding. Dowding thought the *Lotus* captain's decision to rush back into harm's way was "most commendable. Had it not been for his action I doubt that any of *River Afton*'s men would have survived, considering where they were sunk." The commodore left it unsaid that he would not have survived either. The *Lotus* probably would not have found the *River Afton* survivors without the help of an Arctic mirage. The survivors had set off flares to try to attract rescuers, but the flares' thick, reddish smoke never rose more than six feet above the surface of the sea. The mirage inverted the image of the low-hanging smoke and made it appear to the *Lotus* as a red cloud boiling high out of the sea.

THE *TIRPITZ* WAS PASSING 45 miles north of the rock face of the North Cape on its way east when it was spotted by the Soviet submarine K-1, under the command of Captain Second Rank Nikolay Alexandrovich Lunin, one of the Soviets' most decorated submarine commanders.

Lunin could not get close to the *Tirpitz* without being mauled by German destroyers, so the sub fired two torpedoes at the battleship from long range. The K-1's sonar operator detected two explosions, and Lunin reported to his superiors that he thought he had hit the *Tirpitz*. The torpedoes, however, had missed by such a wide margin that the Germans were not even aware of them. Within two hours, however, the *Tirpitz* was spotted northeast of the North Cape by a British submarine and a British plane, both of which radioed the battleship's position to British authorities. German cryptographers decoded those reports and informed the German High Command that the Allies had found the *Tirpitz*.

By then, German planes and U-boats had sunk or disabled twelve merchant ships from convoy PQ-17 in less than twenty-four hours. They were closing fast on other ships. Working together, the planes and U-boats were perfectly suited to the task of hunting down and sinking the scattered ships; the *Tirpitz* was far better suited to attacking an intact convoy. Just before 10:00 p.m. on July 5, Admiral Raeder ordered the battleship and the other German surface warships back to Altenfjord, with the signal *Break. Break. Break.*

The men on the *Tirpitz* could hardly believe it. "They should have let us make one little attack!" one officer wrote. Admiral Schniewind was furious. "Every sortie attempted by our heavy surface units is burdened by the Führer's desire to avoid at all costs the risk of losses or defeats," he complained. Morale on the battleship plummeted. One member of the *Tirpitz*'s crew deserted as soon as the ship returned to port in Norway. After he was caught, he explained, "It's because I am bored and could not stand the monotony. Nothing ever happens on the *Tirpitz*." His unsympathetic superiors ordered him tied to an execution post near the battleship's 15-inch guns and executed by a firing squad. Boredom and thirst for glory aside, it had no longer made sense for the German Navy to risk its most powerful warship, even with no Allied aircraft carriers around. The *Tirpitz* already had wrecked convoy PQ-17 without firing a shot.

Every ship in the convoy either had been sunk or was struggling to escape that fate.

DEEP IN THE ICE FIELD, the *Ayrshire* and the three freshly white-painted freighters resumed their perilous journey north. "Making very slow progress through ice," wrote an anonymous diarist on the *Ayrshire*. "Have to break every inch of way with ships' bows. . . . Ice fields as far as the eye can see. Very cold." There were no more leads, only ice. Soon the ice was so thick that the *Troubadour* and *Ayrshire* no longer could force their way through it with their bows. The four-ship convoy had gone as far north as it could.

The *Ironclad*'s navigator aimed his sextant at the sun and estimated the ships' position at latitude 80°22′ N and longitude 38°E. The vessels had penetrated 25 miles into the ice field. They were roughly 600 miles from the North Pole and more than 800 miles from Archangel. They were midway between the Svalbard island group, which includes Spitsbergen, and the uninhabited Russian archipelago of Franz Josef Land. They were less than 50 miles from a tiny Norwegian island, but they could not possibly reach it, and in any case, Lieutenant Carter wrote, "the principal inhabitants were polar bears and walruses." The most significant calculation was that the four ships were roughly 350 miles from Novaya Zemlya.

The *Ayrshire* and the three freighters maneuvered into a semicircular formation, with the nearest ships about 100 yards apart. "In the sun's glare from the ice, we could barely see each other, even that close together," Carter recalled. Carraway broke into the *Troubadour*'s other two tanks and aimed their turret guns to face outward from the circle of ships. The little convoy looked like an icebound version of Custer's Last Stand. The ships' engineers banked the fires in the boilers to prevent any smoke from escaping through the stacks. The captains refrained from assigning make-work tasks to the crews. Carter decided to catch up on his sleep, in case the following day brought unwelcome surprises. When he woke up, he saw several mariners staring at something in the distance. Carter peered through his binoculars to see what they were looking at. Two of the younger members of the *Ironclad*'s Armed Guard men were "paddling around a patch of open water on some kind of boat." Carter fired three shots with his pistol to call them back to the ship. The men had salvaged a piece of heavy canvas from an old hatch cover and wrapped it around a wooden frame to fashion a makeshift canoe. Carter chewed them out and ordered them to disassemble it. "But they had done a great job of building it," he wrote, "and I let them keep the parts for reassembly at some more appropriate time and place." He was assuming they would survive long enough to reach a more appropriate time and place. First, they would have to reach Novaya Zemlya.

CHAPTER EIGHT
NOVAYA ZEMLYA

The Russian archipelago of Novaya Zemlya—"New Land" in Russian—was a barren Arctic wilderness. It consisted of two long, slender islands forming a crescent-shaped barrier between the Barents Sea and the even colder and more remote Kara Sea. Together the islands extended for more than 600 miles, divided only by a narrow, winding strait named the Matochkin Shar, or Matthew Strait. Novaya Zemlya was an isolated extension of the Ural Mountains. The northern island, Severny, was a mass of rugged peaks mantled with snow and glaciers. The southern island, Yuhzny, was mountainous near the strait but tapered southward into hills and treeless tundra. Novaya Zemlya's climate discouraged all but the hardiest human habitation. Winters brought subzero temperatures and ferocious storms; the brief Arctic summers brought high winds and chill fog.

Russian merchant captains began stopping at Novaya Zemlya in the eleventh century to barter with indigenous hunters for walrus tusks and polar bear hides. The western side of the islands, facing the Barents Sea, was accessible year-round, but the eastern side, facing the Kara Sea, was usually iced in. Novaya Zemlya later became a jumping-off point for Arctic explorers, including the Dutchman Willem Barents, whose ship became trapped in the ice at the islands' northeast tip in 1576. Barents and his men built a crude hut and endured a brutal winter, stalked by polar bears that ransacked their icebound ship and tried to claw their way into the hut. The men ate Arctic foxes they caught in traps and bears they shot with their muskets. They used bear fat to keep their lamps burning throughout the sunless winter. Barents survived the winter but died on the voyage home across the sea that now bears his name. So remote was the site of Barents's hut that it was not rediscovered for 274 years.* By World War II, the only occupants of Novaya Zemlya were a few hardy trappers, hunters, and weather observers.

Few men in convoy PQ-17 had heard of Novaya Zemlya when they left Iceland. Howard Carraway did not even attempt to pronounce the name, which he wrote "sounds like a mixture of a sneeze and a burp." The *Arctic Pilot* described Novaya Zemlya as "little known" and mostly covered by ice, though its coast was "indented with bays, and there are many good anchorages." The only fact about Novaya Zemlya that really mattered to the mariners was that it was Russian soil. The islands beckoned to them like a crooked finger.

Deep in the ice field on the afternoon of July 6, 1942, the captains of the *Ayrshire* and the three freighters felt an ominous shift in the wind. It began blowing out of the south. If it kept up, the 25 miles of ice they had put between themselves and the open sea would be pushed northward toward them, trapping their ships. Every minute they stayed in the ice field could reduce their chances of ever getting out. The captains agreed

---

* The crew of a Norwegian ship discovered the hut—which the men had named *Behouden Huys,* or "the saved house"—in 1871 in much the same condition as it was left by its occupants. Today, some of the artifacts from the hut are displayed in Amsterdam's Rijksmuseum, which is most famous for its wealth of art masterpieces, including *The Night Watch* by Rembrandt.

to leave their hiding place and make for the open water and then Novaya Zemlya.

The men on the four ships could tell that the German assault on convoy PQ-17 was continuing. The airwaves still were full of SOS calls going unanswered. The Liberty ship *John Witherspoon* was torpedoed. The British freighter *Bolton Castle* was bombed. So was the American freighter *Pan Atlantic,* which was packed with explosives and sank in just three minutes, taking twenty-five of its thirty-seven officers and crew to the bottom with it. The *Troubadour, Ironclad,* and *Silver Sword* were certain to join the list of casualties if they were spotted by the Germans on the open sea. That risk seemed preferable, however, to the risk of being trapped in the ice.

The four captains agreed the ships would ease back out of the ice field and then east along its edge, staying as far as possible from the German air bases in Norway. When they reached the northern tip of Novaya Zemlya, they would try to continue east into the Kara Sea and then make their way south along the far side of Novaya Zemlya, keeping the islands between them and the Barents Sea. Their planned route would take the four ships past the point where Willem Barents's hut had stood. Once the vessels reached the southern tip of the island, they would head west toward the entrance to the White Sea, and to Archangel. The trip clearly would be long and circuitous, with ice a constant, threatening companion.

The shifting ice made for a white-knuckle journey toward open water. The *Troubadour* was "grinding steadily on, sometimes north, sometimes east, then again south, when the ice gets too heavy," Carraway wrote. "We have failed to dodge a really big hard cake [of ice] and have to smack her head on." The ice gradually grew thinner and the big bergs less numerous as the ships worked their way south and east. Carraway addressed his writing more directly to Avis: "It's a fairy tale, almost, hard to believe even when I'm seeing it. Here we are within spittin' distance of the North Pole. If anyone had told me a year ago that . . . But you've heard this all before." He wrote that he planned to get some sleep, and possibly even take a bath. "I haven't taken off my shoes in four days. Almost five . . . Well, sweet dreams, Angel, I'm off to the hay!"

The ships finally emerged from the ice into the Barents Sea, although scattered floes and growlers continued to bump against the hulls. The air was cold, but the sun shone brightly in a cerulean sky. Walter Baker on the *Ayrshire* confessed an odd disappointment that the Arctic weather was so mild: "I had always thought that the roof of the world would be continually plunged in gloom by snow blizzards which would blot out the sun, but instead it was just the opposite. Virgin whiteness and brilliant blue sky lit by a sun that did not drop below the horizon. Now that we were out of the ice and all the grinding, rasping and shuddering had ceased, a strange stillness pervaded the air."

Around 7:00 a.m. on July 7, a loud boom to the south made the men on the decks of the four ships jump. A plume of black smoke rose into the sky. It seemed obvious that a ship had blown up. Everyone on the four ships scanned the skies for a German bomber. They watched and listened, but the enemy did not appear. The mariners had no way of knowing that the exploding ship was the American freighter *Pan Kraft*, whose crew had abandoned it the previous day near the ice field after a bomb set it afire. The derelict *Pan Kraft* had smoldered for more than twenty-four hours before the fire reached some TNT in the ship's cargo holds and ignited the explosion. The *Pan Kraft* went to the bottom with 7,800 tons of airplane parts in crates and a deckload of bombers. The *Ayrshire* and the freighters steered as far north of the plume of black smoke as possible. Their hiatus from the war was suddenly over.

A thick band of fog hung over the water several hundred yards south of the ice edge. It apparently marked the invisible line where the warm Gulf Stream water collided with the cold meltwaters of the ice field. The captains hoped the ships could hide in the fog band all the way to Novaya Zemlya. Inside the fog, the air was chill and the ships had to slow down to keep from hitting one another. But the seafarers welcomed the fog, their ancient enemy, as though it were a troop of cavalry with bugles blaring; it offered shelter. No sooner did the ships enter the fog band than the men heard an airplane engine. "The German planes had a very distinctive motor sound," Lieutenant Carter wrote. "[W]e heard one coming up from behind us and going right over us and not very high." Gunners on all four ships manned their guns and swung them upward. The *Ayrshire's* gunnery officer prayed that none of the young Yanks would start shooting. The same thought occurred to Carter. "Don't shoot! Don't shoot!" he shouted at the *Ironclad's* gun crew. Then he offered "a fervent, silent prayer that nobody would send a line of tracers past some startled pilot's nose and give away our presence under that fog." No one fired. "Go away, you dirty German bastard!" shouted one of the sailors on the *Ayrshire*. The sound of the plane faded, and the weird Arctic silence returned. Only a few minutes later, the fog bank parted, leaving the ships sailing under bright sunshine. The plane did not return. "The Lord was with us," Carter concluded. "It just was not our time for catastrophe to strike." Walter Baker on the *Ayrshire* recalled a passage from the Bible's book of Exodus in which God saves the Israelites from the pursuing Egyptians: "And the Lord went before them, to shew the way by day in a pillar of cloud."

The four ships hurried into another fog bank. The water was temporarily clear of ice, so they increased their speed to 10 knots. The *Ayrshire* took the lead, with the *Troubadour, Ironclad,* and *Silver Sword* steaming three abreast behind it. The fog grew so thick that lookouts on the freighters lost sight of the trawler. Ahead in the gloom Carter heard three short blasts of the *Ayrshire's* whistle—the signal for danger. Carter saw the dark shape of the *Ayrshire* swerve sharply to starboard, at almost a 90-degree angle. Then he saw the reason. Directly ahead of the ships, a salient of the ice field jutted far into the sea. The freighters were about to slam into it. "Pandemonium reigned," Carter wrote. The captain shouted orders to the *Ironclad's* helmsman. The *Ironclad* had to cut its speed but maintain steerageway to turn sharply to the right. To the left of the *Ironclad,* the

Silver Sword turned more quickly. She jabbed her bow into the *Ironclad*, opening a two-foot crack in the *Ironclad*'s hull just below the waterline. After several anxious minutes, the *Ironclad*'s chief engineer reported that the ship's pumps could keep up with the water seeping in through the crack. "It was a pretty good jolt," Francis Brummer on the *Ironclad* recalled, "but except for a few dents we were OK. The same was true for the *Silver Sword*." It had been a close call. The captains agreed that from then on they would stay at least a mile from the edge of the ice field.

On the *Troubadour,* Captain Salvesen took the opportunity to get his first serious sleep since before the scatter order. He slept soundly for eight hours and returned to the bridge refreshed. Carraway, who at first had doubted the Norwegian captain, now looked up to him. "He was admirable in the ice, standing in the bitter cold, atop the bridge for a better view, hour after hour, giving commands by the hundreds to the wheel," Carraway wrote of the captain. "We were the only ship of the four to get through the stuff without a bent bow, or dented side, or some small damage."

But Carraway grew increasingly angry at the *Troubadour*'s "black gang," the soot-covered toilers in the ship's engine room. The *Troubadour* kept falling behind the other vessels. It was barely averaging 8 knots. Carraway wrote Avis, "Almost impossible to believe is that even now, when we are practically alone, and in such great danger, this heaven-cursed crew does not do its best. I can't believe that men would be so damned lazy in such a great crisis, and when what we are doing is so valuable to us, as well as to Russia. But there it is. Right now, we're more than a mile behind, and the steam isn't nearly top. . . . But the hell with it. We're jinxed." Salvesen angrily chewed out the firemen and coal passers, and the *Troubadour* briefly caught up, only to fall behind again. Jim North thought the black gang was blameless: Not even the laziest, surliest man on the ship would intentionally slow its flight from the Nazis through the Arctic. North said the problem was the boilers, which had not worked properly since the Italians sabotaged them in Jacksonville.

More SOS calls came over the radios. The World War I–era American freighter *Alcoa Ranger* was torpedoed by a U-boat and then pummeled by the sub's deck cannon. The British freighter *Hartlebury* was sent to the bottom by three torpedoes. The American freighter *Olopana,* whose crew had tried unsuccessfully to pick up lifeboat survivors two days earlier, was torpedoed and then shelled until it sank. All three of the doomed ships radioed their final locations as near the southern tip of Novaya Zemlya. The men on the *Ayrshire* and the three white freighters could only guess at the fates of the rest of the ships from convoy PQ-17. Baker wondered if his trawler and the three freighters were the only ones still afloat.

In the stretches of clear weather between the fog banks, the mariners glimpsed whales and walruses on the still surface of the sea. Small gray seals watched the passing ships from ice floes "like little men with whiskers staring up at us with wonderment in their eyes," Baker wrote. "We were moving in waters rarely sailed in by anyone, even in peacetime." At around 2:00 a.m. on July 9, the lookouts sighted the northern tip of Novaya Zemlya. "This place has snow and glaciers all over it," wrote Brummer. The captains saw immediately that circling around the east side of the island was impossible. The Kara Sea was choked with ice. "So it was back to the drawing boards," wrote Carter, "to devise a new plan of action."

The only real option was to head south through the Barents Sea along Novaya Zemlya's western shore. The island was spectacular but uninviting in the extreme. Its rocky shore rose steeply into a mass of ice-covered mountains. The ships passed a small bay and the *Ayrshire,* which had the shallowest draft of the four vessels, crept into the bay to see if it was deep enough for the freighters. It was. All four vessels dropped anchor, the rumble of their anchor chains echoing through the still bay. The *Ayrshire* tied up against the *Troubadour* to top off its supply of coal. For a change, mariners were eager to help with the coal transfer. The work got their blood pumping. The air felt much colder in the bay. Snow and sleet fell intermittently. The men took comfort in being close to land. If their ships were sunk in the bay, they would have a chance of reaching shore—albeit a desolate shore. For the first time on the voyage, Carraway slept without wearing all his clothes and his life vest. "Pajamas felt good again," he wrote Avis.

Baker wrote that Novaya Zemlya looked otherworldly, primeval. He half-expected to see a woolly mammoth lumbering among the boulders. Carter described his new surroundings with an element of wonder:

> It was a beautiful little bay. At its southern end there was a glacier that I guessed to be about three hundred feet above sea level. A rock spire in the middle divided it into two smaller branches. Then those branches joined into a single glacier making it into the shape of the letter Y at the bottom. As the whole face of the glacier crept toward the sea, the increasing depth of the water created an ice overhang. The weight of this overhang caused pieces of the face of the glacier to break off and fall into the bay, becoming icebergs of various shapes and sizes. The flow of the outgoing tide carried them out, making a beautiful parade of icebergs sparking in the brilliant morning sunlight as they marched one by one to the sea. As I drank in the splendor of this setting, both with the naked eye and my binoculars, a movement on shore just a few hundred yards away caught my eye. A polar bear was standing knee deep in the water fishing for what appeared to be salmon, and doing a good job of it too. I watched him catch two in about five minutes.

The four captains convened on the *Troubadour* to discuss their next move. They could not even agree on where exactly they were. The debate grew heated. Carraway, who was in attendance, wrote that Captain Clyde

Colbeth of the *Silver Sword* "wanted to scuttle the ship and save the crew" and that Captain Moore of the *Ironclad* "didn't disagree," but Salvesen of the *Troubadour* "got heated up about that time" and spoke out:

> He said he was not scuttling his ship. He was going to Arch-angel with the cargo or be sunk on the way there. Lives, he said, could be lost in the attempt. This is a war in which life is pretty cheap. If [any other captains] wanted to go back, or scuttle, or do anything except head for Archangel, they would do it without his company. He would go alone.

The captain's fiery speech "rallied weakening spirits," Carraway wrote, and the other captains agreed to press on. Lieutenant Gradwell later would play down the debate, writing only that the merchant captains were "showing unmistakable signs of strain." The captains decided to keep the vessels in the bay a few hours longer to give the crews more time to rest, and then to head south for the Matochkin Shar, the strait dividing the two islands of Novaya Zemlya. No one knew if the strait was navigable, but given the lack of other options, the Matochkin Shar seemed as good a destination as any.

Carraway got a few hours of sleep, ate dinner, showered, and put on his cleanest uniform. By the time he was finished, he "felt like let's go get 'em." He emerged onto the *Troubadour's* main deck to find the *Ayrshire* just finishing the coal transfer. Gradwell invited him aboard the *Ayrshire* for a drink, which turned into several drinks, and Carraway soon found himself "stewed to the ears." Gradwell did not seem intoxicated. He said his *Times Handy Atlas* showed a remote weather station located at the mouth of the Matochkin Shar. If the station was still there, it surely would have a radio. The radio could provide the ships with a link to Archangel. Gradwell worried, however, that the radio station might have fallen into German hands. If so, the radio could be used to summon U-boats and bombers to destroy them.

Gradwell proposed treating the weather station as a hostile outpost. He asked if Carraway would help organize an armed raid against it. If the raiders found Germans occupying the station, they would try to overwhelm them before a radio message could be sent. If the station was in Soviet hands, the raiders would back off and apologize for the attack. Carraway agreed to Gradwell's plan. So did the merchant captains. Gradwell chose Richard Elsden, his first officer, to lead the raiding party. Elsden decided to take along Carraway, Carter, eight Armed Guard gunners, and a few of the toughest merchant seamen on the four ships. North was not among those.

The ersatz commandos armed themselves with .45-caliber pistols, several hand grenades, a .30-caliber machine gun from the *Troubadour*'s antiaircraft battery, and ten Thompson submachine guns from the *Troubadour*'s tanks. Carraway called the Tommy guns "Chicago pianos," a slang term reflecting their use by Prohibition-era Chicago gangsters such as Al Capone and George "Bugs" Moran. The plan called for the fourteen raiders to row ashore in the *Ayrshire*'s dingy and then separate into three groups. One group would rush the weather station straight on while the two other groups circled around from either side to catch its occupants by surprise. Carraway was leery. "I hope this little adventure doesn't come about," he wrote in his diary, "but if it does, we'll be found ready." He added a personal note to Avis: "So, in case anything happens, remember, darling, that I love you with all my heart and soul, today and forever, will you?"

The ships crept south along the rocky coast, looking for the mouth of the Matochkin Shar. The lookouts saw no sign of activity—no ships, no masts on the horizon, no castaways, no lifeboats, no debris. The only signs of life were birds, which rose from the shore in huge, shrieking clouds only to descend again as the ship passed. Jim North had never seen so many birds. Carter took the time to prepare a coded message for the raiders to transmit by radio to Archangel if the chance arose.

The four vessels arrived at the mouth of the Matochkin Shar on July 10 at around 11:00 a.m.—five hours earlier than the captains had expected. The strait was a gash of dark water lined by steep, barren cliffs shrouded in mist. The mouth of the strait was about a mile wide. A radio tower rose out of a jumble of rocks at the north side. The *Ayrshire* signaled the freighters to prepare for action. Suddenly the *Ironclad* ran aground and lurched to a stop just outside the mouth of the strait. The *Ayrshire* hurried to help but ran onto a submerged rock. The rock tipped the trawler so steeply that some of the crew feared it would capsize and gathered up their possessions. The *Ayrshire* backed off the rock but the collision had dislodged its sonar dome. Gone with the dome was the *Ayrshire's* ability to detect U-boats. Gradwell decided not to mention the loss of the sonar to the other captains. The *Ayrshire* tried to tow the *Ironclad* off the rocks but it was no use. The captain of the *Ironclad* exchanged heated words with Gradwell.

So much for the element of surprise. Carraway noticed gun emplacements among the rocks near the radio tower and wondered if someone up there was getting ready to blow the four vessels out of the water. Finally, the raiding party set out in the *Ayrshire's* 20-foot dinghy. A Polish seaman from the *Ironclad* had been added to the group at the last minute because he spoke a little Russian. The *Ayrshire* kept its stern gun aimed at the radio tower as the dinghy bobbed through a heavy chop toward shore. In addition to the Chicago pianos and the other weapons, the raiders carried an American flag, an English-Russian dictionary, and an assortment of cigarettes and candy bars. This was gunboat diplomacy at its most outlandish.

The water was so rough that the men in the dinghy did not see a rowboat coming out to meet them until they were almost on top of it. Some of the commandos pointed their guns at the rowboat's lone occupant. The Polish seaman shouted at him, asking if he was Russian. "*Da!*" he cried. "*Da!*" Carter noted that the man "looked very Russian, dressed in a padded outfit, with a friendly grin showing two shiny steel front teeth." The Russian motioned for the raiders to follow him. He rowed through a hidden gap in the rocks to a small sandy beach with a floating dock. He tied up his boat and trudged up some stone steps that had been cut into a steep cliff nearly 50 feet high. The raiders "shouldered our two tons of shooting irons" and lugged them up the steps. Scattered among the rocks all around them were large nests full of ducks and eggs. The steps led to a cluster of buildings, and the Russian led the raiders into the largest. Inside were six people—five men and a woman—and three dogs. The Russians greeted the raiders warmly, but the language barrier was formidable. The Polish seaman did not understand the Russians' dialect. The English-Russian dictionary was useless. The groups communicated by gestures and drawings. "After more than an hour of this madhouse, calisthenics conversation, we got what information we could," Carraway wrote. Carter handed the Russians the coded message and asked them to include it in their daily weather report, where the Germans might not notice it.

The raiders were about to depart when the female weather observer spoke a word that sounded like "coffee." The mariners smiled and were ushered into a room with a log table. They sat down to a hearty lunch of baked pastry with duck meat, hard-boiled duck eggs, sliced black bread and butter, and demitasses of thick black coffee. Carraway was amazed to find such delicious coffee "in this rag-tag end of the universe." The well-fed commandos rowed back to the *Ayrshire*. "Well, the landing party has been accomplished, and nobody was killed," Carraway wrote in his diary. "In fact, the only danger there was an overdose of hospitality."

One of the Russians went back in the dinghy to guide the ships to an anchorage deeper inside the Matochkin Shar, where they could not be seen from the sea. The *Ironclad*'s crew refloated the vessel by transferring some of its cargo to the trawler. The *Ayrshire* had just started leading the three freighters into the strait when the Russian mentioned that lifeboats had come ashore on the island south of the Matochkin Shar. Gradwell turned the trawler around and headed it south along the shore of Novaya Zemlya to investigate.

Just south of the strait, the *Ayrshire's* lookouts saw bodies floating in the shallows—Allied mariners from convoy PQ-17. Gradwell recovered the bodies and zipped them into canvas bags. That experience would haunt his dreams for the rest of his life.

Five miles south of the Matochkin Shar, the *Ayrshire* came upon a makeshift camp on the rocky shore. The campers were thirty-four survivors of the American freighter *Fairfield City*, which had been bombed and sunk on July 5, about 250 miles west of Novaya Zemlya. The survivors had stepped the sails on their lifeboats and reached the island in four days, thanks to a favorable wind. They had fashioned tents out of sails and sail covers, built a fire, and boiled the only food they had left: a five-gallon can of hot chocolate. Several men had set out on foot in search of help. They were astonished to meet three Russian Boy Scouts—the Russians called them Pioneers—on a field trip to learn how to forage for food. The Pioneers gave the hungry castaways a large collection of duck, gull, and albatross eggs, as well as a can of corned beef—most likely from a previous Arctic convoy. The Pioneers had reported the castaways to the Russian weather station only hours before the commando raid.

The *Ayrshire* took aboard all of the *Fairfield City* survivors. Some were badly frostbitten. Gradwell arranged for most of them to be transferred to the freighters, which had more room than the trawler did. Then the *Ayrshire* led the *Troubadour, Ironclad,* and *Silver Sword* into the Matochkin Shar. The strait was actually a fjord, scoured out of the rock by glaciers. The deeper the ships got into it, the closer the rock walls seemed to press in. The air grew colder, and the mariners heard the familiar clunking of ice against the hulls. The Matochkin Shar gave the men the creeps. Some wondered if it was a trap. Finally, the vessels rounded a sharp bend and the men saw a small harbor at the base of a massive, snow-covered mountain. Carraway was surprised to see an American Liberty ship anchored there. The *Troubadour* flashed a signal asking the vessel's name. Carraway was even more surprised when the ship identified itself as the *Benjamin Harrison*. He had thought he'd seen her bombed and sunk on the

Fourth of July, when he actually had witnessed the sinking of the *Christopher Newport*. Carraway was thrilled; one of his friends from Navy Armed Guard school was aboard the *Benjamin Harrison*.

After the *Ayrshire* dropped anchor, Gradwell noticed several small buildings on shore. He put on his cleanest uniform and took the dinghy to pay an official visit. Most of the inhabitants of the settlement were rough-looking trappers and hunters. They kept an enormous pack of Siberian huskies as hunting dogs. As soon as Gradwell stepped out of the boat, "I was surrounded by about a hundred huskies, and I wished I had my sea boots on." A tall Soviet naval officer waded through the dogs and led Gradwell to a hut with a man and woman inside. They looked Mongolian to Gradwell. Neither spoke English, but Gradwell was able to determine that they had medical training and that the hut was an infirmary. He resolved to bring some of the most severely frostbitten *Fairfield City* survivors there.

While Gradwell was ashore, Carraway went aboard the *Benjamin Harrison* to visit his friend. On the ship, he found a second Armed Guard buddy who had been rescued by the *Benjamin Harrison* from the sunken *Pan Kraft*. Carraway could hardly believe his Armed Guard training class was holding a reunion in the Matochkin Shar. His friends offered some insight into what had happened to other ships in convoy PQ-17.

AFTER THE SCATTER ORDER, the *Benjamin Harrison* had made a beeline for Novaya Zemlya, along with the *Fairfield City, John Witherspoon,* and *Daniel Morgan*. The four ships had tried in vain to keep up with the antiaircraft ship *Pozarica* and its escort of corvettes, which had refused to slow down for them. Soon, U-boats and bombers had overtaken the merchant ships and sunk all except the *Benjamin Harrison,* which miraculously had arrived at Novaya Zemlya unscathed on July 6. The crew of the *Benjamin Harrison* had been surprised to find seventeen vessels from convoy PQ-17 hiding in the strait. Only four of them were merchant ships; the other thirteen were British escort vessels that had left the merchant ships behind. Soon after the *Benjamin Harrison* steamed into the strait, the corvette *Lotus* had arrived to a chorus of cheers, carrying eighty-one men it had rescued, including Commodore Dowding.

Dowding had immediately organized the ships in the strait into a new convoy and set out for Archangel on July 7—the same day the *Ayrshire, Troubadour, Ironclad,* and *Silver Sword* reemerged from the ice field. Almost at once, the *Benjamin Harrison* had gotten lost in a dense fog and returned to the Matochkin Shar. The men on the ship had no idea whether the rest of their new convoy had made it safely to Archangel after the *Benjamin Harrison* dropped out.

In fact, Dowding had led the rest of the little convoy through fog and ice, stopping to pick up lifeboats full of half-frozen castaways from sunken merchant ships. German bombers had attacked, sinking two of the convoy's four merchant ships before the rest finally limped into Archangel on July 10. Upon arriving in Archangel, Dowding had been pleasantly surprised to find two other merchant ships from convoy PQ-17 already there. The American freighter *Bellingham* and the Soviet tanker *Donbass*—aided by the U.S. Navy Armed Guard gunners it had rescued from the sunken *Daniel Morgan*—had gotten past the Germans and reached Archangel without escorts.

Commodore Dowding found little other good news about convoy PQ-17 in Archangel. Mostly he found confusion. British and American authorities were scrambling to tally up the convoy's losses. Their lists of merchant ships sunk, damaged, or missing changed by the hour. Much of the information filtering into Archangel about convoy PQ-17 was conflicting, wrong, or both. On July 9, U.S. ambassador to the Soviet Union W. Averell Harriman reported that either the British freighter *Hartlebury* or the American freighter *Washington* had been sunk, "but [it's] not definite yet which one." In fact, the *Hartlebury* had been resting on the bottom of the Barents Sea for three days and the *Washington* for four. Admiralty officials kept demanding updates: "It is essential that result of

PQ-17 should be known as soon as possible." But determining the fates of the thirty-three ships was no simple task. Hundreds of mariners were still adrift on the Barents Sea in lifeboats or on rafts, running out of food, water, and body heat.

At first, the Allies' chief source of information about the convoy's fate was the Germans, who knew more about what had happened to PQ-17 than the Allies did, and were eager to tell the world. Here was a victory that did not require the usual lies and half-truths of the Nazi propaganda machine. On July 7, Radio Berlin gleefully reported a "convoy catastrophe" in which U-boats and bombers had engaged in a highly successful "hunt" for helpless merchant ships. The Germans correctly listed twenty-one ships they had sunk, though they erroneously added the Russian tanker *Azerbaijan* and the *Silver Sword*. Radio Berlin even reported some of the sunken ships' tonnages and cargoes. The Germans explained they had gotten their information from mariners captured by U-boats. They added that "more survivors are continually being brought in" and further details "will probably be learnt in the course of a few days." The Nazis ended their press statement with a taunt:

> The British Admiralty and the American Navy Department have so far maintained complete silence on this convoy catastrophe. The above details are therefore published in order to satisfy the British and American public's desire for news.

Three days later, the Germans provided the further details they had promised. This time, they did exaggerate. They claimed to have sunk 37 ships, along with 1,400 tanks, 42,000 tons of foodstuffs, 52,000 tons of steel and other metals, as well as weapons, ammunition, and other materials. They inflated the true total of 22 ships by including the 2 merchant ships that had turned back for Iceland; the 4 merchant ships that had safely reached Archangel; and several vessels whose whereabouts were still unknown to both sides, including the *Troubadour*, *Ironclad*, and *Silver*

Sword. The Germans got one fact dead right: The loss of ships and cargo from convoy PQ-17 "corresponds to the loss of material which would be lost in a great battle." That same day, the Allies released their first public statement about convoy PQ-17, disclosing only that an Arctic convoy had suffered substantial losses.

Soviet authorities complained their Western allies were telling them nothing. The day after the Germans' second press statement, the Soviet Admiral of the Fleet, Nikolay Gerasimovich Kuznetzov, a compact, powerfully built man with a brusque manner, asked the head of the British Naval Mission, Rear Admiral G. J. A. Miles, what had happened to convoy PQ-17. Miles apparently knew few details. He told Kuznetzov what the Admiralty had told him: The convoy had been scattered to avoid destruction by the *Tirpitz.* Kuznetzov "expressed doubt on wisdom of dispersing convoy," Miles wrote to his superiors at the Admiralty. Kuznetzov added that he "considered *Tirpitz* had achieved her object by causing convoy to scatter, thus making it defenseless and easy prey for aircraft and submarines."

Soviet admiral Arseny Golovko, commander of the Soviet Northern Fleet, claimed that one British rear admiral was too ashamed to face him. "Every time we come across each other since PQ-17 he avoids looking at me in the eyes, blushes (yes, yes, blushes!) and avoids meeting with me," Golovko wrote in his memoirs. Stalin would soon express his own views about convoy PQ-17 in person to Churchill, in less cordial terms than the Soviet admiral had used.

For the fifty-one-year-old Commodore Dowding, every day since the Fourth of July had been hard. His flagship the *River Afton* had been sunk with great loss of life. He probably would have died too if the captain of the *Lotus* had not ignored orders and gone back to save him. After arriving in the Matochkin Shar, Dowding had led a second convoy through fog, ice, and fire, losing half the merchant ships in that convoy. The toll from convoy PQ-17 was still rising.

To make matters worse, a horrific blunder by a British officer had brought disaster to homebound Arctic convoy QP-13, which had passed convoy PQ-17 in midocean. The thirty-six ships of the convoy had crossed the Arctic without a scratch and then split into two groups, with one group heading to Scotland and the other to Iceland. The ships in the latter group were only a day out of Hvalfjord when they ran into a storm and then dense fog off the coast of Iceland. An officer on a British escort vessel mistook an iceberg for land and led the ships into a "friendly" Allied minefield. In only minutes, seven ships struck mines and sank, casting hundreds of men into the cold, rough sea. The death toll was 173—more men than would be killed in convoy PQ-17. The dead included dozens of American mariners riding back to the United States as passengers on ships in convoy QP-13 after their original ships had been sunk on the way to Russia.

It seemed that the Allies could do nothing right, and that the news only got worse.

Then Dowding heard that a message had just arrived from Novaya Zemlya: Several of the merchant ships the Germans claimed to have sunk had materialized in the Matochkin Shar, accompanied by the trawler *Ayrshire*. They were requesting escorts to Archangel. Dowding resolved to go back to Novaya Zemlya and get them.

CHAPTER NINE

"WE THREE GHOSTS"

The Matochkin Shar would not remain a refuge for long. The strait was too shallow for a U-boat to enter at periscope depth, but a U-boat could station itself at the mouth of the Matochkin Shar and bottle up the ships inside, where bombers could reach them. Lieutenant Gradwell wondered if the vessels could pass all the way through the strait into the Kara Sea. The *Ayrshire* explored in that direction but found the eastern end of the strait hopelessly blocked by ice. The only way out of the Matochkin Shar was the way the ships had come in. They were hiding in a frozen cul-de-sac that at any moment could turn into a trap.

Two days dragged by after the foray to the weather station, with no sign of help from Archangel. Gradwell began to worry. He thought back to the mariners' confused attempts to communicate with the Soviet weather observers. Had the Russians sent the radio message? Had they even understood they were being asked to? So much had gone wrong for convoy PQ-17 already that it was easy to think the worst.

For the men on the *Troubadour, Ironclad,* and *Silver Sword,* the excitement of reaching Novaya Zemlya had evaporated. On the *Troubadour*, Howard Carraway passed the dreary days reading Thomas Hardy's novel *Far from the Madding Crowd* and playing Hearts with castaways from the *Fairfield City*, whose company he preferred to that of the *Troubadour*'s crew. Four of the *Fairfield City* men offered to help operate the turret guns on the tanks, and Carraway showed them how. He also spent a lot of his downtime sleeping. In his dreams, he and Avis were always together, and usually strolling in Charleston, South Carolina, near his hometown. In one dream, Avis had been sore at him for some reason he did not understand, but at least they had been together, in a warm, lush place that was nothing like the Matochkin Shar.

Late on July 12, Walter Baker spotted what he thought was a plane in the sky to the west and sounded the alarm. The *Ayrshire* weighed anchor and raced toward the mouth of the strait, signaling the freighters to prepare to leave at once. The lookouts on the trawler saw only seagulls. "I got a lot of leg pulling and caustic remarks about 'aeroplanes that flapped their wings,'" Baker wrote.

The next day the sun burned through the fog and the weather turned unexpectedly balmy. The mariners shed their jackets and rolled up their shirtsleeves. Then they saw a plane pass over the mouth of the Matochkin Shar. No one had any doubts this time. The plane circled and then glided into the strait between the canyonlike walls. All the ships' gunners, including the men in the tanks, manned their weapons. The plane, however, was a dark green Catalina seaplane with a red Russian star on the fuselage—"the first Russian plane we had seen," Lieutenant Carter noted. The seaplane touched down in the middle of the strait and the *Ayrshire* went alongside it. In the plane's cockpit was Captain Ilya P. Mazuruk, a famous Russian aviator who had become a national hero for landing a plane near the North Pole. Mazuruk was becoming a hero in the war as well. He had devised a system for flying American fighter planes from Alaska to Vladivostok. Now, on the opposite side of the Soviet Union, he was coordinating Russian efforts to rescue convoy PQ-17 survivors all along the coast of Novaya Zemlya. Word about the convoy's plight *had* gotten through.

Mazuruk, who spoke English, climbed out of the seaplane and went aboard the *Ayrshire*. He told Gradwell convoy PQ-17 had suffered severe losses. Gradwell was surprised to learn the *Tirpitz* had not attacked the convoy. Mazuruk said lifeboats full of castaways from sunken ships had come ashore on Novaya Zemlya, both north and south of the Matochkin Shar. One American freighter, the *Winston-Salem,* was beached in a cove north of the strait. The *Winston-Salem*'s crew had run the ship aground on purpose and moved ashore because they expected the freighter to be bombed. South of the Matochkin Shar, Mazuruk told Gradwell, the British freighter *Empire Tide* was hiding in a cove named Moller Bay. The *Empire Tide* had become a floating refuge for survivors of several sunken merchant ships, who had reached Novaya Zemlya in lifeboats.

Mazuruk told Gradwell an escort force would come from Archangel to collect the *Ayrshire* and the merchant ships, but he did not know exactly when. Gradwell handed the Russian aviator a handwritten summary of the *Ayrshire*'s activities since July 4, and asked Mazuruk to give it to the senior British naval officer in Archangel. Gradwell had begun to wonder what the Admiralty would think of his decision to ignore the scatter order. From what he had observed, the Royal Navy's treatment of men who disobeyed orders depended on the results of the disobedience. If the results were favorable, a man would be praised for showing initiative; if not, he could be severely punished. In his report, Gradwell explained his reasoning after the convoy was scattered:

> I considered that the Northerly route along the ice-barrier might be the safest, and that along that route I might be of assistance as no other escorts had shaped a course in that direction. I also thought that I might escort the one or two ships already heading that way without defeating the object of scattering.

Gradwell wrote a summary of the four ships' flight into the ice field, the white paint job, the ships' arrival at Novaya Zemlya, and the raid on the weather station—although he left out some of the Keystone Cops aspects of the raid. Gradwell ended his report with a plea for escort vessels and air support for the rest of the voyage to Archangel:

> The Masters of the merchant ships (though their behavior has so far been admirable) are showing unmistakable signs of strain. I much doubt if I could persuade them to make a dash for Archangel without a considerably increased escort and a promise of fighter protection in the entrance to the White Sea. In fact, there has already been talk of scuttling the ships while near the shore rather than [continuing on toward Archangel] to what they consider, with only one escort, certain sinking.

British and American authorities in Archangel were still trying to determine the casualty toll for convoy PQ-17. Lists of ships in the convoy were passed back and forth to be marked up with pencil as "Sunk," "Probably Sunk," or "Unaccounted For." The *Ayrshire, Troubadour,* and *Ironclad* were "Unaccounted For," but the *Silver Sword* was listed among the "Probably Sunk." A few pieces of good news trickled in. The rescue ship *Rathlin* reached Archangel with nineteen survivors of the sunken *Navarino* and forty-four from the sunken *William Hooper.* The *Rathlin*'s gunners reported sending a German plane down in flames, "leaving 5 charred bodies floating in the sea." A Russian vessel rescued forty-nine survivors of the *Peter Kerr* who had sailed their lifeboats for hundreds of miles to the Russian coast near the Kola Inlet. But overall the news was disturbing. On July 14, the Admiralty provided an update on the ship losses:

(a) Four arrived in White Sea. BELLINGHAM, SAMUEL CHASE, OCEAN FREEDOM, DONBASS.

(b) Observed in Western Novaya Zemlya. AZBAIDJAN [*sic*].

(c) Fourteen sunk, CHRISTOPHER NEWPORT, EMPIRE BYRON,
NAVARINO, PAN KRAFT, RIVER AFTON, WASHINGTON,
WINSTON-SALEM, PETER KERR, BOLTON CASTLE,
J. WITHERSPOON.

(d) Five presumed sunk, DANIEL MORGAN, EARLSTON, OLOPANA,
SILVER SWORD, EMPIRE TIDE.

(e) Nine unaccounted for, HARTLEBURY, PAULUS POTTER,
ALCOA RANGER, CARLTON, FAIRFIELD CITY, HONOMU,
IRONCLAD, TROUBADOUR, BENJAMIN HARRISON. Of these four
are reported to be in harbours on West Coast Novaya
Zemlya.

(f) Two returned to Iceland, RICHARD BLAND, EXFORD.

(g) One A/S Trawler missing, one rescue ship and RFA Oiler
Sunk.

The missing trawler referenced in section (g) was the *Ayrshire*. The
sunken rescue ship was the *Zaafaran*, and the sunken oiler was the *Aldersdale*. The report did not mention the American freighters *Pan Atlantic*,
Hoosier, *El Capitan*, and *William Hooper*, all of which had been sunk.
The *William Hooper*, in fact, had been sunk ten days earlier, on the
Fourth of July, in the air attacks preceding the scatter order.

THE DAY AFTER THE ADMIRALTY'S update on the sinkings, Churchill
sent a secret message to Roosevelt in Washington, D.C.:

Only four ships have reached Archangel, with four or five more
precariously in the ice off Novaya Zemlya out of the 33 included

in Convoy PQ-17. If a half had got through we should have persevered, but with only a quarter arriving the operation is not good enough. For instance, out of nearly 600 tanks in PQ-17, little over 100 arrived and nearly 500 are lost. This cannot help anybody but the enemy. The Admiralty cannot see what better protection can be devised, nor can they hazard battleships east of Bear Island. . . .

We therefore advise against running PQ-18 which must start [July] 18th at latest. If it were composed only of our merchant ships we should certainly not send them, but no fewer than 22 are your own American ships. We should therefore like to know how you feel about it.

Future prospects of supplying Russia by this northern route are bad. Murmansk has been largely burnt out and there are several signs of an impending German attack upon it. By the time that perpetual daylight gives place to the dark period, Archangel will be frozen. . . . We await your answer before explaining things to Stalin. The message which it is proposed to send to him, if you agree that the convoy is not to go, is being sent to you later today. Meanwhile the convoy [PQ-18] is continuing to load and assemble.

Churchill sent a separate message to Roosevelt in which he fairly insisted the president postpone the invasion of France and invade North Africa instead. "I am most anxious for you to know where I stand myself at the present time," he wrote. "I have found no one who regards [a 1942 invasion of France] as possible." Churchill said the Allies should invade North Africa as soon as practicable, while continuing to build up U.S. troops in England for an invasion of France in 1943. "All this seems to me as clear as noonday," Churchill wrote. Roosevelt replied the next day, July 15, that after consulting with Admiral Ernest King, the operational head of the U.S. Navy, "I must reluctantly agree to the position which the

Admiralty has taken regarding the Russian convoys to the north." Roosevelt added that he wanted to increase the convoys through the Persian Gulf to Russia to make up for the postponement of the Arctic convoys. The president also called Churchill's draft message to Stalin "a good one" and suggested Churchill send it right away, which he did. Churchill's message was lengthy. It retraced the history of the Arctic convoys since 1941 and the Germans' intensifying efforts to stop them, culminating with their determined attacks on convoys PQ-16 and PQ-17:

Before the May convoy [PQ-16] was sent off, the Admiralty warned us that the losses would be very severe if, as was expected, the Germans employed their surface forces to the eastward of Bear Island. We decided however to sail the convoy. An attack by surface ships did not materialize, and the convoy got through with a loss of one-sixth, chiefly from air attack. In the case of PQ-17 however the Germans at last used their forces in the manner we had always feared. They concentrated their U-boats to the westward of Bear Island and reserved their surface forces for attack to the eastward of Bear Island.

Churchill told Stalin the Arctic convoys had grown so hazardous in twenty-four-hour daylight that the Royal Navy simply could no longer protect them without endangering warships vital to other missions, such as protecting Britain's lifeline of supplies from the United States and building up U.S. armies in England for an invasion of France in 1943. The message continued:

My naval advisers tell me that if they had the handling of the German surface, submarine, and air forces, in present circumstances, they would guarantee the complete destruction of any convoy to North Russia. They have not been able so far to hold out any hopes that convoys attempting to make the passage in perpetual daylight would fare better than PQ-17. It is therefore with the greatest regret that we have reached the conclusion that to attempt to run the next convoy, PQ-18, would bring no benefits to you and would only involve dead loss to the common cause. At the same time, I give you my assurance that if we can devise arrangements which give a reasonable chance of at least a fair proportion of the contents of the convoys reaching you we will start them again at once. . . . Meanwhile we are prepared to dispatch immediately to the Persian Gulf some of the ships which were to have sailed in [convoy PQ-18].

Churchill never mentioned the fact that the Admiralty had scattered convoy PQ-17. But Stalin focused on the scattering in his reply to Churchill on June 23. Churchill considered Stalin's reply "rough and surly." Certainly, it was blunt:

I received your message of July 17. Two conclusions can be drawn from it. First, the British Government refuses to continue the sending of war materials to the Soviet Union via the northern route. Second, in spite of the agreed communiqué concerning the urgent tasks of creating a second front in 1942 the British Government postpones this matter until 1943.

Our naval experts consider the reasons put forward by the British naval experts to justify the cessation of convoys to the northern ports of the U.S.S.R. wholly unconvincing. They are of the opinion that with good will and readiness to fulfill the contracted obligations these convoys could be regularly undertaken and heavy losses could be inflicted on the enemy. Our experts find it also difficult to understand and to explain the order given by the Admiralty that the escorting vessels of the PQ-17 should return, whereas the cargo boats should disperse and try to reach the Soviet ports one by one without any protection at all. Of course I do not think that regular convoys to the Soviet northern ports could be effected without risk or losses. But in wartime no important undertaking could be effected without risk or losses.

In any case I never expected that the British Government would stop dispatch of war materials to us just at the very moment when the Soviet Union, in view of the serious situation on the Soviet-German front, requires these materials more than ever. It is obvious that the transport via Persian Gulf could in no way compensate for the cessation of convoys to the northern ports.

With regard to . . . creating a second front in Europe, I am afraid it is not being treated with the seriousness it deserves. Taking fully into account the present position on the Soviet-German front, I must state in the most emphatic manner that the Soviet Government cannot acquiesce in the postponement of a second front in Europe until 1943.

I hope you will not feel offended that I expressed frankly and honestly my own opinion as well as the opinion of my colleagues on the question raised in your message.

Churchill did feel offended. He believed the British and Americans were doing all they could for the Soviet Union. He had little sympathy for Stalin and his fellow Communists, who "had been willing, until they were themselves attacked, to see us totally destroyed and share the booty with Hitler." Churchill did not reply to Stalin's letter, however. He saw no point in inflaming the Soviet dictator just for the pleasure of telling him off.

Roosevelt, meanwhile, had communicated separately with Stalin in a series of letters during the first part of July. The tone of Roosevelt's and Stalin's letters differed markedly from the tone of Churchill's and Stalin's letters. Roosevelt told Stalin he was sending the Soviet Union 115 more tanks than Stalin had requested. Stalin thanked the president but added, "I consider it a duty to advise you that, which our specialists confirm, the American tanks catch on fire very easily from projectiles of anti-tank weapons striking the rear or sides. This results from the fact that high grade gasoline used in American tanks forms a heavy layer of gas vapors creating favorable conditions for catching fire." Stalin went on to explain to Roosevelt that German tanks were designed similarly to U.S. tanks but used lower-grade gas, which did not produce such concentrated vapors. Stalin, unlike many dictators, did a lot of reading and immersed himself in details. Roosevelt and Stalin discussed several other topics, including the pending arrival of a new deputy U.S. naval attaché in Moscow. Stalin said he would extend every courtesy to the young man. Nowhere in the letters did Roosevelt or Stalin mention the Arctic convoys.

For Stalin and the Soviet Union, every day brought a crisis somewhere along the 1,500-mile eastern front. In the south, the Germans were massing their troops for an assault on Stalingrad. In the north, Leningrad remained under siege. For civilians remaining in Leningrad, daily life was hellish. Most of the city's adult males were either at the front or dead. Children had to grow up fast. When the air-raid sirens sounded, the mother of fourteen-year-old Yury Alexandrov sent him to the roof of their apartment building with a shovel. When the German bombers dropped their sticklike incendiaries, Yuri and the other children had to shovel them off the roof quickly before they could ignite and set the building on fire. Sand was piled around the base of the building to extinguish the incendiaries. The system worked. If the Germans ever switched to high-explosive bombs, however, the children on the roof with the shovels would be the first to die.

The siege of Leningrad resonated more with people in the United

States than did the horrors elsewhere on the eastern front. The main reason was the Russian composer Dmitri Shostakovich's Seventh Symphony. Shostakovich, a Leningrad native, had started writing the symphony in the besieged and starving city, where he also dug trenches, watched for fires, and lived in fear of the secret police, who pressured him to write tunes for a song-and-dance ensemble of retired NKVD agents. Shostakovich was evacuated from Leningrad before the brutal winter of 1941–42 and finished the Seventh Symphony in relative safety behind the battle lines. On June 25, 1942, two days before convoy PQ-17 left Iceland, a microfilm copy of the symphony arrived by plane in New York City. The composition was performed at Radio City Music Hall for a radio audience of millions on July 19—while the *Ayrshire, Troubadour, Ironclad,* and *Silver Sword* were waiting to be rescued from the Matochkin Shar.

THE *AYRSHIRE* AND ITS LITTLE convoy, which now included four freighters with the addition of the *Benjamin Harrison,* moved ten miles deeper into the strait on the advice of the Russian officer at the trappers' settlement. The crew of the *Benjamin Harrison* had slathered white paint on their vessel too. At the new anchorage, the strait was so narrow that even the most skilled German pilot might have trouble squeezing a bomb through the gap between the cliffs. The air was even colder deep in the strait. Ice clung to the rocks on shore. When the sun appeared, it threw such a glare off the ice that some of the mariners put on their goggles. Carraway wrote that the inside of the strait was "a perfect wasteland. . . . Other than a few lights and beacons along the channel's more tortuous bends, you'd never know men had ever been here before us." Carraway had hoped to reach Archangel by July 17, his and Avis's six-month anniversary, and celebrate "in grand style, with plenty of vodka and a touch of caviar." But the day passed without any escort vessels arriving in the strait.

The first new arrivals in the Matochkin Shar were not Commodore

Dowding's escorts but a pair of Soviet ships. The first was a formidable-looking icebreaker named the *Murman*. The second was the battered Soviet tanker *Azerbaijan*, which the Western mariners had never expected to see again. They had last seen the *Azerbaijan* on the Fourth of July, emerging from a boiling mass of smoke and flame after being hit by a bomb. Then had come the scatter order. The *Azerbaijan* had fought off Junkers 88s to limp into the Matochkin Shar. Its cargo of linseed oil was long gone. The tanker's hull was riddled with machine-gun rounds, and the deck was warped by the intense heat of the fire that had nearly sunk the ship. She was a floating wreck. But her captain had gotten his ship to Russia. The *Azerbaijan* dropped anchor in the strait at a distance from the Allied vessels. The Soviet vessel sent forth no greetings or representatives. The blond female bosun was nowhere to be seen.

A third Russian vessel, a coal-burning trawler named the *Kirov*, entered the strait and came alongside the *Troubadour* to obtain some coal. While the coal was being transferred, Captain Salvesen went aboard the *Kirov* and drank vodka with the Russian officers. Later, the *Ayrshire* came alongside the *Troubadour* for coal. For all the *Troubadour*'s shortcomings, its generous stores of coal were proving invaluable to the refugees of convoy PQ-17 and their would-be rescuers. The *Troubadour* had in effect become a collier.

After the *Ayrshire* finished taking on coal, two of Gradwell's men stayed aboard the *Troubadour* for dinner and were bowled over by the menu, which included Virginia ham, mashed potatoes, green beans, corn, and apple pie for dessert. It was the best food the Brits had eaten on the entire voyage. They were accustomed to corned beef in cans. The men on the *Troubadour* had never regarded good food as a luxury, but their perspective would change before long.

Gradwell did not join his men for dinner aboard the *Troubadour* because he previously had accepted an invitation to dine with the Russian captain of the *Murman*, who impressed Gradwell as "the first person I had met for nearly a month who did not seem to be in a state of complete jitters." Gradwell and the Russian captain "made great friends," Gradwell wrote. "He played me Russian gypsy music records and I showed him American glossy magazines." Gradwell kept the glossy magazines hidden until the *Murman*'s onboard commissar was not looking. Part of a commissar's job was to protect Soviet mariners from being corrupted by "subversive" Western magazines on Allied ships; commissars were known to confiscate those with photos of fancy cars and lavish meals such as Thanksgiving feasts.

After dinner, the Russians invited Gradwell and First Officer Elsden ashore to watch a movie. Unfortunately, Gradwell wrote, "it was the usual Russian propaganda film showing pre-1914 Russia with Cossacks beating the proletariat with whips. It opened with a scene of two Russian ladies driving in a carriage in St. Petersburg. This is supposed to make you dislike the bourgeoisie but it merely reminded me of my mother and my aunt when I was a small boy and made me more homesick than ever." The shore visit ended on a more enjoyable note with a boisterous singing competition. The Russians won hands down, although Elsden impressed them with a bawdy English drinking song. The Soviet icebreaker tied up alongside the *Ayrshire,* and the Russian crew broke out accordions and concertinas and sang Russian folk songs, their voices echoing through the Matochkin Shar.

The next morning, July 15, Gradwell signaled the American ships to weigh anchor and head toward the mouth of the Matochkin Shar. The *Troubadour* and *Ironclad* immediately plowed into a submerged mud bank and got stuck. The *Ayrshire* and the Russian trawler *Kirov* went back to retrieve them. The *Kirov* maneuvered into position to tow the *Troubadour* free of the mud bank but backed into the freighter with too much force. A depth charge tumbled off a rack on the *Kirov*'s stern and bounced heavily across the *Troubadour*'s deck. Jim North and his shipmates ran for cover. They did not know that depth charges had to be armed before they would explode. The depth charge on the *Troubadour* rolled harmlessly to a stop. Some of the Russian crew retrieved it.

Together, the *Kirov* and *Ayrshire* pulled the *Troubadour* out of the mud. The *Ironclad* worked itself free. The trawlers led the two freighters back toward the mouth of the strait, where the other vessels were getting ready for the 400-mile run to Archangel.

"I hate to go . . . and am pessimistic of our chances," Carraway wrote in his diary. "God or Allah grant us a fog or a snowstorm to hide in, and keep us clear of mines. . . . If we get through, it will be a masterpiece of good luck. But I'm ready to try it, ready to try anything to get there. The Russians need this stuff and I'm getting damn well tired of being 'on the way' there."

The Germans spotted the ships in the Matochkin Shar that afternoon. A little before 6:00 p.m. a Junkers 88 passed over the strait at high altitude. The *Troubadour* and one of the Russian ships shot at it. The German pilot ignored them and circled over the strait as if to confirm "I see you." The plane flew off to the south. Its visit instantly ratcheted up the tension in the Matochkin Shar. Rumors flew that an attack was imminent. Everybody was on edge. Fights broke out. Carraway reflected that "the high seas can hold nothing more terrifying than this inactivity." Another day passed without a rescue, and then another.

Finally, on the morning of July 20, Commodore Dowding arrived at the mouth of the strait with a small escort force consisting of the corvettes *Lotus, La Malouine,* and *Poppy.* On the *Ironclad,* Carter marveled that Dowding was again risking his life to gather up his battered flock: "What an amazingly courageous and resourceful man and Naval officer he was!" At Dowding's signal, the merchant ships emerged from the strait and turned south along the coast of Novaya Zemlya. The corvettes beamed their sonar through the water. A light fog set in.

The mariners looked up to see a small Russian plane passing overhead, flying north along the shore of Novaya Zemlya. At the controls was another celebrated Russian polar explorer, Ivan Dmitriyevich Papanin, whom the Soviets had given the rank of rear admiral and tasked with keeping the North Russia ports open. Sitting next to Papanin in the plane's cramped passenger seat was Commander Samuel Frankel, the U.S. naval attaché for North Russia. The two men were on their way to try to refloat the American freighter *Winston-Salem,* whose crew had intentionally run the ship aground at a place called Goose Earth. Frankel was determined to save the *Winston-Salem.* It was one of the few ships from convoy PQ-17 that could still be saved. The others were in Dowding's new convoy.

Dowding commanded the new convoy from the bridge of the corvette *Poppy.* He had known Gradwell's family for years and invited Gradwell aboard the *Poppy* for a drink. Gradwell felt enormous relief that Dowding had taken over responsibility for the *Troubadour, Ironclad, Silver Sword, Benjamin Harrison,* and *Azerbaijan.* At the same time, Gradwell recalled, "this was the worst part of the journey. I had got my ships so far, and it would have been depressing to lose them at the last lap." It was still a long way to Archangel.

The *Troubadour,* true to form, fell steadily behind the new convoy. Mud from the freighter's most recent grounding clogged its circulating pumps. Several new escorts arrived, however, and three of them dropped back with the *Troubadour.* Carraway joked that the *Troubadour* suddenly had become "the best escorted vessel in the history of convoys." Among the new escorts was the antiaircraft ship *Pozarica,* which after reaching Archangel had been assigned to protect ships on the approaches to the White Sea. The *Pozarica's* captain signaled his congratulations to his counterpart on the *Azerbaijan* for driving the crippled Soviet tanker through ice and fire. Izotov replied, "Thank you very much for congratulations. We are fulfilling our duty on service for our country and our General with you matter for to smash Nazi." The British war correspondent Godfrey Winn, who was aboard the *Pozarica,* wrote that the *Azerbaijan* "epitomized for us . . . the fighting spirit of the Russian people."

About 30 miles south of the Matochkin Shar, the convoy stopped at Moller Bay to pick up the British freighter *Empire Tide,* along with more than two hundred survivors from other ships who had come ashore in lifeboats near the freighter. Sixty-five lifeboat survivors from the sunken American freighters *Alcoa Ranger, Washington,* and *Olopana* had been camping on the rocky shore, subsisting on a thin soup they made from ducks. Nine other men with severe frostbite had been flown to a hospital in Archangel by Mazuruk, the Russian pilot who had spoken with Gradwell in the Matochkin Shar. Soon after the *Empire Tide* joined the convoy, the ships were enveloped by a fog so dense that Salvesen kept blasting the *Troubadour's* foghorn to warn other vessels to keep their distance. Carraway jumped every time the foghorn sounded. He was on edge, waiting for the Germans to attack.

To his great surprise, they never did.

Soon the mariners noticed low, snow-streaked bluffs on either side of the convoy. The ships had entered the Gourlo, a narrow strait connecting the Barents Sea to the White Sea. It was the finish line of their run to Russia. Soviet gun emplacements guarded both banks of the Gourlo. Russian fighter planes roared overhead, distinguishable by their red stars. Soviet destroyers, smaller than American and British destroyers but bristling with guns, came out to meet the convoy. There were no more air raids or U-boat alarms. The only surprise was a grand finale of Arctic mirages, more bizarre than any the mariners had yet seen. "Before our very eyes, other ships took on fantastic shapes," Baker wrote. Ships' superstructures vanished, leaving disembodied masts floating in the air. Baker "watched, fascinated, the tricks that nature, or the atmosphere, played for me."

The Gourlo opened into the White Sea, which the mariners noted was muddy brown rather than white. The ships followed a channel into the southeastern corner of the huge inland sea, where Archangel and its auxiliary ports were scattered along the wide delta of the North Dvina River.

The mariners welcomed the return of a few hours of darkness every day in Archangel, which lies below the Arctic Circle. "First time I saw darkness in 27 days," wrote Francis Brummer on the *Ironclad*. First light on July 25, 1942, revealed a flat, marshy shoreline covered with green—a color the men had not seen in weeks. People came out of wooden houses along the riverfront to wave at the passing ships. "We could relax and smile again," Baker recalled. "We waved happily back to the Russians on the shore. The sun put out its flags in a glorious blaze of color. . . . Four weeks after leaving Iceland, with God as our Pilot and Protector, we reached Archangel." U.S. naval authorities in Archangel reported the ships' arrival in more prosaic terms:

> Following arrive Archangel area 25th Iron Clad [sic], Silver Sword, Benjamin Harrison and Troubadour, American, Empire Tide British, Azerbaijan Soviet. There are now 1200 survivors here of all nationalities, 500 of which are American.

Every eye in the harbor was drawn to the *Troubadour, Ironclad,* and *Silver Sword.* After having been given up for dead, they had materialized, all in white. "We three ghosts," Carraway called them in his diary. Inevitably, mariners in Archangel dubbed them the "the Ghost Ships." Paul Lund and Harry Ludlam wrote, "It was an incongruous sight, with the *Ayrshire* leading her three merchantmen, all still painted a dazzling white." The white-painted *Benjamin Harrison* might have qualified at least as an honorary ghost ship. And even without new coats of white paint, the *Ayrshire* and the *Azerbaijan* deserved consideration for that honor as well.*

The ships passed between banks of flowering potato plants. A few miles upriver, they entered logging country. The banks of the river were lined with shabby sawmills to which wood was delivered by horse-drawn sledges. The hills above the city were densely carpeted with Northern

---

* The Ghost Ships were not the last vessels from convoy PQ-17 to arrive at Archangel. That distinction would belong to the *Winston-Salem*. Frankel and the Soviets managed to refloat the vessel and get it to Archangel three days after the arrival of the Ghost Ships, on July 28.

spruce, pine, and fir. Rafts of freshly cut logs drifted downriver on the outgoing tide. The air was cold, and smelled tart from the pine and the marshes. Salvesen announced that the *Troubadour* had been ordered to dock not at Archangel but at the outlying port of Molotovsk. Carraway was happy to be going to any port. He told his Armed Guard men to clean the tanks' turret guns and get the tanks ready for their new Soviet owners. Carraway could do nothing about the white paint slathered all over the tanks.

A Russian harbor pilot came aboard the *Troubadour* and guided the freighter farther upriver to a wooden dock that looked as though someone had just finished nailing it together. Four armed and uniformed soldiers stood waiting. The pilot misjudged the approach and the *Troubadour* slammed into the dock. "Boards creaked and went flying like match sticks," Jim North recalled. "Soldiers went running." The pilot managed to dock the *Troubadour* on his second try. The soldiers warily returned and stood guard at the gangplanks. Another ship was tied up nearby, being repaired by a throng of workmen clad in what looked like prison uniforms. From the docks a narrow roadway of logs and mud led up a steep hill into a stand of woods. North heard a train whistle from that direction.

The Ghost Ships had left Novaya Zemlya just in time. Two days after their arrival in Archangel, a U-boat attacked the island, using its deck cannon to shell a Soviet camp at Moller Bay, killing one person and injuring four others. Moller Bay was where the British freighter *Empire Tide* had hidden along with the lifeboat survivors of other ships. The U-boat sank Mazuruk's seaplane, which was moored in the bay, though the famous Arctic aviator was not present. After the U-boat attack, the German cruiser *Admiral Scheer* invaded the Kara Sea.

Only eleven of the original thirty-five ships of convoy PQ-17 had reached Archangel. Two had turned back to Iceland; twenty-two lay on the bottom of the Barents Sea with all their cargo. The Germans had also sunk the rescue ship *Zaafaran* and British fleet oiler *Aldersdale*. The human toll from convoy PQ-17 was still being calculated. It hovered somewhere between one hundred and three hundred, with scores of mariners still unaccounted for. Some had been captured by the Germans. Others were still adrift in lifeboats, including the star-crossed survivors of the American freighter *Honomu*.

The *Honomu* had been torpedoed on July 5 in the middle of the Barents Sea, but the Allies had not known of its sinking until July 18, when a ship's bell was discovered in a mass of floating debris. The bell bore the inscription "SS *Edmore*, Seattle," and a check of *Lloyd's Register of Ships* showed that the *Edmore* was the former name of the *Honomu*. No survivors or bodies were found near the bell, although two men in the *Honomu's* engine room had been killed by the torpedo strike. The *Honomu's* captain and four other mariners had been taken prisoner by the U-boat that sank their ship. The other survivors had set out in a lifeboat and four rafts. The nineteen men on the rafts had been rescued by a British vessel, but the fourteen men in the lifeboat were not so fortunate. As the lifeboat drifted through fog, sleet, and snow, they died of exposure one by one. Only four of the fourteen would still be alive on July 31—four weeks after the sinking—when a U-boat crew finally showed mercy on the survivors of the *Honomu* by taking them prisoner.

The Ghost Ships' odyssey to Archangel had taken twenty-eight days—almost three times the normal duration of the voyage. The mariners thought they had seen everything, but their adventure was far from over. The survivors of convoy PQ-17 had entered a nation traumatized by Stalin and Hitler. The mariners would be alternately charmed, threatened, and amazed by the Russians. In the heat of World War II, they would receive an unsettling preview of the Cold War.

CHAPTER TEN

ARKHANGELSK

In the days of the czars, Archangel—Arkhangelsk in Russian—had been a great cosmopolitan city, a jewel of Northern Europe. It was a historic seaport, founded in 1584 by Ivan the Terrible on the delta where the North Dvina River flows into the White Sea, near the site of a twelfth-century monastery dedicated to the Archangel Michael. Peter the Great had built Russia's first state shipyard at Archangel a century later, and for more than three hundred years the city had thrived as an international port, serving as Russia's chief link to Western trade, industry, and culture, despite the considerable disadvantage of being iced in every winter when the White Sea froze over. Merchants and visitors from around the world had strolled Archangel's streets and marveled at the intricate designs of its traditional wooden buildings. The Russian government had even allowed foreign merchants to build Catholic and Lutheran churches in the city. But by the time the survivors of convoy PQ-17 straggled into Archangel in late July 1942, the city was no longer beautiful, prosperous, or welcoming.

Under Soviet rule, Archangel and its surroundings had been transformed into a land of exile and hard labor. Most of the handsome wooden architecture was gone. The bulk of the city's shipping business had shifted to the Baltic Sea port of Leningrad, which could stay open year-round. Archangel, whose population hovered around two hundred thousand, served the Stalin regime mainly as an industrial port, an export hub for the timber industry. World War II transformed it into a vital port for Lend-Lease supplies. Rail lines led straight from its docks to both Moscow and Leningrad. Archangel shared the burden with Murmansk of receiving the Arctic convoys.

While Murmansk was only 35 miles from the German air bases, and thus under constant attack, Archangel was more than 350 miles from the front lines, and barely within range of the German bombers in Norway. The Germans had not yet bombed Archangel by the time convoy PQ-17 arrived, though German reconnaissance planes swooped low over the city on many occasions, pinpointing future targets for the bombers. In addition, German seaplanes dropped mines into the North Dvina River near Archangel to threaten shipping. During the spring thaw in 1942, Soviet icebreakers had found unexploded mines frozen into the ice.

Even without being bombed, Archangel had been traumatized by the war. One out of every three men in the city had been called up to the front lines with the Red Army, and by the summer of 1942 thousands of them had already been killed. By war's end, more than twenty-three thousand men from Archangel would die in combat—one out of every three who went to the front. Working-age women in the city either served in the military or were bused every day to long shifts in factories producing war supplies. Like other Soviet cities, Archangel had been reduced by the Great Patriotic War into a community of the very old and very young.

And Archangel was starving. The Soviet agencies tasked with collecting and distributing food to the citizenry had proven inept and corrupt even in peacetime, and the outbreak of the war caused severe shortages of bread, meat, and other essentials. Archangel was harder hit than most Soviet cities because, as a vital Lend-Lease port, it was largely closed to outsiders and thus more heavily reliant on the state system. Although Soviet officials and others with connections got plenty to eat, food shortages became severe for most of the populace. During the winter of 1941–42, thousands of citizens of Archangel starved to death. People ate their dogs and cats, and when they ran out of pets, they trapped and ate rodents and wild birds. Some ate their own dead. Over the course of the war, more than thirty-eight thousand Archangel residents would starve to death—more than would die from enemy bombs and bullets.

Most food from the Allied convoys merely passed through Archangel on its way to Moscow or Leningrad. Theft of food from the Archangel docks never stopped, despite severe penalties for anyone who was caught. "Impossible to prevent poorly fed local population from theft in spite of locks and armed guards," assistant U.S. naval attaché to North Russia Kemp Tolley wrote. "Sides of warehouses are literally torn down and guards are bribed into blindness." Women sliced open bags of flour and poured it into their galoshes. Men scooped up handfuls of spilled flour and stuffed it straight into their mouths. When thieves were caught stealing cabbages, the Russians forced them to take off their pants and sit on the ice for long hours, which killed some of them. The Americans protested the practice as cruel, and the Soviets agreed to deal with the thieves "some other way," Ambassador Harriman wrote, "and so they took the offenders out thereafter and shot them." The body of a man who had been shot to death on the docks for stealing lay where it had fallen until fresh snow gradually covered it up.

The only alternative to stealing was living by the Soviet government's rules, which seemed more absurd with every new cutback in rations. Howard Carraway wrote:

> Scattered over the city are little stations, soup kitchens, at which a supply of bread and soup is regularly dumped, [where] long queues of workers, ranging from old men and women to dirty little gamins, line up with buckets, pails, bottles, etc.,

and a net bag for the bread. In order to get an issue, they have to produce tickets showing that so much work has been done. No work, no eat.

Archangel's main business district lay along a street that extended the length of the city, dominated by a pagodalike opera house. Another street ran parallel along the riverfront, and several others ran perpendicular to those two. All the streets were cobblestoned, the sidewalks were wooden, and the sewer ditches were covered with wood. "I thought the city of Archangel itself had a relatively pleasing appearance," wrote Brigadier General James O. Boswell, a U.S. military attaché. "The waterfront was lined with stucco and brick buildings. Many river craft were at the wharves." But Tolley saw in Archangel "neither the majesty of a complete ruin nor the hope of a city that would be reconstructed."

Ramshackle, frontier-style log buildings, board sidewalks, unpaved muddy streets . . . Equally a surprise, even shock, was the appearance of the people. Poorly dressed, giving no sign of welcome, unsmiling, they suggested that life in wartime Archangel was scarcely a lark. . . . A few trucks slewed along cobbled streets through the mud and slush of spring . . . sending sheets of spray in all directions. Pedestrians on the rickety board sidewalks made halfhearted efforts to avoid the splash, cursing softly to themselves, most of them too perpetually hungry to show much enthusiasm, even in anger.

The presence of the Soviet government was oppressive. Loudspeakers blared patriotic music and propaganda. Squads of armed soldiers marched through the streets. A curfew was in effect from midnight to 6:00 a.m., although in July those were mostly daylight hours. The radios of visiting ships were sealed, and no small boats were allowed to be launched into the harbor. Any mariner who wanted to go ashore had to present his pass, or *propusk,* to well-armed Soviet sentries at the base of his ship's gangway.

Archangel was Gulag country. The stevedores who unloaded the ships were prisoners overseen by guards with dogs. Seven of the Soviet Union's more than 470 forced-labor camps were located near the port. Most of the prisoners in the camps near Archangel were political prisoners, ranging from writers who had criticized Stalin to "kulaks"—formerly prosperous farmers—whose farms had been seized by the government. But the prisoners also included criminals and captured German and Finnish soldiers. The POWs were being worked to death. They were fed just enough to keep them alive. One of them caught Jim North's eye and tried to trade him what looked like a family heirloom for a bit of food. North had no trouble distinguishing the POWs from the other prisoners. "They were a sad, hollow-eyed, starving bunch," he said. "They were beyond my help, beyond anyone's help. I was too young to comprehend the horror I was witnessing." The Soviet guards watching the POWs were mostly veterans of the eastern front who had been sent behind the lines to recuperate from wounds or emotional trauma. The guards were harder than the prisoners. They did not hesitate to beat or even kill prisoners who talked back to them or who slowed down in their work because of illness, exhaustion, or injury.

Archangel's fourteen hospitals and clinics were understaffed, undersupplied, and overwhelmed by survivors of sunken ships in convoy PQ-17. Most of the survivors suffered from frostbite. Seaman S. J. Flaherty, who had escaped the *John Witherspoon* in a lifeboat, spent two weeks in an Archangel hospital with frostbitten feet, taking antibiotics and wincing anytime his feet so much as brushed against the blanket. "The beds had no springs and the mattresses felt like straw, but we were grateful," Flaherty wrote. "[O]ur hosts were doing the best that could be managed with what was on hand." A man in a bed near Flaherty's had lost both feet, one hand, and part of his other hand.

After a week in Archangel, Lieutenant Gradwell had heard nothing from the Royal Navy about his disobedience to the scatter order. But the story of the Ghost Ships spread along the Archangel waterfront. British seamen on the corvette *Poppy* heard about "a brave and eccentric barrister yachtsman" who had ignored orders and saved lives. The official silence began to worry Gradwell. But as it turned out, he had no cause for concern. Letters of commendation arrived eventually, some from his superiors but others from unusual sources. The formidable, bearlike Admiral Golovko, commander of the Soviet Northern Fleet, wrote:

> With great satisfaction I have noted the persistent, energetic activities of the Captain of the Trawler Ayrshire, Lieut. Leo Gradwell . . . in escorting three Merchant ships during the course of several days and nights on passage under difficult conditions. . . . Please convey to Lieut. Gradwell and the crew of his ship my gratitude and delight at their work.

Captain Colbeth of the Ghost Ship *Silver Sword* wrote that the *Ayrshire* and its crew "were invaluable to our 3-ship convoy. I do not know how we could have ever reached Archangel without their aid." Gradwell eventually would be rewarded for his disobedience with the Distinguished Service Cross, a high British military honor. But the closest Gradwell ever came to bragging about what he had done were a few vague words he wrote in a letter to his mother from Archangel on August 2:

> I have had the worst month of my life but I am very well indeed and am beginning to sleep again. I can't tell you anything, of course, except that I have had my one big opportunity in this war, and that everyone is being very nice about it.

The news that Gradwell and the *Ayrshire* had survived convoy PQ-17 came as a shock to his wife, Jean. She had heard nothing from him and thought the *Ayrshire* was lost. She had gone so far as to organize a memorial service for him. She canceled it at the last moment when she learned he was still alive and might be coming home after all.

Gradwell, in fact, found life in Archangel at least somewhat enjoyable. When the *Ayrshire* was not running errands around the harbor, he organized small boat regattas in the North Dvina River to help the mariners pass the time. He took Godfrey Winn sailing. At night, Gradwell sometimes drank vodka with Russian naval officers. After one such outing, he was making his way back to the *Ayrshire* when he tumbled into an empty cargo hold and suffered minor injuries.

For most mariners in Archangel, a night on the town started with dinner at the Intourist Hotel, the center for foreign visitors in the city. The hotel was housed in a six-story brick building that had once been elegant. While Soviet citizens starved outside, the hotel offered a sumptuous menu, including pink caviar, smoked salmon, crab, meat, and eggs, accompanied always by vodka. A string ensemble played an eclectic set that included both "The Volga Boat Song" and "If You Knew Susie." The building's upper floors were temporary lodgings for shipwreck survivors and Allied military and government officials. A few blocks away, Allied seamen and sailors could also drink and dance at the International Club. Carraway went there to trade sea stories with his Navy Armed Guard friends. The club had a dance floor and a staff of women who swayed listlessly to scratchy records on a hand-cranked gramophone. "A hostess named Tanya . . . discussed the ideals of Karl Marx while dancing with me cheek to cheek," recalled General Boswell.

Another club in Archangel let mariners dance with Russian girls if they first sat through a Soviet propaganda film. The film lasted almost forty minutes and its gleaming images of a Soviet future looked nothing like the world outside the club's doors. The proprietors did not seem to care if the film was unpersuasive; they were just going through the motions of trying to recruit new Communists. When the film ended, the mariners danced with the girls, who were friendlier than the girls at the other clubs, although they would not sleep with the Americans. The mariners, starved for any kind of female companionship, kept going back to the club to see the girls even though they had to sit through the movie every time.

The outlying village of Molotovsk, where the *Troubadour* had been sent, was a creation of the war, hacked out of the forest to support a wharf hurriedly built into the riverbank. More docks were under construction all up and down the shore, along with a huge dry dock just upriver from the *Troubadour*. "It is altogether obvious that this country is in the war," Carraway wrote in his diary. "Every man and many women are in uniform. . . . Everything that is done is for the one purpose of war. I had never imagined that such a tremendous singleness of purpose could be achieved."

CARRAWAY HAD RECOGNIZED a fact Hitler had missed when he decided to invade Russia. Stalin's government, so cruel and indifferent to its people's happiness, was well suited to the single-minded waging of war. The Soviet system's centralized nature, and its prolific use of state terror, enabled Stalin to mobilize the nation in ways few leaders in the world could match. When the Germans started to overrun a Soviet region full of factories that produced war supplies, Stalin ordered entire factories dismantled and moved piece by piece to new locations safely behind the lines. Many of those factories were already operating again, producing guns, planes, and tanks with American steel, industrial chemicals, and other cargo from the Arctic convoys. The Soviet state assigned every citizen and every organization a specific wartime duty. A shipyard in Archangel was ordered to switch from building ships to building motorized sleighs to carry Soviet troops across the snow. The Soviet slogan was "Totally everything—for the front!"

"Totally everything," of course, included human life. The Red Army grew stronger, hardened by rage over Nazi atrocities—the torture and starvation of captured Red Army soldiers, the razing of villages, the assassinations of community leaders, and the mass murder of tens of thousands of Soviet Jews simply for being Jews. The Russian poet Alexey Surkov captured the fury building against the Nazis:

> The tears of women and children are boiling in my heart
> Hitler the murderer and his hordes shall pay for these
> tears with their wolfish blood

Stalin reduced the meddlesome authority of Red Army commissars and relied more on skilled generals such as Georgi Zhukov. Zhukov was popular with his men. He once noticed some officers in a jeep passing wounded men hobbling along the road; on the spot, Zhukov demoted the officers and gave the wounded men their jeep. But Zhukov, like Stalin, did not hesitate to sacrifice troops and call up more when he ran out. Human beings were one resource the Soviets possessed in abundance. Every soldier in the Red Army had come to understand that he or she had no choice but to fight. Capture by the Germans most likely meant torture, slave labor, and death. Retreat most likely meant the same. On July 28, Stalin issued Order No. 227, more commonly known as the "Not a step back" order. It forbade retreat under the penalty of death. It prohibited even displays of fear or doubt: "Panic mongers and cowards must be destroyed on the spot." Commanders "who retreat from battle positions without an order from above [are] traitors against the Motherland." Order No. 227 created penalty battalions of prisoners to be used in suicide missions, such as leading charges against entrenched enemy positions. The order also created patrol units to roam behind the Soviet lines and shoot deserters. Even in the darkest months of the war, the NKVD never stopped hunting for enemies of the state.

It was technically illegal for Soviet citizens even to carry on conversations with foreigners. That meant any Russian who befriended an Allied mariner on the docks risked an interrogation by the NKVD. It was no wonder most Soviet citizens avoided the men who had sailed across the

Arctic to help them. The wonder was that any Russians dared to befriend the Westerners.

SOON AFTER THE *Troubadour* docked at Molotovsk, a commissar with four uniformed soldiers came aboard the ship. The commissar spoke in English with Salvesen. He kept pointing to a manifest in his hand. He wanted to know why the tanks were painted white and why the turret guns had been fired. The captain's explanation did not satisfy him. Salvesen got angry and threatened to drive the tanks into the North Dvina River if the Russians did not want them. The commissar eventually signed the paper. Jim North watched stevedores in prison garb unload the ship. They manhandled the cargo into old, beat-up Model A trucks. The trucks struggled up a hill, pushed along by groups of prisoners, to a rail siding, where the prisoners then transferred the cargo to boxcars. The cabs of the Model A trucks had fireboxes in which wood was burned for fuel. Soviet commissars strutted around inspecting the work, easily recognizable in their green caps. North watched the unloading process in amazement. He wondered how a nation with so primitive a transportation system could hope to beat the highly mechanized Germans.

At the outlying port of Economia, the *Ironclad* was unloaded by a team of husky female stevedores with Asian features. They worked quickly and efficiently, paying the mariners no attention except for occasional disdainful glares. A young Soviet officer oversaw the unloading—"a very pleasant, quiet, almost studious person," Lieutenant Carter wrote. But when the time came to sign the document accepting the cargo, the young officer gave way to "a stern, hard-nosed character." The new commissar spoke impeccable English and made it clear to Carter that "he was looking for some freebies. He had a list of complaints as long as your arm." The commissar pointed to a layer of red rust coating the treads of the tanks lashed to the *Ironclad*'s main deck. Carter assured him the rust would shake off quickly once the tanks were driven. He added that if the Soviets were not happy with the tanks, the United States could take them back.

The tanks were quickly craned from the ship's deck onto the wharf. Russian tank crews climbed into them and test-drove them around a vacant lot, which knocked the rust off their treads. The tanks were driven up a hill and then up a ramp onto flatcars. They might be in combat by day's end. The rest of the *Ironclad*'s cargo took nearly a week to unload. It included fighter planes in crates, trucks and jeeps, guns, ammunition, steel, wire, radios, binoculars, batteries, medical supplies, food, lard, asbestos, copper, phosphorus and other chemicals, blankets, shoes, and a consignment of White Horse Scotch whisky for the U.S. embassy, to replace the whisky the mutineers had drunk in Iceland.

Most of the steel, ore, and other raw materials from the *Ironclad* and the other surviving ships of convoy PQ-17 were transported by rail to Moscow and then farther east, where the factories had been relocated. The ships' cargoes of food and fuel went mostly to Leningrad, along a rail line extending hundreds of miles through remote marsh and forest. The line was so vital to Leningrad's survival that the Germans constantly attacked it. When they managed to close it temporarily, the Soviets ferried the supplies to Leningrad across Lake Ladoga, an immense freshwater lake—roughly the size of Lake Ontario—on the northeast edge of the city. When the lake froze in winter, daredevil Soviet truckers hauled the supplies to Leningrad on sledges across the ice, dodging German bombs and holes in the ice caused by bombs. The truckers called their perilous route the "Ice Road." People in Leningrad called it the "Road of Life."

Carter, like Jim North, marveled at how hard the Soviets had to work just to transport supplies. But unlike North, Carter found the Russians' efforts encouraging: A nation of people willing to endure everything the citizens of Archangel were enduring would be difficult to defeat. Carter also had reached the conclusion that the United States was not doing nearly enough to help the Soviets. He was dismayed to discover that the U.S. military's entire presence in Archangel consisted of Commander

Frankel, an aide, and a clerk—and that the capable Frankel was about to return to the United States.* As far as Carter was concerned, such a meager investment of American personnel in North Russia made it "difficult to believe that Washington placed a very high priority on the Russian convoy operations in general."

Carter was amazed how little the average Russian knew about life outside the Soviet Union. Some of the Russians he met were convinced America was a glittering paradise out of a Hollywood movie. Others believed the United States was a pitiless Darwinian arena where the strong preyed on the weak. One Russian woman told Carter she had learned in school that the twentieth-century West resembled the nineteenth-century London depicted in Charles Dickens's novels about orphans, beadles, and workhouses.

To some American mariners, however, it was the Soviets who resembled characters out of Dickens. North set out on foot from the *Troubadour* one day to visit a dance hall he had heard was near the docks at Molotovsk. He had walked only a short distance when he found himself surrounded by a gang of street urchins whom the mariners had nicknamed "the Gum-Gum Boys."

The Gum-Gum Boys controlled the weedy, trash-strewn no-man's-land between the docks and the town. They were barefoot, filthy, and dressed in an odd combination of military garb and livery from the days of the czars. They hawked crude knives they claimed had been cut from the fuselages of downed German planes. They coveted gum, chocolate, and cigarettes. They crowded around North, not exactly blocking his way but sidling along with him too closely, calling out, "Tovarich, cigarette!" The boys were known to be expert pickpockets and some undoubtedly were worse than that. North was wearing a red sweater with a big letter *N*, which he had earned by running track at Newtown High School in New

---

* Carter was so "by the book" that when he first met Frankel, he apologetically turned over to Frankel a diary he had kept of the voyage, against Navy regulations. Frankel gave the diary back and told Carter to keep it.

York. The Gum-Gum Boys asked if the *N* stood for Nazi. North held his hand over his pocket containing his wallet and turned back toward the ship. The Gum-Gum Boys moved with him, close enough that he felt sure that one of them would dart in and hit him. But he made it back to the *Troubadour* unscathed with his wallet still in his pocket. He never tried to go to the dance hall again.

A few days later, North noticed that a large building near the docks served as some kind of women's dormitory. Hundreds of women lived there at night but took buses to work elsewhere during the day. The women seemed to be prisoners, or at least detainees. Each wore a quilted coat with an inside pocket containing a spoon, dish, and canteen. North found it easy to sneak into the dormitory, where chocolate and cigarettes made excellent icebreakers. Several of the women made it clear they wanted to sleep with him, and North was glad to oblige. He asked them no questions but was told later that the women were trying to get pregnant in order to qualify for more food and easier jobs. North found life at the dormitory so agreeable, he moved off the *Troubadour* and stayed among the women for a week. He returned to the ship just in time to avoid a police sweep of mariners who had abandoned their ships as he had done.

Among those caught up in the police sweep was one of the *Troubadour*'s most notorious brawlers. He picked a fight the moment he was brought back aboard the ship and was locked up in some kind of animal cage near the bow. As soon as he was released from there, he started a fight with Soviet sentries, who threw him in Archangel's jail. The *Troubadour* lost other crew members as well. The troubled Uruguayan seaman who had threatened to kill his shipmates in Iceland had finally been taken off the ship and hospitalized in Archangel. Another mariner had been removed from the *Troubadour* after going "dangerously mad."

The *Troubadour* was not the only ship in Archangel with problems. On the Liberty ship *Israel Putnam*, two brothers were accused of using threats and knives to intimidate the captain and the crew. Frankel ordered the brothers put in irons and sent home to the States on a U.S. warship, although he was not sure it was legal. On other vessels, minor disputes escalated into fistfights. Mariners got so angry at one U.S. Navy officer that they defecated in his jeep and left him a note telling him not to blame the Russians. A new work stoppage on the *Troubadour* prompted Salvesen to order fourteen crew members confined to the forepeak. Jim North was not among the offenders this time. All over the harbor Frankel felt the tension building. There simply was not enough to do in Archangel to keep the mariners out of trouble. Some of them went to great lengths to entertain themselves, creating a White Sea Baseball League, fashioning bats out of fresh-cut logs and gloves out of the heavy asbestos mitts used for handling hot shell casings. Others grew so bored that they risked their lives hitchhiking into Russia's interior. Captain Herbert Callis of Mathews County, Virginia, hitchhiked more than 600 miles to Moscow. "Friendliest town I ever did see," Callis told a Western journalist who showed him around the Soviet capital. The Navy offered to open a club in Archangel for the idle Americans, or at least to provide the International Club with games and magazines, but Soviet authorities refused to allow such an infusion of American popular culture. Stalin, angry over the Allies' refusal to invade France, even rejected a British offer to anchor a fully equipped hospital ship in Archangel, although Admiral Golovko shrewdly arranged for the hospital ship to dock at Murmansk instead.

Frankel generally sympathized with the American merchant seamen. "The majority . . . were, in fact, fine, generous and brave," he wrote after the war. "They were not fighting for money, and they wanted only one thing—to win the war." He was particularly impressed that the merchant crews often took up collections from their own pay to give to their Navy Armed Guard protectors, who were perpetually broke because they were prohibited by the Navy from accepting bonus pay from the Soviets. But the merchant mariners were not saints, Frankel wrote to his superiors. After the initial shock, the survivors of convoy PQ-17 "are well enough to start raising hell, and I fear that if they are here any length of time we will see some unpleasantness."

On August 9, Frankel summoned all the American mariners in Archangel to a meeting at the International Club. He praised their courage
and promised to try to resolve any problems they encountered and get
them home. "You have suddenly been thrust ashore in a country that is
radically different from any place you have ever been before," Frankel
told the mariners. "It is a country which has been hard at war, which has
suffered privations and which needs our cooperation and help." He asked
the Americans to remember they were guests in the Soviet Union and
that they had food and warm places to sleep, which was more than many
of the Russians had. Frankel might have pointed out that the mariners at
least could look forward to going home, whereas the Russians had nowhere else to go. And at least most of the mariners from convoy PQ-17
were still alive.

A relatively low casualty count was the only positive aspect of the debacle of convoy PQ-17. One hundred and fifty-three men had been killed
out of well over 2,500, including the men on the small escort vessels. The
courageous crews of the three rescue ships had saved hundreds of lives.
The Russians had saved hundreds more. Since many of the merchant ships
had been abandoned while still afloat, their crews had had more time than
usual to escape in lifeboats and on rafts. The weather, though cold, had
been calm. From the standpoint of ships and cargo, however, convoy
PQ-17 had been a disaster. More than 120,000 tons of war supplies had
been lost, including 40 American bombers, 200 tanks, 140 trucks and
jeeps, and enormous quantities of arms, ammunition, and fuel.

ON AUGUST 12, Churchill flew to Moscow to tell Stalin to his face that
the Western allies had decided to invade North Africa rather than France
in 1942. Churchill expected the meeting to be "a somewhat raw job."
Stalin surely would be angry over the invasion plan, as well as the postponement of convoy PQ-18 until September. Roosevelt advised Churchill
to handle "Joe" with great care: "We have got always to bear in mind the

personality of our ally and the very difficult and dangerous situation that confronts him. No one can be expected to approach the war from a world point of view whose country has been invaded. I think we should try to put ourselves in his place."

Churchill agreed, although part of him seemed to relish a collision with Stalin. On the plane to Moscow, he wrote, "I pondered on my mission to this sullen, sinister Bolshevik State I had once tried so hard to strangle at its birth, and which, until Hitler appeared, I had regarded as the mortal foe of civilized freedom. What was it my duty to say to them now?" Molotov, the Soviet foreign minister, met Churchill at the airport in a car whose windows had glass two inches thick. Molotov explained that the thick glass was "more prudent."

As Churchill had expected, Stalin frowned at hearing that his allies would not be ready to invade France until at least 1943. Stalin asked if Britain and the United States could at least land a small force in France. Then, Churchill recalled:

> Stalin, who had become restless, said that his view about war was different. A man who was not prepared to take risks could not win a war. Why were we so afraid of the Germans? He could not understand. His experience showed that troops must be blooded in battle. If you did not blood your troops you had no idea what their value was.

Churchill produced a map of North Africa and explained the secret plan for Operation Torch, which would be launched in November. Stalin declared, "May God prosper this undertaking," but made it clear he considered an invasion of North Africa a poor substitute for an invasion of France. Stalin would not drop the subject. The two leaders engaged in what Churchill described as "a most unpleasant discussion . . . during which [Stalin] said a great many disagreeable things." The Soviet dictator brought up the Arctic convoys and then convoy PQ-17. Churchill said

Stalin made "some rough and rude remarks about the almost total destruction of the Arctic convoy in June," asking at one point, "Has the
British Navy no sense of glory?" Churchill declared the Admiralty had
made the right decisions regarding convoy PQ-17. He added that the
British knew how to fight wars at sea. "Meaning that I know nothing?"
Stalin interjected. Churchill replied, "Russia is a land animal, the British
are sea animals." That comment defused the tension.

After returning to Britain, Churchill wrote a letter to Roosevelt assess-
ing the meeting with Stalin:

> On the whole I am definitely encouraged by my visit to Mos-
> cow. I am sure that the disappointing news I brought could
> not have been imparted except by me personally without lead-
> ing to really serious drifting apart. It was my duty to go. Now
> they know the worst, and having made their protest are en-
> tirely friendly; this in spite of the fact that this is their most
> anxious and agonizing time.

Churchill overestimated the calming influence of his visit to Moscow.
After his departure, Stalin put out yet another peace feeler to Hitler, this
time through the German Foreign Ministry in Sweden. Hitler again
showed no interest.

Roosevelt wrote separately to Stalin apologizing for being unable to
travel to Moscow. He vowed to bring all of America's military power to
bear against Germany "just as soon as it is humanly possible to put
together the transportation." He promised a thousand more tanks would
be shipped soon. "The United States understands that Russia is bearing
the brunt of the fighting and the losses this year," Roosevelt wrote. "We
are filled with admiration of your magnificent resistance. Believe me
when I tell you that we are coming as strongly and as quickly as we possibly can." The Soviets already had been locked in merciless battle—"total
war"—against the Nazis for fourteen months.

ON THE NIGHT OF AUGUST 24, the Germans bombed Archangel for the first time. Eighteen Junkers 88s and Heinkel 111s attacked the city. From the deck of the *Troubadour* at Molotovsk, Carraway watched the searchlights and antiaircraft bursts light up the sky over Archangel. The bombs destroyed several homes and factories, and started fires that burned out of control all night. "Air attack on Archangel city of 5 hours duration," the U.S. naval attaché in the city reported. "Fires were started by incendiaries followed up by high explosives. . . . Power and water supply failed but early next day most fires appeared under control due to rain. [Antiaircraft] defenses described as pitiful."

After that night, the German bombers came regularly. Archangel entered a new and harder phase of the war. One night, Carraway was walking through Molotovsk on his way back to the *Troubadour* when the air-raid siren sounded. He was almost to the ship and ignored a Soviet guard who was herding people into an air-raid shelter. The guard fired a warning burst from his submachine gun close enough to Carraway to spray dirt on his boots. Carraway got the message. He walked briskly into the shelter, right past the guard, who "didn't smile or give me any recognition whatsoever. He just stood there like a dummy, a mummy." Although Carraway did not know it, his instincts in bypassing the air-raid shelter had been correct. Few such shelters in North Russia were well designed, particularly in the early years of the war, and several shelters collapsed and killed their occupants.

Carraway had seen all he wanted to see of America's new ally. He was homesick for South Carolina. "At home it's the hot month, hottest of the year," he wrote in his diary. "Tobacco to cut and cure and market. Cotton is laid by and corn is tall and beginning to brown. The grapes are ripe, and the plums. Melons are just past their prime and the sweeter for their age, and the scarcer." He thought about Sunday dinners on his parents' little farm in Olanta, with ham, fried chicken, and his mother's biscuits.

By the final week of August 1942, Carraway could tell that the *Troubadour*'s departure was imminent. The Russians were loading coal into the vessel's bunkers—albeit grainy, low-quality coal that drew worried looks from the ship's engineer. The *Troubadour* had had enough trouble keeping up with its convoys while burning high-quality coal. Salvesen said the ship had been assigned to sail home in convoy QP-14. It would depart as soon as the Allies dared to send convoy PQ-18 from Iceland, since Iceland-bound and Russia-bound convoys always sailed at the same time and passed one another in midocean.

Carraway could not decide if he wanted to leave immediately or endure Archangel for a few more weeks in the hope of a safer voyage home. On one hand, the window was fast closing for the *Troubadour* to get out of Archangel before winter. The sun brought little warmth anymore, and ice had begun to form along shady stretches of the riverbanks. Soon the river and the White Sea would freeze over. But on the other hand, the longer the *Troubadour* waited, the more darkness it would have in which to hide from the Germans during the return voyage. Every succeeding day brought an additional twenty minutes of darkness. From Carraway's perspective, the ideal time to start the trip would be the last day before the ice made sailing impossible.

No matter when the convoy left, the Arctic sea would no longer be the placid, foggy duck pond it had been in June and July. It would show the homebound ships an angrier face. "We're heading into a long and dangerous trip between here and Iceland," Carraway wrote to Avis. "Our exceeding good luck so far . . . gives me confidence and frightens me. But it must be gone through and that's that."

Not all the Ghost Ships would make it home.

CHAPTER ELEVEN
THE KNIFE-EDGE

As the merchant ships languished in Archangel, the crews' behavior grew worse by the day. The vessels' food supplies ran out, and the mariners were aghast at the local fare, which included yak stew and a tough, stringy meat vaguely labeled as "mutton." Some of the *Ironclad*'s crew began stealing emergency food supplies from the ship's lifeboats, including malted milk tablets, whose sweet taste appealed to the Russian women. Lieutenant Carter was appalled that the men were shortsighted enough to deplete rations they might need in order to stay alive. With the captain's approval, Carter posted Armed Guard sentries at the top of the *Ironclad*'s gangplank to search every man leaving the ship. Almost immediately the sentries discovered a package of the malted milk tablets in the possession of the Kid, the ex-prizefighter who had been handcuffed during the mutiny in Iceland.

The Kid started swinging at the sentries and one of them hit him in the head with a billy club, knocking him out cold. He was locked up in a makeshift brig, where he gathered some strands of rope into a pile and set it on fire. "He really was a bastard when he had been drinking," Carter observed. The next day, the Kid sobered up and acted chastened, but when Carter escorted him to a bathroom, he made a run for the gangplank. Carter hit him over the head with the barrel of his .45-caliber pistol and knocked him unconscious again. The Kid was dragged back to the brig. Carter thought he probably had saved the Kid's life: At the base of the gangplank he would have encountered a poker-faced Soviet guard with a submachine gun.

The mood was no better on the *Troubadour*. The steward and the ship's carpenter announced they would not sail home on the vessel. Even the dauntless Captain Salvesen declared he was finished with the *Troubadour*. "He gives no particular reason except that he . . . has had trouble enough," Howard Carraway wrote. "I can see his point." Carraway hoped the captain, the steward, and the carpenter were just blowing off steam. That seemed as good an explanation as any after months of frustration over the ship, the crew, the weird Arctic weather, the abandonment by the British, and the doleful life in Archangel. All three men ended up staying aboard the ship. The edginess on the *Troubadour* was real, however. The order to depart from depressing Molotovsk came just in time, on September 5.

First, Salvesen was ordered to sail the *Troubadour* across the mouth of the North Dvina River to Economia to load cargo for the voyage home. The order came so late in the day that darkness fell before the *Troubadour* got halfway there. The navigator lost his bearings, and Salvesen, worried about running aground again, decided to drop anchor and wait for daylight. The crew spent a frosty night watching the aurora borealis ripple across the sky and listening for the drone of German bombers that did not come. At first light, the *Troubadour* finished the trip to Economia, which looked depressingly like Molotovsk—a few dozen rough-hewn buildings clustered around a rail line and some docks. Several other surviving ships of convoy PQ-17 were already at Economia, including the *Benjamin Harrison*. The *Troubadour* took on a load of chrome ore and asbestos. The loading went smoothly, and on September 10 the *Troubadour* was ordered to Archangel to join homebound convoy QP-14.

The *Troubadour* followed a narrow, 10-mile-long channel to Archangel. The muddy banks on either side were piled high with more freshly cut lumber than the mariners had ever seen. As the ship drew close to Archangel, the mariners saw numerous bombed-out buildings, including a huge masonry structure the size of a hotel, which had been gutted by fire. The Germans had settled into a pattern of bombing Archangel several times a week. A first wave of bombers would appear over the city at dusk and drop incendiaries onto Archangel's mostly wooden buildings. Then a second wave of bombers would pass over the city and drop high-explosive bombs, using the burning buildings as landmarks.

The *Troubadour* edged up to a coal pier in Archangel and topped off its bunkers with the grainy Russian coal, then made its way to the mouth of the North Dvina River. The weather turned colder, bringing rain mixed with light snow, and the wind quavered through the ship's rigging. Soviet authorities came aboard to collect the mariners' *propusks*. A small boat brought the *Troubadour* ten survivors from the sunken convoy PQ-17 freighter *El Capitan* to carry home to the United States as passengers.

On the morning of September 13, the *Troubadour, Ironclad,* and *Silver Sword* joined a line of merchant ships steaming downriver toward the White Sea and then the open ocean. The ships included all the other merchant ships that had survived convoy PQ-17—the *Benjamin Harrison, Bellingham, Winston-Salem, Empire Tide, Ocean Freedom,* and *Samuel Chase*—as well as nine ships from earlier convoys. The *Ironclad* was loaded with Russian manganese ore, which was used to harden steel. The *Silver Sword* carried chrome ore, pulp wood, and animal hides. The indomitable Commodore Dowding led the new convoy, and the escort force included antisubmarine vessels from convoy PQ-17, including the *Ayrshire*. The trawler secretly carried two tons of butter the crew had bought cheaply in Archangel to smuggle back to Britain, where butter was scarce. Lieutenant Gradwell had ordered the butter wrapped in sailcloth and stowed in the *Ayrshire*'s bilges to hide it from customs inspectors.

The *Ironclad*'s voyage with convoy QP-14 lasted only a few minutes. The ship's rudder suddenly quit responding and the *Ironclad* nearly slammed into another vessel. Captain Moore ordered the anchor dropped, and the rest of the convoy passed the *Ironclad* and continued north. On the *Troubadour,* Carraway shook his head at the *Ironclad* and called it a "poor, unfortunate old tub"—a curious insult to be leveled from the *Troubadour.* A tugboat towed the *Ironclad* back to a dock. U.S. naval authorities boarded the ship and arrested five of the crew on suspicion of sabotaging the rudder. If they had done it to avoid sailing back through the Arctic on the *Ironclad,* they achieved their goal. They would be sent home weeks later as prisoners on a Navy warship.

The *Troubadour* immediately fell behind its new convoy. The ship could not keep up enough steam to maintain a speed of 8 knots. The firemen blamed the grainy Russian coal. The captain blamed the firemen. The *Troubadour* plodded along through bitter cold under clear skies. On September 14, the ships passed through the Gourlo into the open waters of the Barents Sea. Convoy QP-14's route led east-northeast toward Novaya Zemlya, then northeast to the edge of the ice field, and then west to Hvalfjord.

The *Troubadour* briefly caught up with the other ships when they slowed to organize into convoy formation. Then the *Troubadour*'s engines inexplicably stopped. By the time the chief engineer got the ship moving again, convoy QP-14 was almost out of sight. One of the escort vessels signaled the *Troubadour* to hurry and catch up, adding that no escorts would drop back to protect it if it continued to straggle. Soon the convoy vanished over the horizon.

The men on the *Troubadour* knew they would never catch up; they would have to sail the *Troubadour* through the Arctic alone. That prospect overwhelmed one mariner, who began muttering to himself and "begging people to kill him," Carraway wrote. The crew kept a wary eye on him, and also on the Uruguayan seaman who had threatened them at the start of the voyage. He was back on the ship after his hospital stay in Archangel. He no longer seemed agitated, and had resumed his shipboard duties, but how he would respond to the *Troubadour*'s latest crisis was anyone's guess.

On the *Troubadour*'s second day in the open sea, a Junkers 88 bomber passed over the ship at high altitude. The pilot did not seem to notice the ship but the encounter reminded Carraway that the *Troubadour* could be attacked at any moment. He quietly transferred some of his personal items and cigarettes to his assigned lifeboat. If the *Troubadour* was sunk while sailing alone through the Barents Sea, the survivors could not count on being rescued quickly. They might be in the lifeboats for a long time.

As the *Troubadour* chugged west, the lookouts scanned the featureless surface of the sea with renewed urgency, looking for the slender wake of a U-boat's periscope. The *Troubadour* was on the home stretch of its voyage, only four days out of Iceland. Stragglers like the *Troubadour* were the U-boats' bread and butter, and the freighter was approaching the remote Norwegian archipelago of Svalbard, which was a known haunt of U-boats. Carraway knew he should be afraid, but after everything he had been through, he could not seem to muster any fear. "I . . . believe that in some way, as in the past, we'll make it," he wrote to Avis, "even if, as before, it takes a sort of miracle to bring us through."

On September 16, two days east of Svalbard, the *Troubadour* was engulfed by an Arctic blizzard. Carraway was delighted: He much preferred nature's violence to that of the Nazis. Gale-force winds plastered ice and snow against the windward side of the hull and the deckhouse. Then the wind abruptly ceased and the snow began "drifting down by the hatful," piling up on the ship's decks. Carraway wished the snow would keep falling until the *Troubadour* reached Iceland, blinding every U-boat captain

for miles around. But after two days, just as the *Troubadour* was passing
south of Svalbard, the storm gave way to calm, hazy weather—not ideal
for U-boats, but suitable enough.

At five o'clock in the morning on September 18, Carraway was jolted
out of his bunk by the hooting of the U-boat alarm. But the lookouts had
merely spotted an ice floe. Carraway went back to sleep and did not
awaken until just after noon. He was making his way across the main
deck to the galley when he noticed a disturbance in the water about two
miles off the *Troubadour*'s port side. The smooth sea erupted in a series of
small bursts. At first, Carraway thought a whale was spouting. Then he
realized the bursts were the splashes of a torpedo. It was heading straight
for the *Troubadour*'s stern. Carraway shouted a warning to the helmsman
to turn the ship. By the time Carraway and two of his Armed Guard men
reached the 4-inch gun on the stern, the torpedo was only 20 yards away.
He yelled at the men to abandon the gun and save themselves. "We all fell
flat on our faces at the starboard rail and waited to be blown to bloody
hell." As Carraway lay on the deck, he looked into the water and saw the
torpedo zoom past: "I could see it entirely too plainly—the markings, the
copper bands about it, the screw spiraling up the water and everything
else, and it didn't miss that rudder more than 18 inches, I don't believe,
and if the rudder hadn't put over when it did it would have gone right up
in my face, that is within 15 feet of my face."

A short distance away from Carraway stood Jim North, who had gone
out to the stern to smoke a cigarette. North had just taken his first drag
when he saw the torpedo churn past the *Troubadour,* close enough that he
could have hit it with a rock. The torpedo was gone before North had
time to be frightened of it. He thought back to his narrow escape on the
outbound voyage, when a torpedo had come straight at him but then
malfunctioned and sunk. Torpedoes seemed to seek him out and then
spare him.

Carraway saw the wake of the U-boat's periscope. He gave the order
to fire the 4-inch gun, but it jammed. By the time his men got it clear, the

periscope had disappeared. Every man on deck scanned the water's surface. The *Troubadour* was in a lonely stretch of ocean. Salvesen swung the *Troubadour* north toward Spitsbergen, whose snowy mountains loomed above the sea mist. The radioman sent a distress call and repeated it over and over. No one responded. The minutes ticked past. Every ripple on the sea looked like the tip of a periscope. Never on the voyage had the *Troubadour* seemed in greater danger. Finally, a message came from Spitsbergen that help was on the way. Some of Carraway's Armed Guard men wept with relief. One seized his hand and would not stop shaking it. Carraway knew exactly how they felt but told them to get back to their guns and keep their eyes on the sea.

Within five minutes, an Allied plane flew in low and circled the spot where the periscope had been seen. There was no sign of the U-boat. The plane dropped a message on the *Troubadour*'s deck saying a British destroyer was coming to escort the freighter to Iceland. The destroyer arrived quickly and led the *Troubadour* to an anchorage at Spitsbergen. Three other destroyers and a British tanker were waiting there. The four destroyers formed a protective screen around the tanker and the *Troubadour,* and the vessels set out for Iceland.

Fifty miles ahead of the *Troubadour,* its former convoy, QP-14, steamed through snow squalls in the darkness, pursued by U-boats. The *Silver Sword*—the only one of the three Ghost Ships still in the convoy— developed engine trouble and fell behind the other ships. The Ghost Ships seemed destined to sail on a knife-edge. On the morning of September 20, a U-boat sank a British minesweeper escorting the convoy, killing six sailors. A few hours later, men on the *Silver Sword* saw a torpedo streak across the freighter's wake. Before they could spread the alarm, three more torpedoes crashed into the ship, mortally wounding a crewman and setting the *Silver Sword* afire. The captain ordered the crew into the lifeboats, where they were quickly picked up by the rescue ships *Rathlin* and *Zamalek.* Later that night, U-boats sank a British oiler and two freighters. One of the freighters was the convoy PQ-17 survivor

Bellingham; the other was the British freighter *Ocean Voice,* which Commodore Dowding had chosen as his new flagship. Dowding survived a second icy dunking. U-boats crippled the British destroyer *Somali,* which was taken in tow by a second destroyer. The *Somali* later broke in half and sank, taking the lives of forty-seven British sailors, after the towline snapped in a storm.

The same storm lashed the *Troubadour* and its escort of destroyers. The freighter rolled in steep, breaking seas. Green water slammed into the bulkhead directly below the bridge. Jim North had to stand lookout on the wing of the bridge because he would have been swept off the bow. The *Troubadour* slid down the backs of huge waves into deep troughs and then climbed up equally huge waves. Carraway went below at the end of his watch and clung to the frame of his bunk to keep from being hurled out of it. His toiletries bag flew across the room and hit him in the face, leaving him with a black eye. He still preferred facing Mother Nature to facing the Germans.

The *Troubadour's* little convoy finally reached Hvalfjord on the night of September 27, exactly three months after setting out from there for Russia. Carraway reflected that convoy PQ-17's departure "seems only a day or so ago, and I can remember every detail of the leaving." He found it strange to see the anchorage in the dark for the first time. Hvalfjord was much less crowded with ships than it had been in June. The *Troubadour's* radio picked up stations from London and Boston. News reports characterized convoy PQ-18 as having been a success, with "most" of the merchant ships getting through. In fact, the Germans had sunk thirteen of the convoy's forty merchant ships, while losing three U-boats and a staggering forty-one planes, most of them dive-bombers. The *Tirpitz* had stayed in port. Raeder had hatched another aggressive plan to attack the convoy with the cruisers *Admiral Scheer, Admiral Hipper,* and *Köln,* while keeping the *Tirpitz* on standby, but he abandoned that plan after a telephone call from Hitler. The British Admiralty reconfigured the escort force to prevent convoy PQ-18 from turning into a disaster like convoy PQ-17. A British escort carrier accompanied convoy PQ-18 as far as Bear Island, keeping the Shad away. Sixteen Allied destroyers, which had been trained to fight as a unit, escorted the convoy all the way to Archangel.

There had been no discussion of scattering convoy PQ-18. The British never scattered another convoy. And although the captains of the small escort vessels of convoy PQ-17 received official commendations, the senior British naval officer in North Russia made it clear he did not think much of their having abandoned the merchant ships and banded together for their mutual safety while fleeing to Novaya Zemlya after the scatter order: "It would be preferable if . . . [the small escorts] had attached themselves singly to the most valuable ships of the convoy and remained with them," he wrote. Another British officer in Archangel wrote that destroyers were the only escorts powerful enough to mount an effective defense for a convoy, and that "the departure of all destroyer escorts of Convoy PQ-17 has had severe damaging effect on morale of British and American merchant crews . . . especially the latter."

ON THE SAME DAY the *Troubadour* steamed back into Hvalfjord, September 27, Roosevelt and Churchill puzzled over how to break the news to Stalin that the next Arctic convoy, PQ-19, would not be sent as scheduled in October. Convoy PQ-18 had needed every one of its seventy-seven escort vessels to reach Archangel without severe losses. Now, most of those escorts would be needed for Operation Torch, the Allied invasion of North Africa, which was scheduled for November 8. Churchill said convoy PQ-19 could not possibly sail as scheduled unless Operation Torch was postponed, which was out of the question. Roosevelt agreed but added that delaying convoy PQ-19 would be "a tough blow for the Russians." The Red Army and the German Sixth Army were fighting house by house in the smoking ruins of Stalingrad. That battle could very well determine the outcome of the war on the eastern front, and perhaps the outcome of the war in Europe. Roosevelt and Churchill were keenly aware that America and Britain were still on the sidelines.

Roosevelt suggested not telling Stalin the bad news about convoy PQ-19 right away: "I can see nothing to be gained by notifying Stalin sooner than is necessary and indeed much to be lost." He suggested that rather than tell Stalin they were postponing the convoy, they should tell him they had decided to divide it into small groups of ships and send them over the next few months. Churchill agreed to try sending smaller convoys, but he persuaded Roosevelt that Stalin should be told the truth: Operation Torch required so many escort vessels that the big PQ convoys could not resume until at least January 1943.

Stalin's reply was curt: "I have received your message of October 9. Thank you." Roosevelt told Churchill not to worry because the Soviets "do not use speech for the same purposes as we do."

Stalin saved his comments for the Soviet public. In an open letter to *Pravda,* the official newspaper of the Communist Party, he criticized the Western democracies for offering Russia little help: "As compared with the aid which the Soviet Union is giving to the Allies by draining upon itself the main forces of the German Fascist armies, the aid of the Allies to the Soviet Union has so far been little effective." Stalin added that America and Britain needed to "fulfill their obligations fully and on time," and berated them for failing to open a second front in France.

Taking Stalin's cue, Soviet military and government officials turned the expression "second front" into a bitter joke. They held up little cans of food delivered by the convoys and said, "Look, here is the second front." In Moscow, they pointed to the second row at the Bolshoi Ballet, which was reserved for senior Allied representatives with complimentary passes. That row of mostly elderly, balding gentlemen was mocked as the "second front" or the "balding front." As far as the Soviets were concerned, they were getting no help from their Western allies except the on-again, off-again Arctic convoys.

AFTER EIGHT DAYS IN HVALFJORD, the *Troubadour* sailed for the United States in yet another convoy. The weather turned rough and the *Troubadour* as usual fell behind. The seas got so big that Salvesen gave up trying to catch the convoy and turned the *Troubadour* into the wind to ride out the storm. So much seawater found its way into Carraway's room that he collected his soggy belongings and moved into one of the crew's common areas. "But just think!" he wrote to Avis. "It's hardly two weeks, with good luck, before I'll be seeing you again. It's so much like a dream that I can't quite fathom it, can't believe that I'm going back to you, and that you're my wife." His diary entry was barely legible because the *Troubadour* was rolling and bucking so wildly.

In the middle of a particularly violent roll, one of two brothers who had joined the *Troubadour* in Archangel as coal passers fell into the coal bunker from the top of a 25-foot ladder, breaking a leg and fracturing his skull. Salvesen immediately ordered the *Troubadour* to leave the convoy and rush the injured man to the nearest hospital, which was in St. John's, Newfoundland. Carraway admired the captain's compassion but reflected that the injured coal passer was only one of seventy-five men on the ship, including the survivors of the *El Capitan,* whose lives the captain was endangering by ignoring orders and pulling the *Troubadour* out of the convoy. Carraway wondered if the captain had disobeyed orders partly out of a festering anger at the British over the abandonment of convoy PQ-17.

The injured man's brother refused to leave his side, so Jim North was ordered to take a shift as a coal passer. The job entailed shoveling coal into a wheelbarrow, steering the full barrow across the dimly lit coal bunker, and then dumping the coal down chutes into piles where the firemen could shovel it into the ship's boilers. When the firemen ran low on coal, they banged their shovels on the coal chutes. North found the work exhausting. Every time the *Troubadour* rolled, his wheelbarrow tipped over and he had to fill it again. He soon fell behind. The firemen banged their shovels and bellowed curses up the coal chutes. North hated being cooped up in the windowless coal bunker, blind to everything around him. Twice on the voyage he had watched torpedoes head straight at him; now he imagined a third torpedo heading at him while he was unable to see it coming. After a few hours, a huge Norwegian seaman squeezed into the coal bunker to tell North to take a lunch break. North misunderstood and cursed at him. The big Norwegian just grinned, picked up North, and carried him to the mess deck.

The *Troubadour* dropped off the injured coal passer at St. John's and resumed its voyage south. The weather turned warmer and calmer. The *Troubadour* was assigned to a slow convoy. For the first time, it managed to keep up. The voyage began to feel almost routine. Carraway concentrated on writing reports, inventorying supplies, and packing up his gear to leave the ship in New York City.

At around 4:00 p.m. on November 3, the *Troubadour* steamed into New York Harbor. There was no cheering crowd to celebrate the end of the ship's extraordinary voyage, which came as no surprise to the crew. The comings and goings of merchant ships, no matter how perilous and dramatic their voyages had been, were largely ignored by the American public. The day's front-page headlines in *The New York Times* announced a naval battle in the Pacific off the island of Guadalcanal, where the U.S. Marines were engaged in a desperate fight with the Japanese; and the equally desperate efforts by the Red Army to hold off the Nazis in the devastated city of Stalingrad. A story inside the paper quoted a Russian academic telling an audience in Moscow that the Soviet Union would have to fend for itself until the West stopped playing political games and opened a second front in France.

But the most significant development in the war was nowhere in the paper. As the *Troubadour* was docking in New York, seventy-five thousand American soldiers were secretly on their way across the Atlantic to launch Operation Torch, the Allied invasion of North Africa. A smaller force of British troops had sailed simultaneously from the west coast of Britain. The invaders would cross the ocean undetected by the Germans and splash ashore on the beaches of North Africa four days after the *Troubadour*'s unheralded homecoming. Operation Torch would open a new, muscular phase of America's war against the Nazis, which ultimately would relegate the Arctic convoys—and the awkward, passive period of U.S. military history they represented—to a footnote in America's history books.

Carraway, of course, knew nothing about Operation Torch as he walked off the *Troubadour* for the last time. All he cared about was finding a pay phone. After a couple of calls, he located Avis in Chicago, where she was staying with her parents. She caught the next train to New York. Carraway would spend a luxurious twenty-four-day leave with her before having to report back to the Armed Guard. The Navy had decided Carraway's experiences in convoy PQ-17 qualified him as an expert. He would spend the rest of the war teaching gunnery to Armed Guard recruits at a training center in Little Creek, Virginia. Carraway would never go back to sea.

Jim North, along with the rest of the *Troubadour*'s merchant crew, stayed aboard the ship until it reached Philadelphia, where its voyage officially ended. North spent his last day on the *Troubadour* reading a stack of letters the captain had picked up for him in New York. The letters were all from North's family, covering the ninety-nine days he had been incommunicado. The letters reminded him that he had been gone a long time. His father had bought a farm in Arkansas, and then joined the Merchant Marine and gone to sea. His little sister had graduated from high school, survived a burst appendix, and gotten married. His grandparents had sold one farm and bought another. Even though North had not written to anyone, his mother had written him faithfully once a week. He decided to visit her in New York as soon as he got off the *Troubadour*. First, he had to figure out how to escape from the ship in one piece.

Merchant mariners such as North were always paid off in cash at the end of voyages. The law required cash payoffs to protect mariners from unscrupulous shipowners offering worthless IOUs. But a mariner getting off a ship in a strange port with a wad of cash was a robbery waiting to happen. North worried mainly about being robbed by his shipmates. He had learned to get along with them but knew better than to trust them. On the night before the crew was to be paid off in Philadelphia, North walked through the city and mapped out the fastest route from the docks to the train station. Then he returned to the *Troubadour* and packed his seabag. Most of his clothes no longer fit him because he had gained weight on the voyage. He discarded all his belongings except a hunting knife, a half carton of Lucky Strike cigarettes, his woolen long johns, his blue watch cap, and the red sweater with the letter *N* that had attracted the taunts of the Gum-Gum Boys in Molotovsk.

The next morning, North collected his pay, which came to $1,500 in cash plus a $500 bonus check from the Soviet government. He shook hands with Salvesen but did not say goodbye to anyone else. He raced off the *Troubadour* "like it was on fire" and ran for the train station, looking back over his shoulder every few seconds. He was pleasantly surprised that none of his shipmates were chasing him. After pausing to catch his breath, North bought a ticket for New York. He would sail cargo ships for the rest of the war, with no real excitement. Before joining any ship, he always made sure it was not going to Russia.

FOR CARTER AND THE *IRONCLAD*, still stuck in Archangel, the worst of the Murmansk Run was yet to come.

The *Ironclad*'s rudder was easily repaired after the sabotage, but getting the old freighter back to the States was a low priority for everyone except its crew. All the dock space in and around Archangel was needed for newly arrived convoy PQ-18 ships, so the *Ironclad* was moved ten miles up the North Dvina River to a dock at a lumber mill. The weather grew colder. Every day more ice filled the river. "Unexpected cold snap has completely tied up large ship traffic in Archangel port for past five days," the U.S. naval attaché in Archangel reported on November 13. Carter knew if the *Ironclad* did not leave Archangel soon it would have to spend the winter there. To his relief, the ship was assigned to homebound convoy QP-15, along with many of the convoy PQ-18 ships. A Russian tanker came upriver to fill the *Ironclad* with fuel oil for the voyage. The *Ironclad*'s chief engineer noticed that the tanker's oil was full of grit and water, which might wreck the old *Ironclad*'s engines. Moore demanded cleaner oil for his ship. By the time the tanker returned, the convoy had sailed without the *Ironclad*.

Soon afterward, British authorities in Archangel decided to move the *Ironclad* to Murmansk, from whose ice-free harbor the ship could sail home at any point during the winter. The North Dvina River was already frozen solid. A tugboat with a reinforced bow for icebreaking arrived to lead the *Ironclad* into the White Sea, which was only starting to freeze. The tug broke a path through the river ice and the *Ironclad* stayed close behind. A few miles downriver from the lumber dock, Carter saw an in- digenous Sami hunter guiding a sled pulled by a caribou. The man tried to cross the frozen river in front of the ships before they broke a path that would block his way. He lost the race but waited patiently as the tug and *Ironclad* passed. Twenty minutes later, Carter looked back and saw the sled gliding smoothly across the ice, which already had refrozen behind the ships. Carter reflected that steamships like the *Ironclad* were mere curiosities to the Sami, who "had been using the same animals to do the same things in the same way for hundreds of years before the steam en- gine was even invented."

At the mouth of the North Dvina River, a Soviet trawler arrived with a pilot to guide the *Ironclad* through the White Sea. Nightfall brought light snow and then heavy snow. A few lighthouses flashed on shore, but no two were close enough together for the *Ironclad* to use their beams to fix its position. The pilot on the Russian tug flashed signals, but Moore could not understand them. No one on the *Ironclad*'s bridge was sure where the ship was. The captain decided to reverse course and wait until the snow stopped. It fell even harder, blotting out the trawler and everything else. "Our world was the *Ironclad,* surrounded by a moving white veil of snowflakes," Carter wrote. He hoped this was "just one more bump in the long bumpy road that we had traveled already." But the *Ironclad* was at the end of that road.

Around 11:30 p.m. on November 24, the *Ironclad* caromed off an unseen rock in the fog, then struck another rock and stopped dead. The captain decided to drop anchor and wait for daylight before trying to assess the damage. In the meantime, a rising tide lifted the ship just enough to bounce it up and down on more rocks. First light revealed to the crew's surprise that the *Ironclad* already had passed all the way through the White Sea and the Gourlo into the Barents Sea. Unbeknownst to the ship's officers and crew, the old freighter had been creeping through a maze of rocks. The rocks that had pierced her hull were only 500 yards from shore. The land rose into a steep cliff with a flat top. Atop the cliff stood dozens of Sami men and women, smiling and waving at the *Ironclad*'s crew as though "delighted we had stopped in for a visit."

There the *Ironclad* stayed through Thanksgiving Day. The steward scrounged together a dinner of canned salmon in lieu of turkey and stuffing. The *Ironclad*'s pumps labored to keep up with leaks that the rocks had opened in the hull. Finally, two tugs towed the crippled freighter all the way back through the Gourlo and the White Sea to an oil dock at Molotovsk. The *Ironclad*'s stern had settled so deeply that men could lean over the ship's rail and dip their hands in the water. The *Ironclad* was running out of fuel to keep up its steam; once she ran out of steam, the pumps would quit working and the ship would fill up with water and sink. The Russians at the oil dock could not find a fuel pipe long enough to extend to the ship. When the fuel started running out, the *Ironclad*'s crew sawed up the ship's wooden hatch covers and threw them into the boilers. It was no use. On December 8, the pumps stopped and the

Ironclad settled onto the bottom with "a great swoosh of air." The main deck was still above water, but the damage to the hull was so serious that it would require repairs in a dry dock. No dry dock on the White Sea would be usable until the ice melted in the spring. The Soviets faulted Moore for reversing the *Ironclad*'s course in the blinding snow, but Carter blamed "whoever arranged the schedule so that we reached the area of maximum danger in complete darkness."

In any case, U.S. naval authorities in Archangel wanted nothing further to do with the *Ironclad*. They suggested turning over the ship to the Russians and bringing home its crew "at the first opportunity before general mutiny or loss of life occurs." The risk was all too real. Only a few days earlier, a fireman on another American freighter in Archangel had hung a weight around his neck and jumped overboard. He was at least the third American mariner to commit suicide in North Russia.

While arrangements were being made to transfer ownership of the *Ironclad* to the Soviets,* the officers and crew were split up and billeted on whatever Allied vessels in Archangel had room for them. Carter and three of his Armed Guard men were sent to the Liberty ship *Richard Bland*. The *Richard Bland* had originally sailed with convoy PQ-17 out of Hvalfjord but had been forced to turn back after hitting rocks. After being repaired, she had arrived in Archangel on Christmas Day 1942, with convoy JW-51A—the first of the small convoys Roosevelt and Churchill had sent in place of PQ-19. The Allies had permanently dropped the "PQ" convoy designations and replaced them with the "JW" designation, which had been chosen at random. The designation for homebound convoys had been changed from QP to RA. Exactly when the *Richard Bland*

---

* The Soviets ultimately repaired the *Ironclad* and returned it to wartime service as the *Marina Raskova,* named for a heroic female Russian aviatrix. In 1944, the ship was transporting people and supplies through the icy Kara Sea to remote settlements on Novaya Zemlya. A U-boat torpedoed the ship and then two vessels that were picking up survivors. More than three hundred people lost their lives.

would sail for home was unclear. For Carter, the cold, gray Russian winter dragged on.

One day in January 1943, Carter was playing bridge on the ship when he heard short bursts of a submachine gun from the direction of the docks. He and his bridge partners leapt up from the game and looked down from the main deck. The body of a work-camp prisoner lay in the snow. The prisoner had been part of a group pushing a railcar when he had slipped on the ice and fallen beneath a wheel, which had severed his leg below the knee. Instead of rushing him to a nearby medical facility, a guard had simply shot him. None of the other guards or prisoners seemed fazed. Carter assumed it was business as usual. "Life in Russia was cheap and uncertain," he wrote. On another occasion, Carter was walking along the dock and saw messmen from an Allied freighter discarding spoiled oranges onto the ice. The oranges were so rotten that they had turned a putrid bluish-gray. Nevertheless, a group of prisoners ran out onto the ice and scooped them up. So many prisoners joined the scramble that the ice cracked beneath their weight and they plunged into the water. They struggled ashore and the guards ordered them back to work, soaking wet in the freezing cold. "From this episode," Carter wrote, "I came to realize that I needed to refine my own definition of 'hungry.'"

To break the monotony, Carter occasionally took the train into Archangel and stayed at the Intourist Hotel, where the food was still good. The hotel proprietors turned off the heat every night at 8:00 p.m. to save fuel, which left the guest rooms freezing cold. Guests congregated in the hotel's large unisex bathrooms, where the heat was kept on. People stood in line to bathe in six large tubs. Privacy was nonexistent. Whoever was next in line for a tub scrubbed the back of the person bathing. Milling around among the bathers were dozens of fully clothed people who were simply enjoying the warmth. "I am unable to summon the literary skills to provide an accurate word picture of that scene," Carter wrote.

Outside, the Russian winter introduced Carter to entirely new forms of cold weather. "The frosts," for example, were dense banks of fog formed by ice particles. The particles attached themselves to ships' rigging in bladelike extensions that grew outward in the opposite direction of the wind. The ice crystals were delicately beautiful but sharp enough at their edges to draw blood. Carter shaved off an incipient beard after a frost transformed it into an uncomfortable mask of ice.

Carter refused to let the Archangel winter get him down. He resolved to learn the Russian language and carried around a spiral notebook so he could jot down new words. Some of the Russians admired his efforts and risked the scrutiny of the NKVD to help him. Within a few months, Carter had a working vocabulary of roughly eight hundred Russian words and could keep up with basic conversations, though the Russian Cyrillic alphabet remained a mystery to him. He was charmed by glimpses of traditional Russian culture amid the Soviet paranoia. Many Russians secretly observed Christmas as a celebration of the New Year. They decorated fir trees with dried flowers. At a "New Year's" party, a young woman steered Carter into the company of an ancient Russian man, who took him by the arm and led him three times around the holiday tree. The ritual symbolized the passing of wisdom from the aged to the young, and the trips around the tree represented wishes for health, wealth, and happiness. The ceremony was especially touching because it was so hard to imagine those wishes coming true for anyone in wartime Archangel.

By mid-January 1943, the ice in the White Sea had frozen solid, but the British decided to move all Allied ships from Archangel to Murmansk, with the help of formidable Soviet icebreakers with powerful engines and propellers on both ends. The *Richard Bland* and a half dozen other vessels followed the icebreakers through the gray, frozen landscape into the Barents Sea and then up the Kola Inlet to Murmansk. The Germans did not bother them on the voyage, but as soon as the *Richard Bland* dropped anchor at Murmansk, German bombers attacked the city. Carter got plenty of practice firing the ship's 20mm antiaircraft guns. He didn't shoot down any planes, but no bombs hit the *Richard Bland*. The British announced she would leave Murmansk for the United States in the last homebound convoy of the winter. Carter and his shipmates thought they had caught a lucky break. They could not have been more wrong.

CHAPTER TWELVE

REINDEER GAMES

On January 14, 1943, Roosevelt and Churchill met in the Moroccan port city of Casablanca to discuss their next steps in the war. Roosevelt's flight to North Africa made him the first president to visit U.S. troops in a combat zone since Abraham Lincoln—who had visited them on American soil in 1865. Stalin declined to join Roosevelt and Churchill in Casablanca, saying he was too busy directing his armies on the battlefield: "Time presses us, and it would be impossible for me to be absent even for a day, as it is just now that important military operations of our winter campaign are developing." Roosevelt was disappointed. He continued to believe that if he could only meet Stalin face-to-face, he could convince him of America's good intentions. Their exchanges of letters did not seem to be achieving that goal. Just before the conference in Casablanca, Roosevelt had written Stalin suggesting U.S. general Omar Bradley visit Soviet military bases. Stalin had written back, "It should be perfectly obvious that only Russians can inspect Russian military objectives, just as U.S. military objectives can be inspected by none but

Americans. There should be no unclarity in this matter." Stalin went on to complain that the slow pace of the Allied offensive in North Africa had allowed Hitler to transfer troops back to the eastern front.

Roosevelt made the biggest headlines in Casablanca by declaring the Allies would insist on "unconditional surrender" by the Axis powers. But the most pressing issue facing Roosevelt and Churchill at the conference was where to point their armies next. Although the North Africa campaign had, in fact, stalled temporarily in Tunisia, the Allies still seemed likely to chase the Germans off the African continent by spring. Some of Roosevelt's closest military advisors wanted him to invade France next. Stalin obviously did. Churchill argued that the Allies' next target should be Sicily, which could logically lead to an invasion of mainland Italy. At the same time, the United States would keep massing troops in England for the eventual cross-Channel invasion of France. Roosevelt went along with Churchill, agreeing to launch an invasion of Sicily in the summer of 1943. After leaving Casablanca, Roosevelt and Churchill drafted a joint statement to Stalin explaining that they were considering an invasion of France in August or perhaps September 1943. Roosevelt added that American shipyards were producing ships so fast that the Grand Alliance soon would have all it needed. In the meantime, Roosevelt and Churchill assured Stalin, the convoys would continue.

ON MARCH 1, 1943, two months after the conference in Casablanca, Lieutenant Carter and the *Richard Bland* sailed out of Murmansk with homebound convoy RA-53. The mariners were relieved to depart from the nervous, apocalyptic world of Murmansk, where the smoke from smoldering buildings irritated their eyes and the screams of the dive-bombing Stukas rang in their ears. The Germans never stopped bombing the place, and ships at the docks were in constant jeopardy. A U.S. Navy report from Murmansk in the first week of March read:

Heavy and continuous night raids plus several daylight raids last 4 days have resulted in:

British ship *Ocean Freedom* 2 direct hits sinking at dock consider total loss and will probably render useless 1 berth.

Soviet steamer *Lena* while being salvaged turned turtle and berth demolished by bomb.

Incendiaries landed on American ships but extinguished without damage.

Several large buildings destroyed by [bombs] and incendiaries with fairly heavy casualties.

Warehouse and tracks 11 marshalling yards partially destroyed.

Germans using delayed action bombs 1 of which exploded Murmansk

As convoy RA-53 sailed out of Murmansk, Carter was pleased to find that the *Richard Bland* was better armed than the *Ironclad* had been. The *Richard Bland* had a 4-inch, 50-caliber gun on the stern, a cannon on the bow, and eight 20mm antiaircraft guns on the upper decks. The ship's Navy Armed Guard commander, Ensign Ed Neely, welcomed Carter's help. He offered Carter command of the stern gun and invited him to direct fire from some of the antiaircraft guns. The *Richard Bland* was assigned to a coveted spot in the middle of the convoy directly behind the commodore's ship.

The convoy steamed all the way across the Barents Sea and past Bear Island unmolested, and then turned southeast toward Iceland. The weather was rough but not ferocious. On the morning of March 5, lookouts on the American freighter *Executive,* sailing next to the *Richard Bland,* saw a torpedo streak past the vessel's starboard side. Moments later, a second torpedo tore into the *Executive*'s engine room. A third torpedo sped past the stricken *Executive* and struck the *Richard Bland* near the bow. The torpedo burrowed into the forward cargo hold before blowing up. The explosion tore holes in the hull and flooded the hold. The *Richard Bland* stayed afloat but fell behind the convoy.

Crew members reported seeing smoke drifting from the lower reaches of the cargo hold where the shells for the ship's cannon were stored. Carter volunteered to go below and check the damage. He and another man climbed down into the hold with flashlights. The only cargo in that part of the ship was Arctic spruce lumber, which was highly buoyant. The torpedo blast had bent a section of the hull outward, where it acted like a second rudder, interfering with the ship's steering. Carter picked up some cannon shells that had been jarred loose from their storage racks and threw them overboard. The magazine containing most of the Armed Guard's ammunition lay deeper in the ship, at the base of a 25-foot ladder that led through a narrow opening into pitch blackness. Carter saw wisps of "pale, yellow smoke" drifting up from the darkness but decided not to risk venturing down there.

Carter had made a more alarming discovery: The torpedo strike had cracked the *Richard Bland* in half. Cracks were a built-in hazard of Liberty ships, whose hull plates were welded rather than riveted together, making the hulls more rigid and thus more susceptible to cracking. The crack in the *Richard Bland* extended all the way across the width of the main deck and then down the hull on both sides. Another Liberty ship in the convoy, the *J.L.M. Curry,* broke apart after a storm opened a crack in its hull. The *Curry*'s crew was rescued from the foundering ship by a British escort vessel.

The *Richard Bland* had no such rescuer standing by, but fortunately the ship held together. The chief engineer shifted oil and water in the *Richard Bland*'s storage tanks to restore the vessel to an even keel and enable it to catch up to the other ships. As soon as it did, a dozen German

Heinkel 111 bombers attacked the convoy. Two bombs bracketed the *Richard Bland* but did no additional damage.

That night, a snowstorm overtook convoy RA-53 and scattered it. Toward first light, the wind rose to a gale as the sky cleared. The *Richard Bland* was alone. Carter suspected the U-boat that had torpedoed it was still nearby, waiting to finish it off. A wounded straggler like the *Richard Bland* was an easy kill. The only question was whether the storm would sink the *Richard Bland* first. The seas grew rougher and the ship's steering mechanism stopped working. The crew jury-rigged a system to move the rudder with winches. The captain gave up trying to find the convoy and turned the ship into the wind to ride out the rising storm. Carter had never seen such waves. Every time the ship crested one, the crack in the hull opened a few inches wide, only to close again when the ship slid into a trough. Carter could not take his eyes off the crack. When the waves twisted the *Richard Bland,* the two sides of the crack scraped past each other with "a horrific noise that sounded like it came directly from the nether regions," Carter wrote. The entire vessel would "convulse with a great shudder that reached into the consciousness of each person on board."

The storm intensified. Carter estimated the biggest waves at 75 to 80 feet. "I had calculated my line of sight from the flying bridge at fifty-five feet," he wrote. "When we were at the bottom of a trough, I had to look up another twenty-five feet or more to see the top of those awesome walls of water." Carter felt oddly calm. He did not pray or see any of his shipmates doing so. "It was as though we recognized that we were beyond any reasonable possibility of help, even from the Almighty," Carter wrote. "It was more a question of which of the mountains we wouldn't get over, and there was no point in speculating about that."

Carter had gone too long without sleep to stay awake. He made his way to his bunk, which was set up in Ensign Neely's cabin. Carter had no sooner dozed off than the ship rolled violently, hurling him out of his bunk and into a drawer, leaving him with a bruised arm. A loud crash outside the cabin brought Carter out onto the main deck, where he was sprayed in the face by a fire extinguisher that had broken loose from its mounting and was rolling around. The wind had let up and the waves were only half their previous size, but the barometer reading of 25.6 inches of mercury was the lowest Carter had ever seen. The sea around the ship was full of ice. Carter described the scene as "pure surrealism beyond imagining":

> As far as the eye could see, the surface of the ocean was covered by huge blocks of floating ice. These massive floes presented an incredible scene of simultaneous chaos. The waves, further compressed by the ice itself, to a height of ten to fifteen feet, were running under the floating ice floes. The action of the waves created a macabre ballet. The dancers were huge blocks of ice, and a collision with any one of them could have dire, possibly fatal results.

The *Richard Bland* weaved its way among the ice floes as the crack in the hull opened and closed and the lookouts searched for the U-boat. A new ice advisory came over the radio, and the captain steered for open water. On March 9, the *Richard Bland* emerged from the ice floes, only 35 miles from the coast of Iceland. The Norwegian Sea was still rough, with 20-foot waves that would have impressed the mariners a few days earlier. Carter took a break and sat in the chart room imagining what he would do when he reached Iceland. But he had gotten ahead of himself.

A lookout shouted, "Periscope on the port quarter!" Carter reached the bridge just as a torpedo exploded into the ship. Carter ran aft to man the 4-inch gun and saw a second torpedo zoom past, narrowly missing the *Richard Bland*. But the first torpedo had done enough. Seawater gushed in through the hole in the hull. The *Richard Bland*'s engines stopped. The ship was listing so steeply that the 4-inch gun was impossible to aim.

Carter decided to fire a few rounds anyway for the sake of the crew's morale, but the gun's firing mechanism was faulty. Carter was no longer surprised to find a useless gun installed on a merchant ship.

Heavy snow began falling again as the *Richard Bland*'s captain gave the order to abandon ship. The crew lowered the lifeboats, a hazardous job in rough seas. Two lifeboats were snatched by the wind and blown away from the ship while men were still waiting to climb into them. The two remaining lifeboats did not have enough room for everyone still on the ship. The captain asked for volunteers to stay aboard the *Richard Bland* and await rescue. That was asking a lot. Carter and some of the Armed Guard men discussed their options. Carter felt certain the ship was about to be torpedoed again. The air temperature was 15 degrees and the water temperature 28 degrees. The falling snow formed an opaque layer of sludge on the sea. Carter and Neely looked up at a wave curling toward the ship and saw a torpedo in the middle of it.

The torpedo burst into the *Richard Bland*'s engine room, blowing up an oil tank and setting the whole middle of the ship afire. Carter and Neely ran for the lifeboats. The dying ship was an obstacle course. They ducked under a jet of scalding steam from the boilers, only to find their way blocked by fire billowing out of the engine room ventilators. Without a word Neely ran straight through the flames. Carter, behind him, dropped down on his stomach and crawled under them. He jumped up on the other side with a blistered forehead and singed eyebrows. He could not see Neely. The *Richard Bland* finally had broken in two, along the seam of the crack in the hull. The smaller bow section was drifting away. The stern section, on which Carter and most of the crew stood, was sinking. One of the lifeboats dangled vertically at the end of a rope, having dumped its occupants into the sea. The only other lifeboat was ready to launch. It looked full, but Carter knew it was his only chance. He asked if there was room for him and someone said yes. Carter jumped into the boat from a height of 10 feet.

The lifeboat passed among floating bodies. The dead men's life vests kept them faceup, but the cold water had killed them. Carter could not see their faces. Someone said Neely was dead. After running through the wall of fire on the ship, he had leapt 25 feet into the ocean near the lifeboat. But men in the boat had been unable to pull him aboard and the current had carried him away. Carter noticed two other men still clinging to the sides of the lifeboat. He tried to pull them in but had no strength left. Neither did the men in the water. Their heavy clothing weighted them down. Soon they lost hold of the lifeboat and were swept away as Neely had been.

Even without them, the lifeboat was crowded with twenty-seven men, several more than its capacity. It rode alarmingly low in the water, with less than a foot of freeboard between the sea and the top of the boat. Waves kept dumping icy water into the boat, and the men took turns pushing a hand pump to keep the boat from being swamped. Carter could not feel his feet. He looked down at them and saw that his knee-high boots were full of freezing water. The water in the boat only came up to his shins. He wrestled off his boots, dumped out the water and put them back on. The freezing spray had encased him in a layer of ice, which paradoxically seemed to insulate him from the cold.

Carter felt uneasy that his Colt .45 automatic was the only gun in the lifeboat. "If we began to run out of food and water, I was not sure what I might do to save myself," he wrote. The gun "gave me an advantage that I was not comfortable with having. I thought that I knew myself quite well, but I had never been in a situation like that before." He threw the gun into the ocean. Some of his boatmates gave him puzzled looks. Carter did not want to explain how desperate he thought their situation might become. He told them he had gotten rid of the gun to prevent him from being identified as a military officer if the U-boat came looking for prisoners.

Carter could make out a second lifeboat in the darkness a short distance away. It was one of the boats that had been blown away from the ship by the wind. Carter was about to signal to it with a flashlight when he heard a gunshot and saw a flash of light. The U-255, which had sunk their ship, had surfaced near the abandoned bow section of the *Richard Bland*. The Germans had fired the shot to catch the attention of anyone who might be stranded on it. The men in both lifeboats stayed low and kept silent. The Germans did not see them. Finally, the U-boat departed.

The lifeboats drifted for thirteen hours before they were spotted by a British destroyer, which took the castaways aboard shortly after dawn on March 11. From the destroyer's main deck, Carter could see the coast of Iceland. The *Richard Bland* had been that close. The destroyer searched for more survivors. At one point it pulled alongside a life raft with three human forms lying motionless across it. The raft and its occupants were completely encased in ice. A British sailor extended a boat hook to pull the raft alongside. To Carter's astonishment, one of the ice-covered figures reached up and seized the boat hook. "It was akin to a religious experience for me," Carter wrote. "I saw an apparently dead body come alive."

The destroyer rushed the half-frozen man to the U.S. Navy base at Seydisfjordur, which was on the opposite side of Iceland from Reykjavik. The ship docked on the morning of March 13. A third lifeboat with several more *Richard Bland* survivors was picked up by another escort ship. Of the sixty-nine men on the *Richard Bland,* thirty-four were dead, including the captain, Neely, and Carter's friend Wayne Baker, who had been second in command of the *Ironclad's* Armed Guard unit. The Red Cross handed out toiletries and decks of playing cards. Carter was especially thankful for the cards: "I played Solitaire by the hour, to take my mind off of other things that were still too painful to contemplate."

Carter caught a ride on an Army transport ship from Seydisfjordur to Hvalfjord. During the trip he picked up a Navy magazine and was surprised to see his name. Without his knowledge, he had been promoted to senior lieutenant and awarded the Silver Star, the Navy's third highest honor after the Congressional Medal of Honor and the Navy Cross, for bravery in convoy PQ-17. Carter savored the thought of Ann, his bride-to-be, watching the medal being pinned to his chest.

Carter and the rest of the *Richard Bland* survivors stayed on the transport ship to be taken to Boston. When the ship docked, he got off and telephoned his parents in Delaware, who told him Ann was waiting to hear from him. She had moved in with her parents in Santa Barbara, California. After several tries, he got her on the phone. Her first words were "What took you so long?" Carter promised to tell her as soon as she met him in New York City to marry him. She got on the first available plane. Carter took a train to New York and settled into the Commodore Hotel. He made a reservation for Ann at the Biltmore Hotel, and set out to arrange the wedding. By the time she got there, he had gotten a blood test, bought her an engagement bracelet at Tiffany's, arranged for a minister, and reserved the chapel of the Church of the Transfiguration for the afternoon of April 12, 1943.

BY THE TIME CARTER SAID, "I do," the entire course of the war on the eastern front had changed. On February 2, the Red Army defeated the Germans at Stalingrad in one of the pivotal battles of the war. The Soviet victory stunned the Germans and cut off Hitler's path to the oil fields of the Caucasus and the Middle East. The Red Army suffered typically horrific losses at Stalingrad—five hundred thousand men, roughly half of those who fought in the battle. But this time the Germans' losses were horrific too. Their three hundred thousand casualties included more than ninety thousand soldiers captured. Most of the German POWs would die in makeshift Soviet prison camps of starvation, exposure, or disease.

The Germans were far from beaten, but the Red Army was growing stronger all along the eastern front. It was fueled by rage over the atrocities the Nazis had perpetrated on Soviet soil. The Red Army would repay the Germans in kind. A Soviet propagandist, Konstantin Simonov, wrote a poem for *Pravda* simply entitled "Kill Him."

If your home is dear to you where your Russian mother
    nursed you;
If your mother is dear to you and you cannot bear the
    thought of the German slapping her wrinkled face;
If you do not want the German to tear down and trample
    on your father's picture, with the Crosses he earned in
    the last war;
If you do not want your old teacher to be hanged outside
    the old school house;
If you do not want her, whom for so long you did not dare
    even kiss, to be stretched out naked on the floor, so
    that amid hatred, cries and tears, three German curs
    should take what belongs to your manly love;
If you don't want to give away all that which you call your
    Country,
Then kill a German, kill a German every time you see
    one . . .

In May 1943, the Red Army retook Sevastopol, a once-elegant Black Sea resort that German bombs had reduced to a shell. In July, the Soviets recaptured Kursk in the largest tank battle in history. Next, they recaptured Kharkov and then Smolensk. By then, American and British forces had captured Sicily and invaded mainland Italy, but Stalin wrote Churchill that "actions in the Mediterranean are no substitute for a second front in France." Even after the Allies invaded Italy, nearly half of Germany's combat troops were still fighting the Soviets on the eastern front.

The resurgent Red Army needed supplies as much as ever. In October 1943, Churchill wrote Stalin that the large Arctic convoys were about to resume as darkness returned to the convoy routes. To cover himself, Churchill added that unexpected events might force the Allies to change plans. He said Stalin should regard the resumption of the convoys not as a promise "but rather a declaration of our solemn and earnest resolve." Stalin replied that Churchill's message "loses its value by your statement that this intention to send northern convoys to the U.S.S.R. is neither an obligation nor an agreement, but only a statement which . . . the British side can at any moment renounce regardless of any influence it may have on the Soviet armies at the front." Churchill forwarded Stalin's message to Roosevelt, with the notation, "About Russian convoys I have now received a telegram from Uncle Joe which I think you will feel is not exactly all one might hope for from a gentleman for whose sake we are to make an inconvenient, extreme and costly exertion."

SIR DUDLEY POUND DIED ON October 21, 1943. He had suffered a stroke the previous month and resigned his position as First Sea Lord of the Admiralty. He was honored for his years of service with a funeral procession through the streets of central London, in which his friend Churchill marched, followed by an elaborate service in Westminster Abbey. Throughout the funeral ceremony, British aircraft patrolled the skies over central London because the Germans had begun launching V-1 rockets at the British capital. Pound's ashes were buried at sea. The official cause of Pound's death was a brain tumor, but the *Manchester Guardian* newspaper called him the last victim of convoy PQ-17. Churchill subsequently described Pound's decision to scatter the convoy as "precipitate"—a word whose meanings can range from "abrupt" to "rash." He suggested, without citing evidence, that Pound scattered the convoy because he did not want to risk losing the American warships that were temporarily under his command in the escort force. Churchill wrote that he never actually discussed convoy PQ-17 with Pound, and suggested that the fault lay with the decision to allow Commander Broome's six destroyers to leave the merchant ships and withdraw with the cruisers. Churchill never took any responsibility for what happened to the convoy.

IN NOVEMBER 1943, Stalin finally agreed to participate in a three-way meeting with Roosevelt and Churchill in Tehran, Iran, to discuss joint war strategy. Roosevelt still believed he could establish a productive relationship with Stalin if he could sit down with him face-to-face. "I am placing a very great importance on the personal and intimate conversations which you and Churchill and I will have," the president wrote Stalin before the conference, "for on them the hope of the future world will greatly depend." During the conference, Roosevelt secretly arranged one-on-one talks with Stalin, while denying to Churchill that he had done so. In one of those talks, Roosevelt told Stalin he did not object to the Soviet Union maintaining control over the Baltic states and part of Poland—the arrangement Stalin had made with Hitler—but that the realities of American politics prevented Roosevelt from saying so publicly. The president also told Stalin he wanted to see the British Empire broken up. Roosevelt declared afterward that he and Stalin had "talked like men and brothers," and that "I called him Uncle Joe." As the conference progressed, the two men acted more and more like the leaders of two great powers discussing the fate of the postwar world, and Churchill felt more and more like a third wheel.

Roosevelt and Churchill departed Tehran with a commitment from Stalin that the Soviet Union would declare war on the Japanese after the Germans were beaten. They promised Stalin they at last would open the second front in the spring of 1944 with an amphibious invasion of France. They kept their word. On June 6, 1944—D-Day—more than six hundred thousand American, British, and Canadian troops surged ashore on the beaches of Normandy, France. Commodore Jack Dowding of convoy PQ-17 served as the main transportation officer for the British part of the invasion. The D-Day assault force was large even by eastern front standards, and Stalin was delighted. He sent Roosevelt a silver-framed photograph of himself in a uniform bedecked with medals, bearing the inscription: "To President Franklin D. Roosevelt in memory of the day of the invasion of Northern France by the Allied American and British liberating armies. From his friend Joseph V. Stalin, June 6, 1944."

Those warm wishes belied rifts in the Grand Alliance that were widening into a chasm. Some of Roosevelt's advisors warned that the Soviets, in the process of routing the Germans, were establishing a zone of occupation in Eastern Europe. William Bullitt, a former U.S. ambassador to the Soviet Union, told Roosevelt the only way to stop the Red Army's advance across Europe was to put American troops in its path. "To win the peace at the close of this war will be at least as difficult as to win the war," Bullitt said. Roosevelt's current ambassador to the Soviet Union, Averell Harriman, saw a growing refusal by the Soviets to cooperate on even small matters. The Soviets interned American bomber pilots who ran out of fuel and landed in Russia after raids on the Japanese in China. Stalin continued to bar American advisors from Soviet bases and factories despite the fact that by 1943 more than five thousand Soviet advisors were in the United States observing the production of everything from aircraft to minesweepers. The Soviets were ordering Lend-Lease supplies that could not possibly be shipped until after the war was over, raising suspicions that they were stockpiling American weapons for possible future use against American troops.* Harriman told Churchill in early 1944, "The Russian bear is demanding much and yet biting the hands that are feeding him."

The growing mistrust between the Soviets and their Western allies was palpable in Murmansk and Archangel. The dining room at Archangel's Intourist Hotel had been equipped by the NKVD with mirrors and microphones to capture every word and glance exchanged by the Allied

---

* American soldiers in Korea in 1951 reported seeing old U.S. equipment in the hands of the North Koreans, who were being supported in their fight against the United States by the Soviets and the Chinese.

patrons. An American merchant seaman who bought a bound copy of Shostakovich's Seventh Symphony at an Archangel music store was surprised when Soviet sentries seized it on the docks. They returned it to him after examining it to make sure no coded secrets were hidden in the sheet music. Stalin brushed aside a request by Churchill to increase the number of British naval staff in Murmansk and Archangel, saying the British officers already in North Russia had little to do except spy on the Soviet military.

In fact, both sides were constantly engaged in intelligence gathering in the ports, though their methods were often ham-handed. Two U.S. Navy officers were sent on a "goodwill" mission to a Soviet destroyer with a bottle of vodka and instructions to learn as much as they could about the Soviet Northern Fleet. They were greeted on the ship by a commissar with his own bottle of vodka. Before they could try to loosen his tongue with a few toasts, the commissar proposed three quick toasts of his own and then asked for the range of the newest American radar. Ceremonial inspections of Soviet warships by Allied officers were often preceded by vodka toasts drunk to the ship, the second front, the Great Patriotic War, and "everything down to and including the ship's cat," wrote Kemp Tolley. "To have refused [any of the toasts] would have been considered a mortal insult. Then the inspection would commence, everything a hazy blur."

Soviet and Allied officials in North Russia had little choice but to work together, and often "friendships broke out," as one retired Russian naval officer put it. But animosity was more common and sometimes took strange forms. The Soviets insisted on presenting gifts of live, adult reindeer to high-ranking Allied officials who were ending their tours of duty in North Russia. None of those officials wanted a reindeer, which Tolley described as a "cow-sized, thoroughly disgruntled, half-wild beast" with a stubborn disposition. But the Russians said gifting reindeer was a time-honored tradition, and the honorees always felt obligated to accept the animals to avoid a diplomatic faux pas. Tolley felt sure the giving of reindeer was no tradition but merely a prank to annoy Western officials the Russians disliked.

One British admiral reluctantly accepted a reindeer in Murmansk and had it loaded aboard a destroyer to be transported to Archangel. The reindeer could not be coaxed off the warship, so British sailors maneuvered it close to the rail and shoved it into the North Dvina River. It swam ashore, where "the spectacle of a large reindeer, digging in its heels every step of the way, being dragged through the streets of Archangel by a posse of straining, swearing British bluejackets was a scene long remembered by the amused residents," Tolley wrote. Most of the gift reindeer ended up in a pen on the edge of the city.

The brutality of Stalin's regime became harder for other members of the Grand Alliance to ignore. In May 1943, the International Medical Commission reported the Soviets had massacred more than four thousand Polish military officers in the remote Katyn Forest near Smolensk and buried them in a mass grave. The Russians insisted until 1991 that the Nazis were responsible for the killings, which was all too plausible a lie in a region where both the Soviets and the Nazis committed mass murders.

The Soviet Gulag continued to swallow people by the hundreds of thousands. Among those imprisoned near Archangel was Aleksandr Solzhenitsyn, a decorated Red Army artillery spotter who was arrested in 1943 after writing a friend a letter in which he criticized the government. Decades later, in *The Gulag Archipelago*, Solzhenitsyn described life in a solitary cell in Archangel, "where the glass had been smeared over with red lead so that the only rays of God's maimed light which crept in to you were crimson, and where a 15-watt bulb burned constantly in the ceiling, day and night."

That same year, three American mariners were thrown into a labor camp near Archangel after a run-in with the NKVD. One of them, Jac Smith, was put to work removing the bodies of new arrivals to the camp who had not survived the long rail journey in unheated boxcars. Most of the bodies "were twisted and warped in the agonizing grotesque positions they assumed as they collapsed dying among the feet of those who could still stand," Smith wrote. "Sometimes there would be a body not quite stiff. Those were the worst." The camp's main security feature was not guards or fences but the vast, snowy wilderness surrounding the place. Smith walked away from it and nearly froze to death before being rescued by a Sami family and smuggled to Britain by Norwegian resistance fighters. One of Smith's shipmates was released from the camp after the war. The other simply disappeared.

Despite the rift in the Grand Alliance, the flow of Lend-Lease supplies continued. More and more of the convoys to the Soviet Union were routed to Iraq through the Mediterranean as the Allies gained control of that region. But the Arctic convoys continued. They had changed since convoy PQ-17. They no longer departed from Hvalfjord but from Loch Ewe in Scotland. They had much less to fear from the German bombers, most of which had been moved out of Norway to face new Allied threats farther south. A failed attack by German cruisers and destroyers on an Arctic convoy in 1943 so enraged Hitler that he threatened to scrap the entire German surface fleet. The Führer's tirade provoked Admiral Raeder into resigning as head of the German Navy. Hitler replaced him with Admiral Karl Doenitz, commander of the U-boat force.

Doenitz's U-boats continued to stalk the Arctic convoys, but the rate of merchant ship losses on the Murmansk Run plummeted from 12 percent in 1943 to 1 percent in 1944. During the second half of 1944, all 159 Allied cargo ships that sailed for North Russia got there safely, and only 2 ships were sunk on the voyages home. The risk had shifted to the U-boats, which were increasingly helpless against new Allied antisubmarine tactics and technology. The number of U-boats sunk in the Arctic rose from zero in 1943 to 25 in 1944.

In November 1944, the British finally sank the *Tirpitz*. Ever since convoy PQ-17, they had kept the battleship in a near-constant state of disrepair with bombing raids and an audacious attack by commandos in midget submarines. After a bomb blew a hole in the *Tirpitz*'s main deck in September 1944, the Germans decided the ship was no longer seaworthy. They towed it to the Norwegian port of Tromso and anchored it as a floating fortress to defend the harbor. The berth at Tromso offered far less protection than the *Tirpitz*'s former berth near Trondheim. On November 12, British Lancaster bombers from Lossiemouth in northeast Scotland scored two direct hits on the *Tirpitz* and the giant battleship took on a steep list and then suddenly capsized, trapping a thousand men inside it. Rescuers cut through the hull with torches but managed to save only eighty-five. The *Tirpitz* never sank an Allied vessel. Its greatest achievement was casting a dark enough shadow over convoy PQ-17 to scatter it.

THE ADMIRALTY MANAGED to hide the details of the scattering from the public until February 1945, when Germany released twenty-five American merchant mariners from the *Carlton* and *Honomu,* who had been taken prisoners of war after their ships were sunk following the breakup of convoy PQ-17. Upon arriving in New York, the men bitterly denounced the British for abandoning the convoy and leaving them to die or be captured. The mariners' account of the breakup of convoy PQ-17 contained inaccuracies—they told reporters, for example, that the British escorts "had been lured off in a wild goose chase of the enemy [warships] *Scharnhorst* and *Gneisenau*"—not the *Tirpitz*—and that every ship in the convoy had been sunk. British naval officers seized on those errors and dismissed the men's entire account as "arrant nonsense." The Admiralty officially stayed mum. The U.S. Navy would neither confirm nor deny the mariners' story, although *The New York Times* noted that the Navy "offered no objection to its publication." The Admiralty later offered a misleading statement that implied that scattering the convoy had averted an attack by German surface ships. Not until 1950 did the release of official documents clarify what actually happened. Broome, who had retired as a captain in the Royal Navy, wrote a letter to the editor of *The*

Times of London saying the ships of convoy PQ-17 were "sunk by our First Sea Lord's signal sent from an armchair some 2,000 miles away. It is to my everlasting regret that I obeyed it."

IN FEBRUARY 1945—around the time POWs of convoy PQ-17 came home—Roosevelt, Churchill, and Stalin met for the second and last time. Stalin insisted their conference take place in Yalta, in the Crimea, which was a 600-mile trip for Stalin and a 6,000-mile trip for Roosevelt. The president was in no shape for such a journey. "I was shocked by Roosevelt's physical appearance," wrote one of his aides, Charles Bohlen. "He was not only frail and desperately tired, he looked ill." The president did not press Stalin on the future of Eastern Europe, although the Soviets had occupied Bulgaria and appeared likely to occupy Czechoslovakia and Hungary. Roosevelt placed his hope for postwar peace in the creation of the United Nations. Stalin regarded the U.N. as a naïve concept but agreed the Soviet Union would participate because Roosevelt considered it so important. Stalin insisted the Soviet Union and other members of the U.N.'s Security Council have veto power over any proposed actions or resolutions—a rule that has severely limited the U.N.'s power and credibility ever since.

Less than a month after the Yalta conference, on April 12, 1945, Roosevelt was recuperating at his spa in Warm Springs, Georgia. He told visitors the Soviets were "quite a nice crowd" except for "a few sinister faces appearing here and there." The president spent part of the morning trying to patch a new crack in the Grand Alliance. Stalin had angrily—and falsely—accused America and Britain of trying to exclude the Soviets from a peace agreement with Nazi Germany. Roosevelt had drafted a message to Stalin saying "minor" disagreements should not distract them from finishing off the Nazis. Ambassador Harriman reviewed the draft and objected to the word "minor," suggesting the dispute was "of a major nature." Roosevelt decided to stick with "minor" and ordered the message sent. He then wrote Churchill that he preferred to minimize such disputes because they tended to work themselves out. Soon afterward, Roosevelt complained of "a terrific pain" in the back of his head and then lost consciousness. He never regained it.

The monumental task of finishing the war and preventing the Soviet Union from dominating Europe fell to former vice president Harry S. Truman. Truman did not share Roosevelt's hopeful view of Stalin and the Soviet Union. Soon after Hitler invaded Russia in 1941, Truman—who was then a little-known U.S. senator from Missouri—had declared: "If we see that Germany is winning we ought to help Russia, and if Russia is winning we ought to help Germany, and that way let them kill as many as possible, although I don't want to see Hitler victorious under any circumstances." Although Truman subsequently expressed a desire to work with the Soviets, he took a dim view of them. The Soviets did not like Truman either. Khrushchev would write in his memoirs, "Stalin had no respect at all for Truman. He considered Truman worthless. Rightly so. Truman didn't deserve respect. This is a fact." After Truman took office, Harriman warned him, "We are faced with a Barbarian invasion of Europe." Soon Truman would halt the convoys of Lend-Lease supplies to Russia.

The last two wartime Arctic convoys, the Russia-bound JW-66 and the homebound RA-66, sailed from Scotland and Murmansk, respectively, in the final week of April 1945. By then, the U-boats had abandoned their traditional hunting grounds near Bear Island and moved to the mouth of the Kola Inlet, where they could attack convoys entering and leaving Murmansk. The Allies countered the U-boats' new strategy by sending escort vessels charging out of the inlet to drive the U-boats underwater. Then the convoys would steam out of the inlet and past the U-boats before they could resurface and give chase. Convoy JW-66 pulled into Murmansk unscathed. Convoy RA-66 lost an escort ship to a U-boat, but another U-boat was sunk with the loss of all hands.

After the Germans surrendered on May 8, 1945, the Allies sent their final convoy to North Russia. Convoy JW-67 comprised twenty-six ships, eighteen of them American. The British sent along an escort force as a precaution against rogue U-boat commanders and other aftershocks of the war. The convoy reached Murmansk without incident. A homebound convoy from Murmansk to Loch Ewe, Scotland, also arrived safely. The Arctic convoys were finished, and so was the illusion of a peaceful postwar world. For the next fifty years, the Barents Sea would serve as a battleground for the Cold War, where nuclear submarines played cat and mouse in the depths. U.S. military based in Iceland helped the Allies monitor Soviet military activity throughout the Cold War.

Carter witnessed the decline of U.S.-Soviet relations from a perspective available only to Arctic convoy veterans. In December 1945, he was surprised to learn that the Soviet government had honored him for his service aboard the *Ironclad*. In fact, the Soviets had awarded 70 medals and 120 "orders" to Arctic convoy veterans from the U.S. Navy and the Navy and U.S. Coast Guard Reserves. Carter received the Order of the Great Patriotic War, First Class, which came with a monthly payment of twenty rubles; free passage on all Soviet trams, trains, and vessels; various Soviet tax exemptions; and discounts on public housing in the Soviet Union. The U.S. Navy sent Carter a letter authorizing him to accept the award and explaining that the Soviets needed a photo of him to include in a booklet that would accompany it. Carter was honored but felt uncomfortable sending a photo of himself to the Soviet Union, so he did not.

A little over a year later, in 1947, the U.S. Navy sent Carter a second letter reflecting a change of attitude about the Soviet medals. The Navy's earlier instruction to send a photo to the Soviets was "canceled"; any awards from Stalin's government were to be kept solely as "mementos" of the fraught, perilous, eye-opening voyage through the Arctic to Russia.

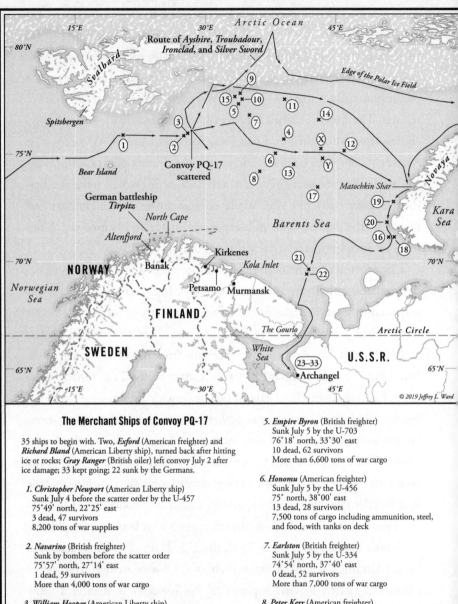

Route of *Ayshire, Troubadour, Ironclad,* and *Silver Sword*

Arctic Ocean

15°E   30°E   45°E

80°N

Svalbard

Edge of the Polar Ice Field

Spitsbergen

⑨
⑮ ✕✕ ⑩
⑤ ✕
③ ⑦ ⑪
② ✕✕ ⑭
① ✕ ✕ ④ ✕
75°N *Bear Island* ✕ Ⓧ ⑫
Convoy PQ-17 ⑥ ✕
scattered ⑧ ⑬ Ⓨ

Novaya

Matochkin Shar

⑲ ✕
Kara
Sea
⑳ ✕

Barents Sea ⑯ ✕✕
⑱

German battleship
Tirpitz
North Cape
Altenfjord
Kirkenes
NORWAY **Banak** *Kola Inlet*

70°N ✕ ⑰ 70°N
⑯
Petsamo **Murmansk** ㉑ ✕
㉒

*Norwegian
Sea*

FINLAND

The Gourlo Arctic Circle

SWEDEN White Sea **U.S.S.R.**

65°N ㉓–㉝ 65°N
•**Archangel**

-15°E 30°E 45°E © 2019 Jeffrey L. Ward

The Merchant Ships of Convoy PQ-17

35 ships to begin with. Two, ***Exford*** (American freighter) and
Richard Bland (American Liberty ship), turned back after hitting
ice or rocks; ***Gray Ranger*** (British oiler) left convoy July 2 after
ice damage; 33 kept going; 22 sunk by the Germans.

1. Christopher Newport (American Liberty ship)
Sunk July 4 before the scatter order by the U-457
75°49' north, 22°25' east
3 dead, 47 survivors
8,200 tons of war supplies

2. Navarino (British freighter)
Sunk by bombers before the scatter order
75°57' north, 27°14' east
1 dead, 59 survivors
More than 4,000 tons of war cargo

3. William Hooper (American Liberty ship)
Sunk before the scatter order by the U-334
75°57' north, 27°15' east
3 dead, 55 survivors
8,600 tons of ammunition, food, and steel, with tanks and
trucks on deck

4. Carlton (American freighter)
Sunk July 5 by the U-88
72°50' north, 24°35' east
3 dead, 42 survivors
5,000 tons of war cargo including ammunition, food,
and 200 tons of TNT, with tanks on deck

5. Empire Byron (British freighter)
Sunk July 5 by the U-703
76°18' north, 33°30' east
10 dead, 62 survivors
More than 6,600 tons of war cargo

6. Honomu (American freighter)
Sunk July 5 by the U-456
75° north, 38°00' east
13 dead, 28 survivors
7,500 tons of cargo including ammunition, steel,
and food, with tanks on deck

7. Earlston (British freighter)
Sunk July 5 by the U-334
74°54' north, 37°40' east
0 dead, 52 survivors
More than 7,000 tons of war cargo

8. Peter Kerr (American freighter)
Bombed and sunk July 5
74°30' north, 35°00' east
0 dead, 48 survivors
6,600 tons of trucks, steel, and food, with four
bombers on deck

9. Washington (American freighter)
Bombed and sunk July 5
76°14' north, 33°44' east
0 dead, 46 survivors, many frostbite injuries
5,500 tons of ammunition, steel, and food, with tanks and
truck chassis on deck

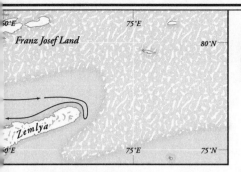

 50°E   75°E

Franz Josef Land

80°N

Zemlya

0°E   75°E   75°N

THE FATE OF CONVOY PQ-17
July 4–28, 1942

10. Paulus Potter (Dutch freighter)
Bombed July 5 and then sunk July 13 by the U-255
75°57' north, 40°10' east
0 dead, 76 survivors
More than 7,000 tons of war cargo

11. Pan Kraft (American freighter)
Bombed and sunk July 5
76°50' north, 38°00' east
2 dead, 45 survivors
5,000 tons of TNT, ammunition, steel, and airplane
parts in crates, with bombers on deck

12. Daniel Morgan (American Liberty ship)
Bombed and then sunk July 5 by the U-88
75°08' north, 45°06' east
3 dead, 51 survivors
7,176 tons of cargo including steel, explosives, and food,
with tanks and other vehicles on deck

13. Fairfield City (American freighter)
Bombed and sunk July 5
74°40' north, 39°45' east
17 dead, 34 survivors
7,400 tons of war supplies

14. River Afton (British freighter)
Sunk July 5 by the U-703
75°57' north, 43°00' east
23 dead, 33 survivors
More than 5,000 tons of war cargo

15. Bolton Castle (British freighter)
Bombed and sunk July 5
Near 76°14' north, 33°44' east
0 dead, 70 survivors
More than 5,000 tons of war cargo

16. John Witherspoon (American Liberty ship)
Sunk July 6 by the U-255
72°05' north, 48°30' east
1 dead, 49 survivors
8,575 tons of mostly ammunition, also high-test gasoline,
with tanks and trucks on deck

17. Pan Atlantic (American freighter)
Bombed and sunk July 6
271 miles off Cape Kanin, U.S.S.R.
26 dead, 23 survivors
8,000 tons of TNT, steel, and food, with tanks on deck

18. Alcoa Ranger (American freighter)
Sunk July 7 by the U-255
71°38' north, 49°35' east
0 dead, 40 survivors
7,200 tons of cargo including steel, armor plate, and flour,
with 19 tanks on deck

19. Hartlebury (British freighter)
Bombed and then sunk July 7 by the U-355
72°30' north, 52°30' east
38 dead, 20 survivors
More than 5,000 tons of war cargo

20. Olopana (American freighter)
Sunk July 8 by the U-255
72°10' north, 51°00' east
7 dead, 34 survivors
6,000 tons of cargo including explosives and high-test
gasoline, with trucks on deck

21. Hoosier (American freighter)
Bombed and then sunk July 10 by the U-376
69°25' north, 38°35' east
0 dead, 53 survivors
5,029 tons of machinery and explosives, with
tanks on deck

22. El Capitan (Panamanian-flagged freighter)
Bombed and then sunk July 10 by the U-251
69°23' north, 40°50' east
0 dead, 67 survivors
More than 5,000 tons of machinery, metals,
ammunition, food, and leather, with tanks and
airplanes on deck

Also Sunk

X. Aldersdale (British fleet oiler)
Bombed and then sunk July 7 by the U-457
75°00' north, 45°00' east
0 dead, 54 survivors

Y. Zaafaran (British rescue ship)
Bombed and then sunk July 5
75°05' north, 43°40' east
0 dead, 97 survivors

11 Merchant Ships Reached Archangel

23. Donbass (Soviet tanker)
More than 7,000 tons of oil
24. Bellingham (American freighter)
More than 5,300 tons of war cargo
25. Samuel Chase (American Liberty ship)
More than 7,500 tons of war cargo
26. Ocean Freedom (British freighter)
More than 6,500 tons of war cargo
27. Empire Tide (British freighter)
More than 6,500 tons of war cargo
28. Azerbaijan (Soviet tanker)
Carrying linseed oil—entire cargo lost on voyage
29. Benjamin Harrison (American Liberty ship)
More than 7,000 tons of war cargo
30. Silver Sword (American freighter)
Nearly 5,000 tons of war cargo
31. Ironclad (American freighter)
More than 5,000 tons of war cargo
32. Troubadour (Panamanian-flagged freighter)
More than 6,000 tons of war cargo, with three tanks
and numerous trucks on deck
33. Winston-Salem (American freighter)
More than 6,000 tons of war cargo

CHAPTER THIRTEEN

RECKONING

If the Ghost Ships fled into the Arctic waters in summer today, they most likely could steam all the way to the North Pole unimpeded. Thanks to global warming, convoy PQ-17's route from Iceland to Archangel has been free of ice in summer for more than thirty years. A twenty-first-century ship might encounter some ice at the point between Spitsbergen and Franz Josef Land where the Ghost Ships halted their northward flight because the ice was too thick to break. But the ice in that part of the Arctic today is no longer thick enough to resist ships with reinforced bows. It is first-year ice, formed only the previous winter, slushy in spots and so loose that a ship could simply push it apart. Between 1980 and 2017, the Arctic ice field has shrunk from 2.7 million square miles to less than 1.8 million square miles. Scientists predict it will be gone entirely by the end of the twenty-first century, and perhaps as early as 2040 if the process of global warming keeps accelerating.

The vanishing ice is only the most visible of the changes taking place along the route of convoy PQ-17. The ice's retreat has opened vast reaches of the Arctic to shipping, fishing, oil and natural gas drilling—and possible military confrontations. Russia staked its claim to the lion's share of the Arctic and its resources in 2007 when a Russian submarine symbolically planted a Russian flag in the seabed at the North Pole. Russia is expanding its military bases in the Arctic and building lighthouses and other infrastructure along stretches of coastline that had long been considered hopelessly remote. In the summer of 2017, a newly built Russian tanker longer than a football field made history by hauling a cargo of liquefied natural gas (LNG) across the Arctic from Norway to South Korea without the help of an icebreaker. Russian president Vladimir V. Putin called the LNG tanker's voyage "a big event in the opening up of the Arctic." Russia's potential competitors for Arctic resources include Norway, the United States, Canada, Finland, Iceland, Sweden, and China. The former head of the U.S. Coast Guard suggested that competition for sovereignty over the Arctic may soon resemble the current fight over the South China Sea, where China has built artificial islands to try to assert control over those waters.

AFTER WORLD WAR II gave way to the Cold War, the Arctic became a different kind of high-stakes battleground. The Soviets, gaining precious knowledge from the designs of German and Japanese submarines awarded to them as war reparations, quickly upgraded their submarine fleet and then developed a fleet of nuclear subs to compete with America's. They fortified the Kola Peninsula near Murmansk with bases for nuclear subs and surface warships, as well as shipyards, air bases, and air-defense facilities, and built a huge shipbuilding facility at Severodvinsk on the White Sea near Archangel. Because the Soviets were usually playing catch-up to the U.S. Navy, they often rushed newly designed subs into service without adequate testing, which led to fatal accidents in the depths of the Barents and Norwegian seas. Since the Arctic was the fastest route by which nuclear missiles could streak from the United States to the Soviet Union, and vice versa, American and Soviet subs often played cat and mouse to get within striking range of each other's major cities and to spy on each other. No fewer than twenty-five collisions between American and Soviet subs are believed to have occurred during the Cold War.

Novaya Zemlya, the onetime refuge of the Ghost Ships, became one of the Soviet Union's main sites for nuclear tests. Between 1954 and 1990, the Soviets conducted at least 240 nuclear tests on or near the archipelago, including the most powerful nuclear blast in history, a hydrogen bomb nicknamed the "Tsar Bomb," which created a 50-megaton fireball with a diameter of five miles. The Soviets also dumped nuclear waste in the waters around Novaya Zemlya. Today, the Russian government says the area is free of nuclear pollution. Novaya Zemlya is home to several secure military bases, and in 2009 Putin declared part of the island a national park. Novaya Zemlya is closed to most visitors. In February 2019, a small village on the archipelago was invaded by more than fifty starving polar bears whose seal-hunting territory—the pack ice—had significantly melted.

After the collapse of the Soviet Union in 1991, the Russian Federation began dismantling its fleet of nuclear subs but lacked the resources to complete the costly and complex task of disposing of their nuclear components. The problem of how to properly dispose of nuclear materials and waste from the Soviet era has persisted through the twentieth century into the twenty-first.

Iceland, the starting point for convoy PQ-17, was transformed by the Arctic convoys and the Allied occupation. Iceland began the war as a neglected rural outpost of Denmark and ended it as a prosperous independent nation. Many Icelanders initially resented the British and American troops who occupied their country, and feared reprisal by the Nazis. More than 230 Icelandic mariners were killed at sea by German bombers and U-boats—roughly one of every six hundred people living in Iceland during the war. In Reykjavik and other communities, romantic trysts between Allied soldiers and Icelandic girls were so numerous that they became known collectively, and disapprovingly, as "the Situation" or "the Condition."

But the Allied occupiers enriched Icelandic businesses and industries.

They built roads and other infrastructure, including the Keflavik Airport, which remains Iceland's largest. Many Icelanders ended up calling World War II "the blessed war." The U.S. military maintained a base in Iceland until 2006. Iceland's years of prosperity came to a jarring halt in 2007–2008, when its three main banks failed after racking up enormous debt. Iceland's economy has still not fully recovered, but it has benefited from a surge in tourism, which has become the country's largest industry. Since 2016, the number of American tourists visiting Iceland every year has exceeded the number of Icelanders. In a sense, Iceland has been reoccupied.

Hvalfjord, the "Whale Fjord" from which convoy PQ-17 departed for Russia, remains isolated even though it is only an hour's drive north of Reykjavik. The fjord looks empty except for wandering sheep, a scattering of farms, an aluminum smelter, and a commercial whaling operation. On a hillside deep in the fjord stands the homespun War and Peace Museum, which displays photographs and artifacts from the Allied convoy years. One huge photo shows the *Tirpitz* at the ready in the Norwegian fjords. Hvalfjord is starkly beautiful on a sunny day, but when the wind picks up and the clouds move in, it's easy to see how the place looked so forlorn to the men preparing to sail across the Arctic for Russia.

Norway has become one of the world's wealthiest nations by shrewdly managing a windfall profit from offshore oil and natural gas fields in the Norwegian and Barents seas. The author Michael Booth called Norway "the Dubai of the north." But even casual tourists can still see scars of the Nazi occupation in the tidy, prosperous cities along the Norwegian coast. Among the warehouses on the busy Bergen waterfront stands a concrete U-boat bunker, which remains a sobering sight even though it has been repurposed for a modern business. In Trondheim, a lovely hilltop park on the grounds of a seventeenth-century fortress features a Frisbee golf course but also the remains of an execution post where the Gestapo shackled captured Norwegian resistance fighters before shooting them. Just down the hill from the fortress, a museum contains a diorama exhibit of a notorious Gestapo chief who operated a torture chamber in the basement of a local villa. Northeast of Trondheim, near the *Tirpitz's* former berth, a granite memorial honors the British bomber crews who died trying to destroy the ship. Farther north along the Norwegian coast, near the North Cape, the tiny picture-postcard cities of Hammerfest and Honnigsvag were rebuilt from ashes after 1944, when the retreating Nazis burned them to the ground. The Germans were so determined not to leave any shelter or food for the advancing Red Army that they even burned the sod huts of the indigenous Sami people and slaughtered their reindeer herds.

Murmansk today is the largest city north of the Arctic Circle, with a population of more than 350,000. It is a gritty place, marked by World War II, the Cold War, and the collapse of the Soviet Union in 1991. Towering over Murmansk's harbor is a massive 130-foot concrete statue of a Red Army soldier in a greatcoat with a submachine gun slung over his shoulder. The statue, nicknamed "Alyosha," represents the Soviet fighters who held off the Germans in order to keep Murmansk open as a port for the Arctic convoys. Another monument in Murmansk honors the crew of the Soviet submarine *Kursk,* which sank in the Barents Sea in 2000 with the loss of 118 lives, as well as the victims of other Russian submarine accidents.

The *Kursk* sinking epitomized the poor state of the Soviet military after the Soviet Union's collapse. The Soviet government had sustained Murmansk, offering rich incentives for workers to move there. When those incentives vanished, Murmansk fell into a decline that is evident today in its potholed streets and blocks of neglected, crumbling buildings. The Murmansk skyline is an ugly wall of gray nine-story apartment buildings erected by the Soviet government to house workers. The city waterfront is dominated by a busy open-air coal pier that locals complain is a constant source of windblown coal dust and respiratory problems. Although Murmansk boasts the world's northernmost McDonald's fast-food restaurant, the city has struggled to attract Western tourists. When the first cruise ship docked at Murmansk in 1991, a Russian tour guide recalled, "it was like aliens coming to town." Murmansk's fortunes seem almost certain to improve, however, as Russia extracts oil and natural gas from under the Barents Sea and strengthens its military. Murmansk is just up the Kola Inlet from the Russian naval base at Severomorsk, the headquarters of the Northern Fleet and most of Russia's submarines.

Archangel today feels more vibrant and cosmopolitan than Murmansk. Its population exceeds 390,000. A wide pedestrian walkway follows the downtown riverfront—the Embankment—past a nautical park, a statue of Peter the Great, and a floating restaurant. Tugs pull rafts of logs downriver. A few blocks inland, touristy Chumbarova Street is lined with traditional wooden houses and unusual statues, including a fisherman riding a huge cod as though it were a bucking bronco. Archangel is full of statues, including some of the last remaining ones of Lenin in Russia. A statue of a woman holding her young daughter stands on a spot where a German bomb exploded. Across town is a carefully tended cemetery for British soldiers who died in Archangel of Spanish flu and other noncombat causes during the brief Allied intervention in 1919. Two modern museums in Archangel offer exhibits on the Great Patriotic War, focusing on the Soviet Union's victory on the eastern front.

THE SOVIET UNION'S DEATH TOLL in World War II almost defies belief. The nation is estimated to have lost more than 23 million lives—roughly 14 percent of its prewar population—and almost two thirds of the victims were civilians.* German losses on all fronts of the war are estimated at 6.6 to 8.8 million, about one third of them civilian. Britain suffered a total of 450,700 deaths in the war, including 116,000 civilians. American losses in the war totaled 418,500, including fewer than 2,000 civilians. It

---

* The only nation to suffer anywhere near as many deaths during World War II was China, which lost roughly 20 million civilian and military lives at the hands of the Japanese.

does no disrespect to the American and British dead to note that nearly twenty-three times as many Soviets died.

The Grand Alliance collapsed after Germany's defeat, which was the alliance's only unifying goal. Stalin had no interest in a closer relationship with the West. Keeping the Soviet Union isolated was vital to his retaining power. After Stalin's death in 1953—probably of natural causes—Khrushchev publicly condemned his mass murders and dismantled his legacy, though he seems not to have destroyed it. In 2017, a public opinion survey in Russia rated Stalin the "most outstanding figure in world history," just ahead of Putin and the nineteenth-century poet Alexander Pushkin.

Churchill's inspirational leadership had carried Britain through the hardest years of World War II. But he was voted out of office soon after Germany's surrender in 1945 (and before Japan's surrender). When his wife, Clementine, suggested the defeat was a blessing in disguise, Churchill replied, "At the moment it seems quite effectively disguised." Churchill regained the prime minister's post a few years later and finally resigned it for good in 1955 at age eighty. He never stopped warning about the evils of Communism. Paradoxically, his legacy is tied to a war in which he had to cultivate Communists as his allies.

Roosevelt has been criticized for not adopting a harder line with Stalin, possibly by tying Lend-Lease aid to postwar borders in Europe. But it's impossible to know whether Stalin would have accepted Allied aid with strings attached, or whether he would have forged another pact with Hitler. By 1945, with the Red Army controlling much of Eastern Europe, Roosevelt had little leverage against Stalin short of threatening to go to war against the Red Army.

Roosevelt obviously misread Stalin and overestimated his own powers of persuasion. In his eagerness to please Stalin, Roosevelt bears a significant share of the responsibility for sending convoy PQ-17 across the Arctic in twenty-four-hour daylight. But from a wider perspective, the president had the wisdom to recognize the Soviet Union as a necessary ally and to use the Arctic convoys to buy time and fortify the Red Army until U.S. troops were ready to fight the Germans.

Kemp Tolley, who grew cynical about so much of what he witnessed in North Russia, nonetheless came home believing in the value of the Murmansk Run: "The bottom line on convoys to the north is that though it was costly, sometimes exasperating, always dangerous, and to a certain degree bumbling, it worked. Conceivably it saved the war. . . . The bad things were outnumbered by the good things: sincere, desperate efforts by the Russians to get the job done; kind, generous, cooperative people in most of the ships who were grateful for the help received from those ashore, whether Russian, British or American, recognizing the difficulties under which they operated."

Between 1941 and 1945, the Arctic convoys delivered to the Soviet Union more than 4 million tons of war supplies worth more than $12.4 billion, which corresponds to more than $180 billion in today's dollars. Those supplies represented roughly one third of the total Lend-Lease shipments to Stalin's regime; the remaining two thirds reached the Soviet Union via the southern convoy route through Iraq in the last two and a half years of the war. But the Murmansk Run was the Soviets' main lifeline from the West early in the war, when the Red Army and Soviet industries were on the brink, and Russia's survival—and possibly Europe's fate—hung in the balance.

Together, the northern and southern convoys delivered more than 10,000 Allied tanks, 10,000 artillery pieces, 14,500 planes, and 450,000 trucks, along with fuel to operate them. They delivered enough state-of-the-art radio and radar equipment to modernize the Soviet military. They delivered 100,000 tons of rubber, as well as huge quantities of steel, aluminum, and chemicals to jump-start Soviet factories after the shock of the Nazi invasion. (Some entire American factories were dismantled and shipped to Russia, including the Ford Motor Company's River Rouge tire factory in Dearborn, Michigan.) The convoys delivered 2.3 million tons of food, ranging from canned meat to salted fish, powdered eggs to beans, dried vegetables to sugar, tea, and coffee. They brought the Soviets medical supplies, clothing, and a wide array of miscellaneous cargo including toys, fishing tackle, and false teeth.

Of the roughly 1,400 Allied merchant ships that set out for North Russia, 104 were sunk while en route to North Russia, while moored at the docks of Murmansk or Archangel, or while sailing home, with the loss of 829 Allied merchant seamen. That total does not include the loss of 29 Soviet ships and their uncounted casualties. In addition, 18 British warships were sunk while protecting the Arctic convoys—including the cruisers *Trinidad* and *Edinburgh*—at a cost of 1,944 lives. (The Germans' attacks on the Arctic convoys cost them 5 warships, 31 U-boats, dozens of planes, and several thousand lives.) While the Allied losses on the much busier North Atlantic convoy routes were higher in sheer numbers, the Murmansk Run was proportionally the deadliest convoy route of World War II. And the costliest Arctic convoy by far, in terms of ships, tonnage, and cargo, was convoy PQ-17. The distinguished American naval historian Samuel Eliot Morison wrote of the scattering of convoy PQ-17: "There has never been anything like it in our maritime history." The Seafarers International Union (SIU), an American union representing unlicensed mariners, called the convoy "the most tragic episode of the war at sea." Churchill called it "one of the most melancholy naval episodes in the whole of the war."

The story of convoy PQ-17 joined a long list of cautionary tales, dating as far back as warfare itself, in which distant commanders erred by substituting their judgment for that of the men risking their lives on the front lines. Modern historians still look to the convoy for lessons in leadership. In 2015, Milan Vego, a professor at the U.S. Naval War College in Newport, Rhode Island, argued that while the decision to send convoy PQ-17 was justified, Pound violated the basic principles of naval command by usurping the most critical decisions from his commanders on the scene. On a more fundamental level, Vego wrote, "No convoy should be left to proceed independently without its direct and distant covers."

THE MEN WHO SAILED IN convoy PQ-17 came home both haunted and inspired by the experience.

Leo Gradwell suffered for years from night terrors. He could not forget retrieving the dead bodies of mariners from the shallows off Novaya Zemlya. Like many men of his generation, Gradwell did not talk about the war to his family. His oldest son, Christopher, did not hear of PQ-17 until he was sixteen years old, when his mother encouraged him to ask his father about it. Gradwell responded by retrieving a file of Admiralty records, which he said were rife with errors. He added that most books written about convoy PQ-17 were full of errors too. He told Christopher that scattering the convoy was "a terrible mistake." He did not mention Sir Dudley Pound but expressed anger at Jack Broome for having withdrawn the six destroyers from the convoy's core escort force. Christopher suspected his father's resentment of Broome sprang from a dispute unrelated to convoy PQ-17. "It was certainly possible to have a spat with Dad," Christopher said, "and he never took prisoners." Gradwell never expressed anything but empathy for the Americans in the convoy, who he felt had been sent across the Arctic unprepared. He treasured an American flag one of the Yanks on the Ghost Ships had given him. Every year he arranged the flag around the base of the family's Christmas tree.

For years after the war, Gradwell spent his vacations aboard fishing trawlers with his old *Ayrshire* shipmates, pursuing cod off Bear Island. He worked as an ordinary crew member, taking his turns hauling nets, gutting fish, and passing around a bottle when the day's work was done. If he ever spoke with anyone at length about convoy PQ-17, Christopher said, it was surely with his old *Ayrshire* shipmates on calm, foggy days while fishing in the Barents Sea.

Gradwell resumed his legal career after the war. He had lost all his former clients while he was chasing U-boats, but was appointed a magistrate in London, deciding civil and criminal cases in the lower courts.

Gradwell had a reputation as a shrewd jurist with little patience for ill-prepared lawyers or arguments based on loopholes.

In 1951, soon after turning fifty, he was stricken with polio. He apparently caught the virus from his mother or brother, who had gone swimming in a local pool and returned complaining of stiff necks. They suffered only brief, flulike illnesses, but Gradwell awoke one morning paralyzed from the chest down. Fifty was late in life for a person to contract polio, and Gradwell's doctors feared he would die. He spent five months in quarantine, and almost two years in the hospital. He made the most of his forced inactivity by teaching himself Greek, Latin, French, German, and Spanish, although he had a tin ear and pronounced every foreign word in an upper-class British accent. Gradwell resolved to learn to walk again, and slowly graduated from calipers to crutches to walking sticks to a cane. He returned to the magistrate's bench and even resumed his summer vacations on the trawlers in the Barents Sea, scooting and crawling across the decks in order to keep up with his share of the work.

Gradwell's time in Archangel after convoy PQ-17 had left him with a deep affection for the Russian people. He thought Russia was the only nation other than England to produce great literature. He set out to learn Russian and was known to conjugate Russian verbs on a notepad in court when the testimony in a case grew tedious.

By no means were all of Gradwell's cases tedious. In 1963, he found himself in the middle of the notorious British Cold War political scandal known as the Profumo affair. British secretary of war John Profumo had carried on a brief affair with a nineteen-year-old showgirl named Christine Keeler, whose other beaus included a Soviet military attaché suspected of being a spy.* Although British intelligence concluded Keeler

---

* Keeler, who died in December 2017, also claimed to have had liaisons with Ringo Starr and the actors Warren Beatty, Peter Lawford, and George Peppard. Another woman caught up in the Profumo case, Marilyn "Mandy" Rice-Davies, claimed to have had a liaison with the actor Douglas Fairbanks Jr., who had served on the cruiser USS *Wichita* while it was escorting convoy PQ-17.

was no traitor and had passed no secrets to the Russians, the scandal consumed Britain. Gradwell's role in the case was to determine whether sufficient evidence existed to send Stephen Ward, an artist and osteopath who had introduced Keeler to the Soviet attaché, to trial in a higher court on charges of pimping Keeler and other women. Gradwell listened to days of sensational tabloid testimony and then sent the case forward for trial by another judge at London's famous Old Bailey court. Ward ended up committing suicide by an overdose of sleeping pills on the eve of his conviction in absentia on two counts of living off "immoral earnings." The scandal ended up forcing Profumo to resign and led to the resignation of Prime Minister Harold Macmillan.

Three years after the Profumo case, Gradwell was called upon to decide whether Hubert Selby's gritty novel of working-class Brooklyn, *Last Exit to Brooklyn,* violated Britain's obscenity laws. A writer who covered the trial for the weekly magazine *New Society* described Gradwell as "benign, genial, tolerant and humane," and noted that he "repeatedly showed a wide knowledge and appreciation of literature, and made some genuinely funny remarks." Gradwell eventually ruled that the book was obscene, citing a particularly raw chapter that described the gang rape of a young prostitute. His ruling was overturned by a higher court.

Gradwell retired from the bench the following year at the age of sixty-eight. He died two years later with his family at his side. *The Times* of London headlined his obituary "Magistrate and Sailor."

Jim North quit sailing when the war ended. He had been certified as an Able Seaman, which spared him from the worst chores on his ships, but he never really liked shipboard life. Unlike most of his shipmates, he had managed to save money. He took a train to Arkansas, where his father had bought him a small farm, and set out to build a house. He married a young woman his parents had found for him while he was at sea, and they had a son. Everywhere North went, he met military veterans attending college for free via the G.I. Bill, which excluded merchant mariners. North had not come home expecting a free college education, but he could not understand why merchant mariners were denied such benefits while Armed Guard men on the same ships received them.

North certainly could have used a free education. He quickly discovered he hated farming. He tried peddling watermelons. He applied for a job as a caddy at a golf course but was rejected because he knew nothing about golf. North moved to Santa Barbara, California, where his sister lived, and was surprised when his experience splicing cables on ships landed him a factory job as a rigger, fastening cables to heavy objects so they could be picked up by cranes. He got a real estate license and then a contractor's license. He built houses and also bought run-down houses and refurbished them—flipped them, in modern parlance—and then expanded into apartment buildings. The Santa Barbara real estate market took off, and North prospered. He built a house vaguely shaped like a ship, anchored into the hills overlooking the Santa Barbara Channel. North came to regard his nation's ingratitude for his wartime service as a gift. "It made me more independent," he said. "Instead of becoming somebody's employee, I became an employer. I've been able to go from one interesting thing to another without going broke doing it."

North read everything he could find about convoy PQ-17. He decided that if anyone was to blame, it was not Sir Dudley Pound but the people in the highest reaches of the British government who had left a sick and exhausted man to make impossible choices. North joined a group of American survivors of the Arctic convoys. At one of the reunions he shook hands with Carraway but still could not bring himself to like him.

North remained convinced that God had spared his life in convoy PQ-17. Until his early nineties he took part in annual church mission trips to rebuild out-of-town churches that had been damaged or in some cases burned down by racists. He supported a large family, which at last count numbered thirteen grandchildren and thirty-two great-grandchildren, a number of whom he helped send to college. North said he likes to think he has justified God's decision to spare his life, although "I know I should probably be more religious." In 2017, at the age of ninety-five, he was one of the last living survivors of convoy PQ-17.

Howard Carraway went home to South Carolina in 1945. He returned to civilian life but remained in the Naval Reserve for decades. His experiences in Archangel convinced him America needed a strong military to keep the Soviet Union in check. He became an ardent anti-Communist and did volunteer work for the Republican U.S. senator Strom Thurmond, who spent much of his forty-nine-year Senate career railing against Communism and the civil rights movement.

Carraway turned his love of writing into a career. He and a friend bought a weekly newspaper in tiny Pageland, South Carolina, "the Watermelon Capital of the World," where Carraway wrote columns on local, national, and global issues. After the paper was sold in 1958, Carraway moved his family to Florida, where Avis died of cancer in 1961. Carraway remarried and went to work for the daily *Fort Pierce News Tribune* in Fort Pierce, Florida, where he won a National Headliner Award for investigative stories exposing bid rigging in the trucking industry. Soon after, he left journalism to work for a state utility regulatory agency in Tallahassee. His last job was working for a telephone industry trade group .

Carraway wrote a brief history of his experiences in convoy PQ-17 for the U.S. Navy, and later shared his diary with the author Theodore Taylor, who used it as the primary source for a young adult book entitled *Battle in the Arctic Seas*. Like many of his contemporaries, Carraway did not talk about the war at home. He had told Avis the story of convoy PQ-17 by handing her a box containing his diary and saying, "Here." Years later, his son Mac had to coax the story out of him. Carraway described the *Troubadour*'s crew as a rogues' gallery of work-averse misfits. He felt he owed his life to the professionalism of Captain Salvesen and the incompetence of German torpedo manufacturers. Carraway harbored no ill will toward Sir Dudley Pound or the British in general. "He looked back on PQ-17 with a sense of wonder that he had made it back," Mac Carraway recalled, "and he was grateful for his life. Any hardships he encountered after that were always measured up against the experience of PQ-17. How hard could it be after PQ-17 if your business had a little hiccup?"

All his life, Carraway remained "Humble Howard" to his friends. He often told Mac, "Never take yourself too seriously." Not long before his death from Alzheimer's disease, Carraway started across the street one day without looking both ways and was nearly hit by a motorist who whizzed past him shouting, "Look out, you old fart!" Carraway threw back his head and roared with laughter. He died on March 19, 2003, at the age of eighty-five, and is buried at the National Cemetery in Bushnell, Florida.

William Carter came home with a different perspective from his time in Russia with the *Ironclad*. He too held no grudges over the scattering of convoy PQ-17, although of Sir Dudley Pound he wrote that "the kindest epitaph that I can manage is, 'I never walked a mile in his shoes.'" While Carter was shivering in the half-swamped lifeboat of the torpedoed *Richard Bland,* he had promised God that if he survived he would dedicate his life to public service. He and Ann settled in Dagsboro, Delaware, where Carter worked as an executive in a basket mill and then started an insurance agency he would run for nearly fifty years. His true vocation, however, was what he called his "nonpaying jobs" on volunteer boards and commissions. Carter was instrumental in establishing Delaware's system of technical and community colleges. He oversaw a commission that evolved into the state's environmental office. He served on a state college scholarship board whose beneficiaries included a young man from Wilmington named Joe Biden.

After the Soviet Union collapsed in 1989, Carter saw a chance to undertake a new kind of public service: improving relations between America and Russia. He had never forgotten the Russians in Archangel who had befriended him despite their own misery and the mortal threat of the NKVD. He attended events at the Russian embassy in Washington, D.C., sponsored by the Russian American Cultural Center, to commemorate events such as the meeting of U.S. and Soviet troops at the Elbe River in Germany in 1945. In his spare time, Carter earned a doctorate in higher education and government at the age of seventy-nine, and then wrote a book about convoy PQ-17 that he titled *Why Me, Lord?* The title was not intended as a lament but as a question to God about why his life had been spared. A Russian friend got the book translated into Russian and published there. In 2010, the Russian American Cultural Center invited Carter to Moscow for a celebration in Red Square marking the sixty-fifth anniversary of Victory Day, the day Germany surrendered. (That anniversary is largely ignored in America and Britain because the war with Japan was still raging.) Carter was thrilled. He obtained a passport and made plans to go. But his health failed too quickly for him to make the trip. He died on September 11, 2010, and is buried in a family cemetery in Delaware.

SEVEN YEARS AFTER Carter's death, his son Richard Carter set out to complete his father's journey as a tribute to him. The occasion was Dervish 2017, the latest in a series of reunions of Russian and Western convoy veterans organized by the Polar Convoy Social Group, a nonprofit organization of Russian veterans and history enthusiasts formed in the early 1990s. Dervish 2017 was to be held in St. Petersburg, Russia, which in 1942 was known as Leningrad. Carter knew his father would have been saddened by the direction in which Russia was heading, with Putin consolidating power, amassing personal wealth, and stifling political opposition. Carter also knew his father would have wanted him to go.

Convoy veterans from the United States and Britain have kept traveling to Russia even as the relations between their government and Putin's have deteriorated into a state reminiscent of the Cold War. At times the old veterans have gotten entangled in politics. In 2015, after Russia seized the Crimea and intervened militarily in eastern Ukraine, President Barack Obama and British prime minister David Cameron boycotted a celebration in Red Square to mark the seventieth anniversary of Victory Day. Putin offered Obama's and Cameron's seats on the grandstand to British veterans of the Arctic convoys. The old vets sat behind Chinese president Xi Jinping and listened to Putin give a speech thanking the West for its help against the Nazis but accusing it of trying to impose a "unipolar world order" in the twenty-first century. A British newspaper said the convoy veterans had helped Putin score "a cunning propaganda initiative," but the veterans were unrepentant. One of them accused British officials of behaving like "spoilt children" by skipping the ceremony. The following year, *The Guardian* newspaper opined that Russian celebrations of the Arctic convoys fit into Putin's efforts to stoke Russian nationalism. Russia's role in defeating the Nazis "deserves honor," the paper said. "But it does not justify the actions or the policies of Mr. Putin's regime today."

The Dervish 2017 conference in St. Petersburg included no high-level political games or grand parades. It attracted only eight Arctic convoy veterans—five Brits and three Russians—which was hardly surprising, given that the age of the youngest Arctic convoy veteran now exceeds ninety. The American attendees included me, Carter, and two brothers whose father had survived convoy PQ-18. One of the brothers, a rugged Western rancher, ambled around St. Petersburg in a cowboy hat and a belt with a thick metal buckle. He could not have looked more American if a U.S. flag had been draped around his shoulders.

The conference began with a wreath-laying ceremony at the Admiral Makarov State University of Maritime and Inland Shipping, at the base of a bronze statue of a Russian, a British, and an American sailor standing shoulder to shoulder at the bow of a ship. Several hundred Russians gathered, including uniformed cadets from the college, elderly war survivors, and government officials. Smiling young Russian women in brightly colored dresses presented long-stemmed red chrysanthemums to the veterans, a couple of whom were napping in their chairs.

A few minutes before the ceremony was to start, the U.S. consul general in St. Petersburg, Thomas Leary, took me and the other Americans aside. He thought we should know that the United States and Russia were in the midst of their most serious diplomatic rift since the Cold War. Putin's government had forced the United States to cut hundreds of employees from its diplomatic staff in Russia, including seventy in St. Petersburg whom Leary had personally had to lay off. Leary had just sent an email notifying the Russians that the United States would close the Russian consulate in San Francisco as well as Russian trade offices in Washington and New York. He felt certain the Russians would retaliate. Even before the consulate battle, he said, U.S. State Department relations with the Putin government had turned as cold as the White Sea in January. The convoy ceremony was the first event of any kind to which Leary and his staff had been invited in months. At this low ebb of U.S.-Russia government relations, Leary said, celebrations of better times when relations were warmer "are about all we have left in common."

To me and the other Americans, Leary's comments felt like a bucket of cold water being dumped on us in the middle of a balmy day at the beach. But we all appreciated it. And Leary certainly was not exaggerating. Six months later, the Russians closed the U.S. consulate in St. Petersburg.

The wreath-laying ceremony began with a series of speakers from the Russian government thanking the old veterans for risking their lives for Russia. One speaker ended his remarks with a call to set aside twenty-first-century politics: "The memory of the friendship between nations of the anti-Hitler coalition still unites us today and helps us during modern times," he said. "No complexities are able to erase the memory of the heroes." After laying the wreath, cadets at the maritime college presented an elaborate ninety-minute program commemorating the Arctic convoys. It included poems, dramatic readings, video clips, dancing, and songs, such as this:

> *Legendary northern convoy!*
> *You were born from sea and war,*

With confidence protecting the cargoes
From the enemy fire attacks,
Leading them home behind the Arctic doors,
Legendary northern convoy!

We were amazed that the Russians considered the Arctic convoys so important in the history of World War II. The story of the convoys is far better known in Russia than in the United States, or even in Britain. Russian children are taught about the convoys, including convoy PQ-17, in school. The lessons often emphasize the Russian heroics in dispatching Soviet ships, rescuing Western mariners, and keeping the North Russia ports open despite constant German attacks. Convoy PQ-17 is the subject of a widely read Russian historical novel, *Requiem for Convoy PQ-17,* by the late Valentin Pikul. In 2004, a Russian TV miniseries about convoy PQ-17 introduced the story to a younger generation of Russians. In one way or another, the story of the convoy has helped shape Russian views of the West for three quarters of a century. Over that time, the official Russian interpretation of the Arctic convoys has changed as Russia's relationship with the West has changed.

DURING AND AFTER THE GREAT Patriotic War, Stalin tried to boost Soviet pride and demonize the West by downplaying the convoys' importance. He suggested the Soviet Union would have beaten Hitler without the West's help, but accepted it when it was offered. The official Soviet line was that Lend-Lease supplies from the convoys amounted to only 4 percent of total Soviet war production, and thus played a minor role. Stalin never changed his view that the West tried to provide only enough help to prop up the Red Army so that the Soviets and Nazis could keep slaughtering one another—the scenario described by Harry Truman. Khrushchev, who led the Soviet Union through some of the most anxious years of the Cold War, between 1958 and 1964, wrote that while America and Britain provided valuable aid in World War II, they were not true friends of the Soviets: "[T]hey . . . wanted the Soviet Union to be considerably weaker after the war so that they could dictate their will to us."

Many conservative Russians still hold that view today. "I don't go in for conspiracy theories, but it makes sense," said Maksym Melnikov, a Russian cruise ship captain in his fifties. "I don't blame America for acting in its self-interest. But America is not a shining city on a hill." Melnikov, who grew up in Southern Russia, studied the polar convoys and convoy PQ-17 as a schoolboy and then in the maritime academy. "The convoys were important, and the Russian people are very grateful, very grateful," he said, "but the convoys were not crucial. We could have won the war without you, although it would have taken longer and we would have lost more people."

In the late 1980s, scholars in both Russia and in the West began reassessing the role of the convoys after many long-sealed Soviet files were opened for scrutiny. Russian historians such as Boris Sokolov and Mikhail Suprun concluded that the convoys provided more help than the Soviet government was willing to acknowledge. Suprun, in an interview for this book, said Allied Lend-Lease supplies accounted for as much as 20 percent of Soviet war production, not 4 percent. And every piece of cargo on the ships had been specifically requested by Stalin—right down to the caliber of the ammunition and the caloric content of the foodstuffs—to fill the Soviet Union's most desperate needs.

Suprun said the conflicting views of the Arctic convoys in Russia are generational. "It basically depends on when you grew up, whether you grew up with propaganda or have been allowed to talk openly." His college students hear a very different assessment of the convoys from him than their parents and grandparents heard from their teachers. The window for reassessing the convoys in Russia may be closing, however. For years, the Russian government supported Suprun's efforts to dig beneath the propaganda version of the Great Patriotic War. But recently, he said, "I have gotten some complaints." That was a quite an understatement: In

2009, Suprun was charged with a criminal offense of "invasion of privacy" for researching the fates of ethnic Germans in the Soviet Union who were sent to work camps in North Russia. The charge against him was dropped after a trial behind closed doors. Suprun's lawyer told reporters the government had pursued the case to scare him and other historians into leaving the past alone.

Regardless of the official government's position, Russian rear admiral Alexander Konayev said, "[M]illions of Soviet people at the front and the rear realized they were not struggling with fascism on their own." They were fighting the Nazis with Western weapons and fighting off hunger with Western food. They did not need Stalin or his commissars to tell them whether or not to be grateful.

John Le Cato, the third officer of the Liberty ship *Thomas Hartley,* had an especially moving encounter while he and some shipmates were touring a Russian school near Archangel in 1943. A kindergarten teacher asked them to stand before her class and introduced them to the children:

> These are your uncles from America. They have left their
> homes and their families and crossed the ocean to bring food
> for you and guns for your daddies in the Red Army. That is
> who they are.

Seventy-four years later, those memories are still vivid for many survivors of the Great Patriotic War in North Russia. In the summer of 2017 an elderly tour guide leading a group of Westerners through the Museum of the Northern Fleet in Murmansk stopped in front of a map of the route of convoy PQ-17. Speaking through an interpreter, she recounted the story of the Ghost Ships, describing how a British commander named Gradwell—she pronounced the name "Grade-well"—had led white-painted ships into the Matochkin Shar on Novaya Zemlya and ultimately to Archangel.

She said food from the Arctic convoys helped keep her and her family alive. "I still remember the paper bags with words in English typed on them: 'Dry onions, carrots, potatoes.'" She remembered especially the "rhombus-shaped tin cans"—the cans of Spam processed meat—and the clever way the Americans attached little metal keys to the cans for opening them.

She said she and her family ate food from the Arctic convoys until 1955. Holding her hand over her heart, she looked into her listeners' faces and said softly, "*Spasiba*"—"Thank you."

AUTHOR'S NOTE

I first learned about convoy PQ-17 while researching the Arctic convoys for my previous book, *The Mathews Men,* which chronicles the struggle between Hitler's U-boats and the tiny maritime community of Mathews County, Virginia. Since no Mathews men were in convoy PQ-17, I mentioned it only briefly in the book. But it intrigued me, and I started reading all I could find about it. The story had everything—an exotic, perilous setting; dramatic twists; moral quandaries; heroic deeds; not-so-heroic deeds; and political intrigue at the highest levels. The more I learned about convoy PQ-17, the more I wondered why I had never heard about it before.

The story of convoy PQ-17 is far better known in Britain and Russia than it is in the United States, which strikes me as odd. Most of the men and ships in the convoy were American. The decision to send them into harm's way originated with President Franklin D. Roosevelt, who regarded the Arctic convoys as vital to maintaining a fragile wartime alliance with Joseph Stalin and preventing World War II from evolving into the Cold War. I view the story of convoy PQ-17 as a forgotten chapter of American history with implications for the twenty-first century, and I have tried to tell it in that context. But at its most basic level, it is a tale of survival. To me, the most compelling part of the story is the voyage of the Ghost Ships, which fled into the polar ice to escape destruction by the Nazis. The odyssey of the Ghost Ships is the focus of this book.

Seventy-five years after convoy PQ-17 set out across the Arctic for North Russia, I was lucky to find detailed accounts of the Ghost Ships' adventure.

I am indebted to James Baker North III of Santa Barbara, California, a survivor of convoy PQ-17. Jim, who in 1942 was an ordinary seaman on the freighter *Troubadour,* recounted his experiences to me in a series of interviews. At age ninety-five, he is still a feisty character and a lively raconteur. Jim also shared various documents and photos he had collected over the years.

Mac Carraway of Bradenton, Florida, whose father, Howard, commanded the Navy Armed Guard unit on the *Troubadour,* told me about his father's life and provided me with a copy of a diary his father kept of the voyage of convoy PQ-17. I was astonished to find that the diary was 320 handwritten pages long, and was delighted to discover that Howard Carraway was an excellent writer. It's hard for me to imagine a more complete and revealing record of the Ghost Ships' voyage than his diary. Mac Carraway also gave me other documents related to his father, and directed me to a section of the National Archives in College Park, Maryland, that contains his father's official reports about the convoy, as well as photos he took on the voyage.

Richard E. Carter of Dover, Delaware, whose father, William, commanded the Navy Armed Guard unit on the freighter *Ironclad,* told me his father's story and graciously allowed me to quote at length from his father's self-published book, *Why Me, Lord?* The book contains countless details of the Ghost Ships' adventures that are not available anywhere else. While I was working on the book, Richard and I traveled together to Russia and to Hvalfjord in Iceland, the starting point of convoy PQ-17. Richard, who is a historian, also helped me find additional sources of information about convoy PQ-17.

I am grateful to the three children of Lieutenant Leo Gradwell, the commander of the British trawler HMT *Ayrshire*. Stephen Gradwell, Mary Corrigan, and the late Andrew Gradwell all gave generously of their time to tell me about their father's life, and how his healthy distrust of authority made him one of the true heroes of convoy PQ-17. Mary Corrigan sent me a trove of photos and documents, including her father's handwritten official reports and his decidedly unofficial account of the final stages of the voyage.

I'm indebted to Clare Howard, the granddaughter of Walter John Baker, a young sailor on the *Ayrshire* in 1942 who wrote a wonderfully detailed and lyrical account of the voyage. After her grandfather's death, Clare self-published his account in a book, *The Convoy Is to Scatter*, which is another rich source of details about the Ghost Ships' adventures. She was kind enough to allow me to quote from the book at length, and to provide me with photos of her grandfather and the *Ayrshire*. Thanks to Elise McDonald for allowing me to use photos taken by her grandfather Arthur McDonald of his fellow survivors from the freighter *Washington* on the rocky "beach" of Novaya Zemlya.

My thanks to Yury Alexandrov, Igor Kozyr, and Sergei Aprelev of the Polar Convoy Social Group, an organization of Russian military veterans and history enthusiasts devoted to preserving the memory of the Arctic convoys. Yury, Igor, and Sergei were my hosts for the Dervish 2017 conference in St. Petersburg, Russia, in August 2017. They helped explain to me how the supplies delivered by the convoys were handled and transported once they reached the Soviet Union. I also learned a great deal from Dr. Mikhail Suprun, a prominent Russian historian in Archangel, about life in wartime Archangel and how the Russian perspective on the Arctic convoys has changed over the years. Captain Maksym Melnikov, who was master of the cruise ship M/S *Nautica* during my voyage to Archangel, took time out from his busy schedule at sea to talk with me about sailing in the Arctic and about his own view of the Arctic convoys. Like many Russians, he learned about the convoys in school. Ivan

Katyshev, the department head of Scientific Research at the Northern Maritime Museum in Archangel, helped me obtain Russian documents and photos related to convoy PQ-17.

Maya Crank, Irina Tsyroulieva, and Iryna Pugachova of Virginia Beach translated dozens of pages of Russian documents for me. Hilde Oppedal, a friend from Norway, translated Norwegian documents and showed me around Bergen, Norway. Simon Fowler, a researcher in London, gathered information for me from British sources and also helped me navigate the U.K. National Archives at Kew. Dr. Victoria Hill, an Arctic researcher at Old Dominion University in Norfolk, Virginia, educated me about the Arctic environment and its ongoing transformation due to global warming.

My friends Paul Tyler and Bill Graves pored over drafts of the manuscript and greatly improved it. Rex Bowman provided me with Admiral Arseny Golovko's memoir and other documents, along with advice and encouragement. Kayla Kipps, a librarian at Virginia Tech (Go Hokies!), and my son Cody, a recent graduate of the University of Virginia (Go 'Hoos!), tracked down hard-to-find reference books in the universities' libraries for me. Dave Schwind provided help and advice. Vikki Camp helped me with travel arrangements to Norway, Russia, and London.

I'm grateful to my agent, Farley Chase, who encouraged me to pursue the convoy PQ-17 story, and to my editor at Viking, Wendy Wolf. Others at Viking I'd like to thank include Bruce Giffords, Jane Cavolina, Roland Ottewell, Lorie Young, Terezia Cicel, Matt Varga, Lucia Bernard, Fabiana Van Arsdell, Tricia Conley, Jason Ramirez, Claire Vaccaro, and the marketing and publicity teams. Thanks also to Jeff Ward for his excellent maps.

I could not have written *The Ghost Ships of Archangel* without the love and support of my family. My wife, Kema, was involved in virtually every phase of the book, from discussing the concept with me to assisting me with my research, taking photographs, and reading drafts of the chapters.

NOTES ON SOURCES

PROLOGUE: THE SPINNING NEEDLE

My description of the news of the scatter order reaching the *Troubadour* was based mainly on interviews with James Baker North III, a survivor of convoy PQ-17. I interviewed North at his home in Santa Barbara, California, in 2017. He also provided me with a copy of a 33-page account he wrote in 1992 of his experiences in convoy PQ-17. North, as the story explains, prospered after the war in real estate in Santa Barbara, where he now lives in a house anchored like a ship into the dry hills overlooking the Santa Barbara Channel. He was gracious enough to spend two days talking with me and share documents and photos relating to convoy PQ-17.

North's descriptions of the events immediately after the scatter order jibe with those of the *Troubadour*'s Navy Armed Guard commander, Ensign Howard Carraway, who chronicled the voyage of convoy PQ-17 in a diary he kept aboard the ship. Carraway's diary entries for the voyage of the *Troubadour* in convoy PQ-17 extend for more than 320 handwritten pages, and were provided to me by his son Mac Carraway of Bradenton, Florida. Mac also shared his father's story with me in interviews by phone and in person in Bradenton in 2017.

The background material about the dangers posed by the Germans and the Arctic environment and the involvement of Franklin D. Roosevelt, Winston Churchill, and Joseph Stalin in the Arctic convoys came from numerous sources that are described later in these notes on sources.

Captain Maksym Melnikov, a Russian merchant captain, confirmed North's description of the behavior of magnetic compasses near the Magnetic North Pole.

CHAPTER ONE: THE ENEMY OF MY ENEMY

My description of the scene at Hvalfjord and the mood of the men on the ships was drawn from my own visit to Hvalfjord in August 2018, Ensign Howard Carraway's diary, and other accounts by survivors of convoy PQ-17 and other Arctic convoys that set out from Iceland. Those accounts include the former merchant mariner Robert Carse's *A Cold Corner of Hell* (1969), which I think is one of the best books on the Arctic convoys in general. Carse wrote lively, no-nonsense descriptions of the mariners and their ships. It's hard to single out a particular section of his book, but pages 25–30 are a good place to start. Other descriptions of Hvalfjord are on pages 19–20 of Bernard Edwards's *The Road to Russia* (2002); pages 15–19 of Paul Lund and Harry Ludlam's *I Was There: On Convoy PQ-17, the Convoy to Hell* (although the book's title initially put me off, I found the authors' account extremely well researched and highly informative); and pages 5–6 of Walter John Baker's wonderful book *The Convoy Is to Scatter* (2011). Baker compares Hvalfjord to a Gustave Doré drawing of hell. Michael Walling's *Forgotten Sacrifice* (2012) contains good details about the rigors of sailing the Arctic.

The brief account of a storm blowing the cruiser USS *Wichita* around the harbor at Hvaldfjord came from Walling's *Forgotten Sacrifice*, page 46.

My description of Carraway's personality and his life up until convoy PQ-17 came from my interviews with his son Mac.

The checkered history of the *Troubadour* came from Carraway's diary; Carraway's reports to the Navy in the National Archives and Records Administration (NARA) Record Group 38, kept at the Archives II branch in College Park, Maryland. Records Group 38 contains the files of the chief of naval operations and the Tenth Fleet antisubmarine command, and thus many of the documents relating to merchant ship sinkings in World War II; other records on individual ships in NARA Records Group 178, which also is kept in College Park; and from a feature article in the *Times-Union and Journal* of Jacksonville, Florida, on December 12, 1976, which recounted the ship's history in considerable detail. The occasion for the article was the publication of a young adult book on convoy PQ-17 by Theodore Taylor, *Battle in the Arctic Seas,* which drew from Carraway's diary. Taylor was a fine writer. He is probably best known for his young adult novel *The Cay,* which concerns the U-boat war in the Caribbean.

The description of the *Troubadour*'s Captain Salvesen and the Norwegian third officer's vow to seek revenge against the Germans came from Carraway's diary.

I got my information about the crew of the *Troubadour* from a crew manifest I found online at Ancestry.com, from Carraway's diary, and from James Baker North III, whose rich and often hilarious descriptions of his shipmates were indispensable to me.

My account of North's life before convoy PQ-17 and his early experiences on the *Troubadour* came from my interviews with North and from North's 1992 written account of the voyage.

Although the history of America's long relationship with Russia is available from numerous sources, I found a very helpful synopsis of it on pages 55–64 of Albert L. Weeks's *Russia's Life-Saver: Lend-Lease Aid to the U.S.S.R. in World War II* (2004). Weeks's slim book offers valuable perspective to anyone trying to understand the Arctic convoys.

My brief account of the feckless Allied intervention in the Russian Civil War in 1918–19 was based primarily on E. M. Halliday's *When Hell Froze Over* (2000), which manages to convey the absurdities of the enterprise without ever making light of it. I also examined government documents on the intervention at www.dtic.mil/dtic/tr/fulltext/u2/b063276.pdf.

Churchill's comment that the West would regret not strangling Bolshevism at birth came from Halliday's *When Hell Froze Over,* page 284, as did Khrushchev's comment on how the intervention affected U.S.-Soviet relations in the Cold War.

My descriptions of Joseph Stalin and his history leading up to Operation Barbarossa in 1941 came from numerous sources, including three biographies of Stalin, Robert Service's *Stalin* (2005), Oleg Khlevniuk's *Stalin: New Biography of a Dictator* (2015), and Stephen Kotkin's *Stalin: Waiting for Hitler, 1929–1941* (2017), which is the second volume of a planned three-volume biography. Two books by British authors, Catherine Merridale's *Ivan's War* (2006) and Richard Overy's *Russia's War* (1997), offer great perspective and vivid details about Stalin and his rule of the Soviet Union before (and during) World War II. The quote about Stalin's penchant for butchery came from Service's *Stalin,* page 12. Stories about Stalin's cruelty abound. On page 47 of *Ivan's War,* Merridale quotes a woman who knew Stalin as a boy describing how she recalled watching him swim a swollen river to a small island where a calf was marooned by the floodwaters. The woman had expected Stalin to rescue the calf, but instead he broke its leg.

Merridale also uncovered a suicide note written by a young Red Army officer that vividly illustrates the horror and despair Stalin wrought with the purges of the Great Terror: "I love my country and would never betray it. I believe in an even better future, when a bright sun will shine on all the world. But here there are enemies who sit and threaten every step an honest commander tries to take. I have decided to take my own life, even though I am but twenty-one years old."

My big-picture explanation of how Stalin's rule created opportunities for some Soviet citizens is based on Merridale's *Ivan's War,* pages 35–37. Almost every Russian I met told me a family story of suffering or advancement as a result of the changes Stalin forced on Soviet society.

The Gulag had absorbed 1.67 million people by the time the Soviet Union entered the war, Merridale writes on page 145 of *Ivan's War.* I've seen conflicting figures but choose hers.

Churchill's comment about Poland and Romania not knowing whether they feared the Nazis or the Soviets more came from the first volume of Churchill's history of World War II, *The Gathering Storm* (1948), page 313. Reading Churchill's account of the war was one of the great pleasures of researching this book. Overy's *Russia's War* (1997) further addresses the difficulties of the West forming an alliance with Stalin, on pages 44–46.

My description of the signing of the nonaggression pact and of Hitler's purported boast that "Europe is mine" came from Overy's *Russia's War,* page 49. Stalin's aside to Khrushchev that he had outsmarted Hitler came from the same book, page 50.

Churchill's "sinister news" quote, along with his expression of doubt about the staying power of the nonaggression pact, came from his *The Gathering Storm,* page 351.

My point about the Soviets and Germans working together on a mobile poison-gas wagon came from Weeks's *Russia's Life-Saver,* page 90. The fact that the Soviets gave weather reports to German bombers over Britain came from Overy's *Russia's War,* page 53. Charles Emmerson's *The Future History of the Arctic* (2010) points out that remote Arctic weather stations were critical to both the Allies and the Germans in predicting the weather over the battlefields of Europe.

Jak P. Mallmann Showell's *Swastikas in the Arctic: U-boat Alley Through the Frozen Hell* (2014) describes some of the grim battles over those weather stations. Showell's book describes the war in the Arctic from the U-boats' perspective. At least half a dozen books about the Arctic convoys have "Hell" in their titles.

The report of Stalin "cursing like a cab driver" after hearing of France's defeat and Britain's retreat came from Overy's *Russia's War,* page 59.

My description of Stalin's multiple warnings about a German invasion and his too-late decision to act on them is recounted in numerous books. The most detailed account I found was in Kotkin's *Stalin: Waiting for Hitler, 1929–1941,* pages 895–99.

The detail about the wiring of the Bolshoi Theater to explode came from Merridale's *Ivan's War,* page 128. The details of the German occupation of Tolstoy's and Tchaikovsky's properties came from Overy's *Russia's War,* page 124.

My description of Churchill's efforts to extend a hand to Stalin came from his *The Gathering Storm.*

I reviewed the letters between Churchill and Stalin and between Churchill and Roosevelt at the U.K. National Archives at Kew in southwest London. Other excellent sources of letters written by the three men to one another are the compilations *Roosevelt and Churchill: Their Secret Wartime Correspondence* (1975), edited by Francis L. Loewenheim, Harold D. Langley, and Manfred Jonas; and *My Dear Mr. Stalin: The Complete Correspondence of Franklin D. Roosevelt and Joseph V. Stalin* (2005), edited by Susan Butler. Churchill also includes many of his letters to Roosevelt and Stalin in his five-volume history of World War II.

Roosevelt's emissary Harry Hopkins not only was impressed with Stalin's determination but with Stalin personally. "No man could forget the picture of the dictator of Russia," Hopkins wrote, "an austere, rugged, determined figure in boots that shone like mirrors, stout baggy trousers, and a snug-fitting blouse. He wore no ornament, military or civilian. He's built close to the ground, like a football coach's dream of a tackle. He's about five feet six, about one hundred and ninety pounds. His hands are huge, as hard as his mind. His voice is harsh but ever under control. What he says is all the accent and inflection his words need." I found Hopkins's description of Stalin in Butler's *My Dear Mr. Stalin,* pages 35–36.

The references to *Life* magazine's optimistic portrayal of the NKVD and another magazine's likening Stalin to an Italian gardener came from Amos Perlmutter's *FDR & Stalin* (1993), pages 105–6.

Former president Herbert Hoover's disparaging comments about America forming an alliance with the Soviet Union came from Dennis J. Dunn's *Caught Between Roosevelt and Stalin: America's Ambassadors to Moscow* (1998), page 127.

My information about Stalin's continuing overtures to Hitler after Operation Barbarossa came from my correspondence with Dr. Mikhail Suprun, a Russian historian in Archangel, in March 2018.

The detail about the Soviets turning churches into barns and pigsties came from Merridale's *Ivan's War*, page 33.

I stumbled onto the movie *Days of Glory* while channel surfing one night and watched it almost in disbelief. *Pravda*'s about-face was described in Merridale's *Ivan's War*, page 132.

Roosevelt's "Step on it!" memo came from Butler's *My Dear Mr. Stalin*, page 39.

The statistic of the Soviets losing twenty men for every German they killed came from Overy's *Russia's War*, page 137.

The Grand Alliance was the title Churchill gave to the third volume of his five-volume history of World War II.

The Leningrad diary entry came from Merridale's *Ivan's War*, page 98.

CHAPTER TWO: HELLISH GREEN

My account of the White Horse whisky mutiny came from pages 131–46 of Lieutenant William Carter's *Why Me, Lord?* (2007).

Particulars of Carter's background came from interviews with his son Richard Carter of Dover, Delaware, and from *Why Me, Lord?* My description of the *Ironclad*'s history came from NARA Records Groups 38 and 178 and from *Why Me, Lord?*

The rigors of the Persian Gulf route to the Soviet Union were described to me in an interview in May 2017 with Captain Hugh Stephens, a professor at State University of New York (SUNY) Maritime Academy in the Bronx, who twice during World War II made voyages to the Soviet Union, once via the Persian Gulf and once through the Arctic.

My descriptions of the landmarks along the Arctic convoy route, such as Jan Mayen Island and Bear Island, are based partly on David McGonigal and Dr. Lynn Woodward's *The Complete Encyclopedia of Antarctica and the Arctic* (2001), pages 178–83. I also found a great deal of information about the Arctic climate

and ecology in E. C. Pielou's *A Naturalist's Guide to the Arctic* (1994); John Mc-
Cannon's *A History of the Arctic: Nature, Exploration and Exploitation* (2012);
and Charles Emmerson's *The Future History of the Arctic* (2010).

My description of the foul weather on the Barents Sea came from Chris
Mann and Christer Jörgensen's *Hitler's Arctic War* (2002), page 9.

The account of the Arctic storm and its "grey pavements of water" came from
B. B. Schofield's *The Russian Convoys* (1964), page 197. Schofield's book is another one of my favorites about the Arctic convoys.

Stephens described the wind sounding like a shrieking woman. My descriptions of the impact of the bitter cold on men and ships came from numerous
sources, including interviews with James Baker North III, Stephens, and other
survivors of the voyage, as well as from several books. Michael Walling's *Forgotten Sacrifice* (2012) offers several unusual details on page 48, including the fact
that the extreme cold could freeze nose hairs into needles of ice. Robert Carse's
A Cold Corner of Hell (1969) describes on page 17 how the cold could cause
eyelashes and eyebrows to freeze and fall off.

The capsizing of a British escort vessel from ice buildup on the superstructure is described in numerous books. Walling's account on pages 66–67 of
Forgotten Sacrifice is more detailed than most.

Everyone I asked gave me a slightly different answer about how long a mariner could survive in the icy Arctic waters. I used Russian cruise ship captain
Maksym Melnikov's estimate that a person would be incapacitated in twenty
minutes and dead in thirty because Melnikor, as master of a cruise ship carrying
hundreds of people through those waters, had to make it his business to know.
In addition, accounts from the rescue ships in convoy PQ-17 suggest that survivors pulled from the water within twenty minutes had a much better chance of
surviving than those who had been immersed longer.

My information about Arctic mirages came from Pielou's *A Naturalist's
Guide to the Arctic* (1994), pages 20–23, and also from personal observation.
While sailing through the Arctic in July 2017, I saw numerous such mirages,
which were unlike any I had ever seen elsewhere.

The British mariner's description of the changing balance between light and
darkness in the Barents Sea came from Carse's *A Cold Corner of Hell,* page 18.

The mariner Donald Murphy's description of the "hellish green" Arctic light
came from *Eyewitness Accounts of the World War II Murmansk Run 1941–1945*
(2006), a collection of firsthand accounts edited by Mark Scott. I first heard

about this book from Dr. Mikhail Suprun in Archangel, who highly recommended it. It's a wonderful collection of accounts, and I too recommend it to anyone with a keen interest in the Arctic convoys.

Churchill's *The Gathering Storm* (1948) provides an excellent summary of the Germans' invasion of Norway and the belated British effort to dislodge them. For a more detailed reading of the Nazi invasion of Norway, I suggest Chris Mann and Christer Jorgensen's *Hitler's Arctic War* (2002), pages 32–62.

My description of the *Tirpitz* came from David Brown's *Tirpitz: The Floating Fortress* (1977), Leonce Peillard's *Sink the Tirpitz!* (1968), Vice Admiral Friedrich Ruge's *The Sea War: The German Navy's Story 1939–1945* (1957), and Niklas Zetterling and Michael Tamelander's *Tirpitz: The Life and Death of Germany's Last Super Battleship* (2009).

I visited the otherworldly North Cape of Norway in July 2017. While the North Cape is a touristy place in summer, standing at the edge of the cliff and gazing north across the Barents Sea toward the North Pole is still an extraordinary experience.

Anyone looking to reconstruct the history of the early Arctic convoys probably ought to start with Bob Ruegg and Arnold Hague's *Convoys to Russia 1941–1945* (1992), a no-frills, authoritative listing of the convoys, the ships participating in them, and their fates. B. B. Schofield's *The Russian Convoys* (1964) and Paul Kemp's *Convoy! Drama in Arctic Waters* (2004) also are good sources of information about the early PQ convoys.

Negley Farson's observation about the polar ice hemming in the convoys came from the *Daily Mail* of London on June 16, 1942. Farson had sailed on a merchant ship in Arctic convoy PQ-12 and homebound convoy QP-10.

Hitler's changing attitudes toward the Arctic convoys are reflected in the German Navy's summaries of the Fuehrer Conferences on Naval Affairs for 1941 and 1942, which I reviewed at the U.K. National Archives. Kemp points out on pages 25–27 of *Convoy!* that Hitler's initial lack of interest in stopping the convoys was based on his thinking that the Soviets would be conquered quickly and that the convoys could not save them.

The best account I found of the horrific HMS *Matabele* sinking was in Frank Pearce's *Running the Gauntlet* (1989), pages 30–33.

My account of the *Tirpitz*'s fruitless attempt to attack convoy PQ-12 came primarily from Zetterling and Tamelander's *Tirpitz: The Life and Death of Germany's Last Super Battleship*, pages 37–44.

The description of the frostbitten mariner who had his legs amputated without anesthetic came from Walling's *Forgotten Sacrifice,* page 83.

The story of convoy PQ-14's struggles in the storm came from a report of the British vessel *Hopemount* at the U.K. National Archives.

Admiral Sir Stuart Bonham-Carter's warning about sending convoys through the Arctic in twenty-four-hour daylight came from Pearce's *Running the Gauntlet* (1989), page 79.

Admiral Sir Dudley Pound's comment about the Arctic convoys being a "millstone" came from Robin Brodhurst's biography of Pound, *Churchill's Anchor* (2000), page 238.

Roosevelt's stinging reply to Churchill's message to Harry Hopkins came from Jon Meacham's *Franklin and Winston* (2004), page 210.

Churchill rather dispassionately described being pressured by Roosevelt to send convoys through the Arctic despite the growing danger in *The Hinge of Fate* (1950), pages 258–60.

The brief description of the failed Soviet offensives against the Nazis in February and March 1942 and the German gains in Ukraine came from Richard Overy's *Russia's War* (1997), page 122, and Catherine Merridale's *Ivan's War* (2006), pages 150–52.

Captain S. W. Roskill's assessment of the Soviet's indifference to the dangers of the Arctic convoys and the political pressure on Churchill came from Roskill's definitive Royal Navy history of the war, *The War at Sea 1939–1945,* volume II (1956), page 397.

Ensign Howard Carraway's diary described the betting pool organized by the *Troubadour's* Armed Guard unit.

North told me the story about his ill-fated shore visit in one of our interviews. Talking with North reminded me that no matter how many written accounts exist of an event, there is really no substitute for talking with someone who was there. Sadly, that soon will no longer be possible for the events of World War II.

Carter's explanation of how fallout from the White Horse whisky mutiny kept the *Ironclad* from sailing in convoy PQ-16 came from page 145 of *Why Me, Lord?*

CHAPTER THREE: KNIGHT'S MOVE

My recounting of the *Carlton's* previous attempts to reach Russia is based on documents in NARA Records Group 38. Theodore Taylor's *Battle in the Arctic*

Seas (1976) describes the ship's reputation among mariners as a "Jonah" on page 7.

The description of the relentless air attacks on the Liberty ship *Richard Henry Lee* in convoy PQ-16 came from John Gorley Bunker's *Liberty Ships: The Ugly Ducklings of World War II* (1973), pages 63–64.

Ensign Howard Carraway described his worries about his emotionally troubled shipmate in his diary.

My information about Lieutenant Leo Gradwell came primarily from telephone interviews and email exchanges with his three children, Mary Corrigan, Christopher Gradwell, and the late Andrew Gradwell, who died in January 2018. Each of Gradwell's children remembered something different about their unique father. Mary Corrigan sent me a large trove of photos and documents relating to her father's wartime experience, including copies of his Certificate of Competency as a Master of Pleasure Yachts and a handwritten, unpublished account by Gradwell of the latter part of convoy PQ-17's voyage.

Carraway described in his diary how he received news reports about the fate of convoy PQ-16 and the American victory at the Battle of Midway.

Both sides in the Atlantic war used coded birth notices to inform men at sea that they had become fathers. Timothy P. Mulligan notes on page 184 of his book *Neither Sharks Nor Wolves* (1999) that the commander of the German U-boat force, Admiral Karl Doenitz, personally sent coded birth announcements to his submariners at sea, referring to a newborn son as a "U-boat with periscope" and a newborn daughter as "a U-boat without periscope."

I found the information about the ships and structure of convoy PQ-17 from NARA Records Group 38, which has a large file on the convoy as well as an oral history by Carraway and photographs he took on the voyage, some of which are included in this book.

The footnoted reference to "Roosevelt's eggs" came from Albert L. Weeks's *Russia's Life-Saver: Lend-Lease Aid to the U.S.S.R. in World War II* (2004), page 122.

I obtained records about the never-say-die Soviet tanker *Azerbaijan* from the Northern Maritime Museum in Archangel, Russia, through the museum's department head of Scientific Research, Ivan Katyshev, whom I met briefly in Archangel and corresponded with afterward. The British war correspondent Godfrey Winn's comment about the blond female bosun came from his book

PQ-17 (1948), a very personal account of his experiences on the voyage aboard a British antiaircraft ship.

Admiral Sir Dudley Pound's instructions to his commanders to keep convoy PQ-17 moving even if it was suffering losses came from Robin Brodhurst's *Churchill's Anchor* (2000), page 240.

Captain Jack Broome described the Royal Navy's success in scattering a convoy in the North Atlantic in his informative book *Convoy Is to Scatter* (not to be confused with Walter John Baker's *The Convoy Is to Scatter*), pages 81–82. Broome used the signals exchanged by the British during the convoy as the basis of his book, which provided a good perspective of how the disaster unfolded.

My description of Admiral Sir John Tovey's suggestion that convoy PQ-17 be used as bait for the *Tirpitz* came from David Irving's *The Destruction of Convoy PQ-17* (1968), which is one of the best-known British accounts of the convoy. After the first edition was published, Irving and his publisher were sued for libel by Broome, who argued that the book cast him in an unfairly bad light. A court found in Broome's favor and awarded him substantial damages. Since then, Irving has become better known as a denier of the Holocaust. But his extensive research and legwork in tracking down and interviewing key figures in the story of convoy PQ-17 while they were alive makes *The Destruction of Convoy PQ-17* valuable in understanding the disaster.

The Admiralty's plan for protecting convoy PQ-17 through three separate escort forces makes for confusing, jargon-heavy reading for laymen. I found one of the clearest descriptions of the plan on pages 88–89 of David Wherrett's *From Yorkshire to Archangel: A Young Man's Journey to PQ-17* (2017), which Wherrett wrote as a tribute to his father, who survived the convoy.

German admiral Erich Raeder described his dealings with Hitler about Operation Knight's Move in the Fuehrer Conferences on Naval Affairs for 1942, which I reviewed at the U.K. National Archives. My background information about Raeder and his relationship with Hitler came mainly from page 5 of Anthony Martienssen's *Hitler and His Admirals* (1948) and from page 115 of Leonce Peillard's *Sink the Tirpitz!* (1968). Hitler's comment about being a hero on land but a coward at sea came from page 2 of Martienssen's book.

Raeder expressed his loathing of Hermann Goering at the Nuremberg war crimes trials after the war, saying of him: "The personality of Goering had a disastrous influence on the fate of the German Reich. Unimaginable vanity and unrestrained ambition were two of his principal characteristics; he had a craving for cheap popularity and effect, and was distinguished for dishonesty, ignorance and selfishness. He ignored the interests of State and people, and was both avaricious and extravagant—an effeminate and unsoldierly character." Goering was sentenced to death at Nuremberg but committed suicide on the eve of his scheduled execution by ingesting a cyanide capsule; Raeder was sentenced to life imprisonment, but was released after nine years at the age of seventy-nine, due to his deteriorating health.

Churchill described his bizarre visit from the suspicious Vyacheslav Molotov in *The Hinge of Fate* (1950), pages 331–37. Readers unfamiliar with Molotov the person may be familiar with a crude weapon named for him, the Molotov cocktail—a container of flammable liquid stuffed with a burning fuse and hurled at the enemy. The Finns invented the Molotov cocktail during their brief war with the Soviet Union in 1939–1940 and named it for Molotov as a taunt. The Soviets subsequently made wide use of Molotov cocktails against the Nazis.

The description of the "hammer" as a "schoolmasterish" figure came from a story on Molotov's resignation as foreign minister in *The New York Times,* June 2, 1956.

My account of Churchill's second wartime visit to America came primarily from *The Hinge of Fate,* pages 374–86. Churchill described his discussion with Roosevelt about the atomic bomb on pages 374–75, his wariness about Roosevelt's car with hand brakes on page 377. Churchill's books on the war make it clear that he had a habit of offering advice to his pilots, ship captains, and drivers. He spent part of his visit to Hyde Park riding with Roosevelt in the president's car, which was rigged with special equipment to allow Roosevelt to control the brake and gas pedal with his hands. Roosevelt kept stopping at scenic overlooks on cliffs overlooking the Hudson River, and Churchill kept glancing nervously at the hand brakes, hoping they were reliable. He refrained from mentioning his concerns to the president.

Churchill described receiving the shocking telegram about Tobruk on pages 382–83 of *The Hinge of Fate.* He described his and Ismay's discouraging look at live-fire exercises by green U.S. troops in South Carolina on page 386.

Jon Meacham's *Franklin and Winston* (2004) added several telling details to Churchill's description of his visit to America, on page 187, and described the apparent assassination attempt on the prime minister in Baltimore.

Wartime Murmansk was described by numerous mariners who spent time there. The author and former mariner Felix Riesenberg offered a wonderful description on pages 131–32 of *Sea War* (1956): "Ten patched docks creaked and groaned under a glut of war cargo; sidings were walled by high stacks of bales, cases and barrels; overloaded freight trains were backed up for miles. The waterfront became a dirty sludge at noon when snow melted under the blast of bomb explosions and the grind of heavy machinery; at night it refroze into deep warped ruts of ice and shale. Soot and oil smudged the city, then blizzards howled down out of Barents Sea to whiten it again."

The description of the thunderous Russian antiaircraft barrage from Murmansk came from page 123 of Graeme Ogden's *My Sea Lady* (2013). Ogden was the commander of the HMT *Lady Madeleine,* an armed trawler similar to the *Ayrshire.* Ogden's book described his own convoy experience, which did not include convoy PQ-17, but he did include a short description of the *Ayrshire*'s adventures in convoy PQ-17, as told to him by Gradwell and the *Ayrshire*'s first officer, Richard Elsden. Before he died, Gradwell told his children that Ogden's account of convoy PQ-17 was the only accurate one he ever read in a book. *My Sea Lady* also provides a great deal of background on armed trawlers.

The information about Swedish intelligence sources giving the British a copy of the Knight's Move plan came from Brodhurst's *Churchill's Anchor,* page 238. The officer's comment that the Royal Navy regarded the plan as merely a "rumble of distant thunder" came from Wherrett's *From Yorkshire to Archangel,* page 111. The officer he quotes is Broome.

Carraway's description of the "mutiny" on the *Troubadour* came from his diary. James Baker North III, who was a participant, gave a very different account of the work stoppage in his interviews with me. Carraway's account of his and the captain's efforts to have the troubled Uruguayan seaman removed from the ship came from Carraway's diary.

The account of the final convoy conference in Hvalfjord came from several sources, but primarily from Irving's *The Destruction of Convoy PQ-17,* pages 69–72, and from Broome's *Convoy Is to Scatter* (1972), pages 107–9.

Theodore Taylor's evocative description of the convoy's departure came from page 47 of *Battle in the Arctic Seas.* North's description of missing the departure while stowing the anchor chain came up in one of our interviews. Carraway's reflections on the convoy's departure came from his diary.

CHAPTER FOUR: FIRST BLOOD

I found a reference by Caesar to convoys in his account of the invasion of Britain. The account I read is on page 4 of a collection of war stories edited by Ernest Hemingway and entitled *Men at War: The Best War Stories of All Time* (1955).

The description of the convoy sailing out of Hvalfjord came primarily from Ensign Howard Carraway's diary. Douglas Fairbanks Jr.'s comparison of the merchant ships to "dirty ducks" came from his war diary, part of which is reprinted in his book *A Hell of a War* (1993), on pages 132–33. Fairbanks was a Hollywood screen idol serving as a flag lieutenant on the American cruiser USS *Wichita,* which was part of convoy PQ-17's distant covering force. Although Fairbanks understood Iceland's strategic importance to America and Britain, he did not like the place. He quoted a fellow U.S. Navy officer as saying, "Well, I can understand why we are here in Iceland, and I can understand why the British are in Iceland, but I'll be goddamned if I understand why the Icelanders are in Iceland!"

The mariner's view that people on shore were happy not to be accompanying convoy PQ-17 came from Paul Lund and Harry Ludlam's *I Was There: On PQ17, the Convoy to Hell* (1968), pages 26–27.

Maksym Melnikov talked with me about fog while he was guiding the cruise ship M/S *Nautica* through fog on the way to Murmansk in July 2017. The description of the Arctic fog as "slimy" came from an oral history by the *Ayrshire*'s first officer, Richard Elsden, which I accessed on the website of the Imperial War Museum in London, at www.iwm.org.uk/collections/search?query=pq-17. The museum, which I visited in July 2017, contains other oral histories by men in convoy PQ-17, as well as a diary kept by an anonymous crew member of the *Ayrshire*. One of the things I liked best about the museum was that it includes many physical remnants of the sea war in World War II, including a pair of imposing 15-inch guns like those on the *Tirpitz;* one of those guns' man-sized shells; and a cluster of incendiary bombs similar to the ones German bombers dropped on ships and on Murmansk and Archangel.

Commander Jack Broome's assessment of the Arctic fog came from his *Convoy Is to Scatter* (1972), page 185.

David Wherrett's *From Yorkshire to Archangel* (2017) was a great source of details about the operation of the convoy PQ-17 rescue ships, mainly because Wherrett's father served on one of those vessels, the *Zamalek*. Wherrett provides a good general description of the ship's operations on page 67. The detail about the Admiralty sending three rescue ships along with convoy PQ-17 mainly so that they could bring home a large number of Allied mariners already stranded in North Russia came from a document I found at the U.K. National Archives. The detail about the *Zamalek* putting to sea with dockyard workers still laboring to get it ready came from David Irving's *The Destruction of Convoy PQ-17* (1968), page 70.

Carraway described engaging the tanks in the *Troubadour*'s deck cargo in the defense of the ship in his diary. He was not the only Navy Armed Guard commander to recognize that tanks offered a chance to improve a ship's weaponry. David A. Schwind's *Blue Seas, Red Stars: Soviet Military Medals to U.S. Sea Service Recipients in World War II* (2015) describes how the Armed Guard commander of the Liberty ship *Benjamin Harrison* removed some machine guns from the tanks on his ship and mounted them on the vessel where they would be more effective against planes. Schwind offers detailed descriptions of the brave acts that earned Soviet medals and orders for 217 members of the U.S. Navy, Coast Guard, and Merchant Marine during the Arctic convoys.

Lieutenant William Carter described the *Ironclad*'s inadequate guns on pages 104–8 of *Why Me, Lord?* (2007). He described his approach to shooting at planes on pages 158–59.

Walter John Baker's reflections on the weird beauty of the ice came from his *The Convoy Is to Scatter* (2011), page 10. Godfrey Winn's "batik" comment about the ice came from his book *PQ-17* (1948), page 76.

My account of the *Richard Bland* and the *Exford* being forced to turn back after hitting ice and rocks, respectively, came primarily from NARA Records Group 38, and from Commodore Jack Dowding's extensive and fact-filled final report on convoy PQ-17, which I found at the U.K. National Archives.

The description of the antiaircraft ships serenading the Americans with "Deep in the Heart of Texas" and "Pistol Packin' Mama" came from Carter's *Why Me, Lord?*, pages 154–55.

My account of the bombing of Murmansk came from Maksim I. Starostin's *Krigsdagbok fra Murmansk (War Diary from Murmansk)* (2017), pages 274–77, which was translated for me from Norwegian to English by my Norwegian friend Hilda Oppedal. Hilda, an experienced tour guide, also showed me around Bergen.

The senior British naval officer's warning on Murmansk is at the U.K. National Archives.

Francis Brummer's description of the first German plane locating convoy PQ-17 came from his diary, printed in Donald Vining's *American Diaries of World War II* (1982), page 134.

Winn's colorful description of the Shad came from *PQ-17*, page 76.

My description of the U-boats' challenges in operating in calm seas and twenty-four-hour daylight came from pages 71–73 of Jak P. Mallmann Showell's *Swastikas in the Arctic: U-boat Alley Through the Frozen Hell* (2014).

Carraway wrote in his diary about his initial fear at manning the *Troubadour*'s guns during the first air-raid alarm.

Carter's observations about the sun's movement came from *Why Me, Lord?*, page 150.

Admiral Raeder's instruction that the U-boats ignore homebound convoy QP-13 and concentrate on convoy PQ-17 is among intercepted German signals at the U.K. National Archives.

The message concerning the "whale without a tail" came from NARA Records Group 38. In my research for this book and my previous book, *The Mathews Men* (2016), I found numerous reports of whales being mistaken for U-boats and bombed.

My description of the first attack by German aircraft on the convoy came mostly from Carraway's diary and Carter's *Why Me, Lord?* Winn's comment that he reluctantly admired the German pilot's rescue effort came from *PQ-17*, page 85.

Carraway's assessment of the *Troubadour*'s performance during the first air attack and his description of the aftermath of the attack came from his diary.

Baker's description of his argument with a shipmate over Communism and Stalin came from *The Convoy Is to Scatter*, pages 21–22.

My description of Churchill's defeat of the no-confidence vote in Parliament came mainly from *The Hinge of Fate*, pages 391–409.

I found the detail about Roosevelt taking along *Jane's Fighting Ships* as reading material at Shangri-La in Jon Meacham's *Franklin and Winston* (2004), page 188.

The account of the *Tirpitz* moving through the Inner Leads came from Niklas Zetterling and Michael Tamelander's *Tirpitz: The Life and Death of Germany's Last Super Battleship* (2009), pages 121–24. My background about Admiral Schniewind came from Anthony Martienssen's *Hitler and His Admirals* (1948), page 15. The detail that Schniewind was nicknamed "the Undertaker" by his men came from Theodore Taylor's *Battle in the Arctic Seas* (1976), page 34.

I found helpful descriptions of the various German aircraft that attacked convoy PQ-17 in John C. Fredriksen's *International Warbirds: An Illustrated Guide to World Military Aircraft, 1914–2000* (2002).

My information about the challenges of flying in the Arctic came from page 198 of Adam R. A. Claasen's *Hitler's Northern War: The Luftwaffe's Ill-Fated Campaign, 1940–1945* (2001), which examines the war in the Arctic from the perspective of the German air force.

The quote about the majestic icebergs and polar bears came from an account by John Beardmore, the navigating officer of the British corvette HMS *Poppy*. I found Beardmore's account online at www.cbrnp.com/RNP/Flower/ARTI CLES/Poppy/Beardmore-1.htm, a website devoted to Flower-class corvettes.

Carraway's observations of the icebergs and pancake ice, as well as the ominous sight of the wreckage in the water, came from his diary. Several mariners described seeing the bomber frozen in a mass of ice, but their accounts varied as to whether it was a British or German plane.

My information about Lord Haw-Haw's July 3 taunt of convoy PQ-17 came from Irving's *The Destruction of Convoy PQ-17,* page 116. Mariners on many ships in the convoy listened to Lord Haw-Haw's broadcasts, although some captains forbade it. Lord Haw-Haw's real name was William Joyce. A New York native, he had spent much of his young life in Ireland and Britain. He joined the British Nazi Party and later emigrated to Germany, where he began his propaganda broadcasts. After the war, Joyce was captured and then hanged.

Carraway's comments on the *Ayrshire* and the comfort of the fog came from his diary. So did my account of Carraway's unsuccessful effort to catch a glimpse of Bear Island.

CHAPTER FIVE: FIREWORKS

S. J. Flaherty's quote came from his book *Abandoned Convoy* (1970), page 20. The information and quote about men accepting discomfort in order to protect their lives came from Walter John Baker's *The Convoy Is to Scatter* (2010), pages 34–35.

Ensign Howard Carraway's account of the Heinkel 115s' attack on the convoy came from his diary.

The description of the sinking of the *Christopher Newport* came primarily from the reports of survivors and of the ship's Armed Guard commander in NARA Records Group 38. The Armed Guard commander's report contains details of the heroics of the gunner Hugh Wright, as does David A. Schwind's *Blue Seas, Red Stars: Soviet Military Medals to U.S. Sea Service Recipients in World War II* (2015), page 133. *Blue Seas, Red Stars* also describes Paul Webb being hurled against a smokestack by the force of the torpedo explosion. My account of the *Christopher Newport*'s captain trying to bring a gun aboard the rescue ship *Zamalek* came from Paul Lund and Harry Ludlam's *I Was There: On PQ17, the Convoy to Hell* (1968), page 47.

Baker described how Gradwell was tempted to try to board the abandoned *Christopher Newport,* and how the crew of the *Ayrshire* was glad he reconsidered, on pages 29–30 of *The Convoy Is to Scatter.* The British submarines were unable to sink the derelict *Christopher Newport;* a U-boat finally did.

Godfrey Winn described the practice of marking off a sunken ship on the convoy chart in *PQ-17* (1948), page 93.

Lieutenant William Carter described the unsettling "bombs through the fog syndrome" and his discovery that he could handle the rigors of combat on page 163 of *Why Me, Lord?* On the following page, he described approaching his traumatized shipmate but not knowing how to help him.

Men on several different ships in convoy PQ-17 recounted the story of the German pilot of the Shad obligingly reversing course when men on the ships complained to him that watching him circle them made them dizzy. I thought the story was apocryphal at first but decided to include it after reading so many accounts of it. Baker wrote about the Shad firing a burst into the water near the *Ayrshire* on page 24 of *The Convoy Is to Scatter.*

Carter and other mariners described the hoisting of new American flags to celebrate the Fourth of July. My description of the initial British confusion over the lowering of the old flags came from Winn's *PQ-17,* page 96. Lund and Ludlam's praise for the raising of the new flags as a "splendidly defiant gesture" came from *I Was There: On PQ17, the Convoy to Hell,* page 48. Winn reflected on the newness of war to the Americans in *PQ-17,* page 96. Carraway reported in his diary having "a wee drop" of Scotch with Salvesen to celebrate the Fourth.

The congratulatory holiday messages between the American and British warships came from the Arctic convoys files of NARA Records Group 38 and the U.K. National Archives.

The messages from the Admiralty to the commanders in the field came from the files of the U.K. National Archives.

The Germans' initial confusion over the whereabouts of the Allied carriers is described in the final German report on Operation Knight's Move, a copy of which is contained in the files of the U.K. National Archives.

My accounts of the determined attack by the Heinkel 111 bombers came mostly from Carraway's diary and Carter's *Why Me, Lord?* Several mariners said the planes looked like a swarm of bugs when they first appeared on the horizon.

Much of my description of the USS *Wainwright*'s assault on the Heinkel 111 bombers came from my interviews with James Baker North III, and from Carraway's diary. The diary also described the Armed Guard men on the *Troubadour* cheering the destroyer as it passed the *Troubadour*.

My background information about the courageous German pilot Lieutenant Hennemann came from David Wherrett's *From Yorkshire to Archangel* (2017), pages 128–29. Dowding's comment about Hennemann came from his final report on Convoy PQ-17 in the UK National Archives.

The details about the optimistic castaway shouting "On to Moscow!" and some of the *Navarino* survivors originally thinking they had been left behind came from Paul Kemp's *Convoy! Drama in Arctic Waters* (2004), pages 71–72. The detail about the surgeon on the rescue ship *Zamalek* completing an operation under fire came from Lund and Ludlam's *I Was There: On PQ17, the Convoy to Hell,* pages 60–61; the detail of the young Filipino seaman claiming to have been blown high enough into the air that a plane passed beneath him came from the same book, page 63.

Kemp's excellent summary of the first-aid treatment for men pulled from the freezing water came from pages 131–32 of *Convoy!* Robert Carse's *A Cold Corner of Hell* (1969) also provides great details about the operation of the rescue ships on pages 146–48, including the detail that the *Rathlin*'s rescue swimmer was a peacetime swimming champion who always carried a knife for self-protection when he entered the water.

The mariner's description of the frostbitten seamen recuperating in Archangel came from an account by American seaman Donald Murphy, on page 136 of *Eyewitness Accounts of the World War II Murmansk Run 1941–1945* (2006), edited by Mark Scott.

Richard Elsden's account of the trawler *Ayrshire* dropping back to pick up survivors came from his oral history, which I accessed online from the website of the Imperial War Museum in London. I found Lieutenant Leo Gradwell's flippant comment to the corvette officer in David Irving's *The Destruction of Convoy PQ-17* (1968), page 149. Irving interviewed Gradwell before the latter's death.

I told the story of the *Azerbaijan*'s phoenixlike resurrection by examining a variety of sources, including documents I obtained from the Northern Maritime Museum in Archangel; Carraway's diary; Lund and Ludlam's *I Was There: On PQ17, the Convoy to Hell,* pages 63–64; Winn's *PQ-17,* 101–2; and Irving's *The Destruction of Convoy PQ-17,* page 150.

Baker's reflection after the air attack is from *The Convoy Is to Scatter,* page 33.

Carter's assessment of the convoy's effort against the German bombers came from page 171 of *Why Me, Lord?* Carraway's assessment came from his diary. The details about the Icelandic seamen's activities during the air raid on the *Ironclad* came from Richard Carter, who met children of two of the men during a visit to Iceland in 2018. North offered his views during my interviews with him. Baker recounted the "splicing of the main brace" and the dinner of corned beef on page 42 of *The Convoy Is to Scatter.* Francis Brummer's confession that he forgot to swallow his food came from one of his three entries in Scott's *Eyewitness Accounts,* page 49. Commander Jack Broome's assessment that convoy PQ-17 could get anywhere as long as the ammunition lasted came from his *Convoy Is to Scatter* (1972), page 167.

CHAPTER SIX: SCATTERED

My account of Pound's fateful decision to scatter the convoy was pieced together from a number of sources, starting with the Admiralty files at the U.K. National Archives. The most complete account I found was in Robin Brodhurst's biography of Pound, *Churchill's Anchor* (2001), pages 242–48, including on page 246 the colorful description by Admiral Eccles of how Pound announced the decision. The British author Hugh Sebag-Montefiore helped me understand how the time lag in breaking the Germans' Enigma-coded messages in the summer of 1942 played into Pound's decision.

The description of Pound's background came from Brodhurst's book and also from Pound's entry in the *Oxford Dictionary of National Biography*.

I was in the seventh grade when I first read Sir Arthur Conan Doyle's Sherlock Holmes story "Silver Blaze," but I've always remembered its lesson of paying attention to the absence of clues as well as the presence of them. I thought of the story immediately the first time I read in detail about the information Pound had at his disposal when he made the decision to scatter the convoy. In "Silver Blaze," Holmes deduced—SPOILER ALERT!—that the murderer who stole a famous racehorse was the horse's trainer. Holmes reasoned that the trainer's familiar presence would not have caused the stables' watchdog to bark, whereas a stranger's presence would have.

Pound's fateful series of three signals is at the U.K. National Archives.

I focused on Commander Broome's reaction to the signals because he explained it so clearly in his *Convoy Is to Scatter* (1972), and because his decision to withdraw the six destroyers from convoy PQ-17's core escort force seems so critical to what happened. Of course, it's impossible to say with certainty how the scattered ships of the convoy would have fared if Broome's destroyers had stayed with them rather than racing west with the cruisers. I also relied on *The Times* of London's accounts of the trial of Broome's libel case against David Irving in January and February 1970. Broome and other key figures in the convoy PQ-17 disaster testified during the trial.

The story of the Walrus's flight is from *Convoy Is to Scatter*, pages 175–76.

Broome's quote about the hoisting of the pennant meaning the end of the convoy came from page 187 of *Convoy Is to Scatter*.

My account of Broome's conversation with Commodore Dowding about the scatter order came mainly from *Convoy Is to Scatter*, pages 187–93; Dowding's final report on the convoy, in the Admiralty files of the U.K. National Archives; and *The Times*'s coverage of the libel case in 1970. Broome's farewell message to Dowding and Dowding's reply message are in the Admiralty files at the U.K. National Archives.

Lieutenant Douglas Fairbanks Jr.'s reaction to the scatter order and his quote about the "frightened chicks" came from *A Hell of a War*, pages 140–41.

My description of the difficult choices faced by the commanders of the small escorts, and the anger that resulted, came from several sources, including Irving's *The Destruction of Convoy PQ-17* (1968), pages 175–76; Paul Lund and Harry Ludlam's *I Was There: On PQ17, the Convoy to Hell* (1968), pages 99–100;

and Godfrey Winn's *PQ-17* (1948), pages 107–9 and 113–15. Winn had a front-row seat for this drama-inside-a-drama because he was aboard the antiaircraft ship *Pozarica*. The detail about the anger of the *Poppy*'s officers came from Winn's *PQ-17*, pages 99–100. The detail about an officer on another corvette hurling a chair in anger came from Irving's *The Destruction of Convoy PQ-17*, page 176.

I read Jan de Hartog's novel *The Captain* after Broome recommended it in his book *Convoy Is to Scatter*. On pages 357–58 of *The Captain*, de Hartog's Dutch protagonist engages in a furious, angry argument with a subordinate about whether or not to go back for the survivors. (The Scottish author Alistair Mac-Lean wrote his debut novel, *HMS Ulysses* (1955), about a convoy on the Murmansk Run, though his book is not based on convoy PQ-17.)

Walter John Baker's "Devil . . . take the hindmost" comment is from *The Convoy Is to Scatter* (2011), page 44.

The poignant words from the sailor on the trawler *Northern Gem* came from an account of the convoy by the trawler's coxswain S. A. "Sid" Kerslake, at www.pq17 .eclipse.co.uk. The website offers a number of firsthand accounts of the convoy.

Lieutenant William Carter's description of the reaction to the scatter order on the *Ironclad* and the process of scattering came from page 174 of *Why Me, Lord?* The account of the *Ironclad* captain's reasoning for heading north into the ice field is based on pages 175–76.

My account of the reaction to the scatter order on the *Troubadour* came from my interviews with James Baker North III and from Ensign Howard Carraway's diary.

The description of Gradwell's and Elsden's response to the scatter order came from Elsden's oral history, which I accessed online from the website of the Imperial War Museum in London; and from Graeme Ogden's *My Sea Lady* (2013), pages 155–56.

My description of how Lieutenant Leo Gradwell's response to the scatter order grew out of his healthy skepticism of official decisions came from interviews in 2017 with his children. Mary Corrigan said the Americans on the *Troubadour*, *Ironclad*, and *Silver Sword* were fortunate that, of all the British escort commanders they might have encountered when convoy PQ-17 broke up, they encountered her father.

Gradwell's quote about heading "to hell" came from Irving's *The Destruction of Convoy PQ-17*, page 177.

The account of Gradwell's approaching the *Troubadour* to propose a partnership came primarily from Carraway's diary.

Walter Baker's quote about the partnership came from *The Convoy Is to Scatter,* pages 47–48.

The details about Gradwell's preparations, including stacking the depth charges on the trawler's bow in order to attack the *Tirpitz,* came from Ogden's *My Sea Lady,* page 156.

The description of how the restless crew of the *Tirpitz* spent the night of July 4 came from page 110 of Leonce Peillard's *Sink the Tirpitz!* (1968).

My account of the Germans' reaction to the scattering of convoy PQ-17 is based on the German Navy's report on the attack on convoy PQ-17, which is at the U.K. National Archives; Jak P. Mallmann Showell's *Swastikas in the Arctic: U-boat Alley Through the Frozen Hell* (2014), pages 68–71; Adam R. A. Claasen's *Hitler's Northern War: The Luftwaffe's Ill-Fated Campaign, 1940–1945* (2001), pages 214–15; and Lawrence Paterson's *Steel and Ice: The U-boat Battle in the Arctic and the Black Sea 1941–1945* (2016), pages 103–8.

CHAPTER SEVEN: INTO THE ICE

James Baker North III described steering the *Troubadour* into the ice in his interviews with me.

I based my description of the Arctic ice field on information in E. C. Pielou's *A Naturalist's Guide to the Arctic* (1994), pages 65–69; the U.S. Hydrographic Office's *Arctic Pilot* (1917); and David McGonigal and Dr. Lynn Woodward's *The Complete Encyclopedia of Antarctica and the Arctic* (2001), pages 66–71. I also interviewed Dr. Victoria Hill, an Arctic researcher at Old Dominion University in Norfolk, Virginia, who has made several trips into the Arctic and once was briefly trapped by the ice while aboard a U.S. Coast Guard icebreaker. The *Arctic Pilot*'s warning about the dangers of sailing into leads in the ice came from page 26 of that publication; its advice about shooting into the fog to detect icebergs appears on page 31.

The *Arctic Pilot* describes the phenomena of ice blink and water sky on page 31. Harold Gatty's *The Raft Book* (1943) also describes them on page 42. Gatty's book is full of fascinating facts about using clues from nature to navigate and survive in all latitudes.

I elaborated on the particulars of Arctic mirages in this chapter using Pielou's *A Naturalist's Guide to the Arctic*, pages 20–23, as well as my own experiences while sailing in Arctic waters. Pielou notes that a rare form of mirage sometimes enables people to see objects on the horizon that are, in fact, much farther away. The mirage was first noticed by sailors near Novaya Zemlya, who saw the sun a full two weeks before it crested the horizon at the end of a long, dark Arctic winter. For that reason, the rare mirage is known as the Novaya Zemlya effect.

I obtained the information about the seal-hunting casualties from an exhibit at the museum of the Royal and Ancient Polar Bear Society in tiny Hammerfest, Norway. As far as I'm concerned, no one visiting Hammerfest should miss this quirky, hole-in-the-wall museum.

The description of the four vessels' entry into the ice field came mostly from Carraway's diary but also from Graeme Ogden's *My Sea Lady* (2013), pages 155–56. My description of the SOS calls crackling over the *Troubadour*'s radio came primarily from Carraway's diary, though other survivors of the convoy recounted the experience of listening to those calls.

The chilling plea of the mariner on the *Empire Byron* whose legs were trapped in the wreckage came from Paul Lund and Harry Ludlam's *I Was There: On PQ17, the Convoy to Hell* (1968), page 83. The detail of the British seaman whose life was saved by the intense cold came from Lawrence Paterson's *Steel and Ice* (2016), page 106. The message from the commander of the U-703 to his headquarters came from David Irving's *The Destruction of Convoy PQ-17* (1968), page 190. The description of the *Empire Byron* lifeboat survivors' ordeal came from Lund and Ludlam's *I Was There*, pages 158–159.

I found a description of the encounter between the *Empire Byron* survivors and the commander of the U-703 in Robert Carse's *A Cold Corner of Hell* (1969), pages 162–63.

Commander Jack Broome described his and other British officers' slowly dawning realization that they were not racing toward a fight with the *Tirpitz* but racing to try to avoid such a fight in *Convoy Is to Scatter* (1972), pages 203–11.

My information about the debate among the junior officers on the British destroyer *Offa* came from Lund and Ludlam's *I Was There: On PQ17, the Convoy to Hell*, pages 72–73. The passage from the USS *Wichita*'s onboard newspaper came from page 77 of the same volume.

Details of the *Peter Kerr*'s and *Honomu*'s sinkings came from their respective files in NARA Records Group 38.

Hitler's decision to finally unleash the *Tirpitz* is described in Anthony Martienssen's *Hitler and His Admirals* (1948), pages 152–53; in the German documents in the U.K. National Archives; and in Niklas Zetterling and Michael Tamelander's *Tirpitz: The Life and Death of Germany's Last Super Battleship* (2009), pages 135–36. Martienssen's account is by far the most detailed.

Brummer's comparison of the icebergs in the polar ice field to the mountains of northern Arizona came from one of his entries in *Eyewitness Accounts of the World War II Murmansk Run 1941–1945* (2006), edited by Mark Scott, page 40. Carraway's observations about sailing in the ice field came from his diary; North's observations came from my interviews with him. Elsden's account of his "morale-boosting" mission came from his oral history, which I accessed online from the website of the Imperial War Museum in London; Walter John Baker's comment about the can opener came from page 51 of *The Convoy Is to Scatter* (2011).

North explained to me in our interviews why the *Troubadour* carried such a large quantity of white paint. He also described the painting process, the messmen's complaining, the problems with the goggles, and his narrow escape when an ice floe upset the scaffolding on which he was standing. Carraway also described the painting of the ships at length in his diary.

Carraway's diary described Lieutenant Leo Gradwell's visit to the *Troubadour* and Gradwell's suggestion to further camouflage the ships by spreading white linens across the decks and tying them to the masts.

I obtained the SOS messages from the various ships from John Gorley Bunker's *Liberty Ships: The Ugly Ducklings of World War II* (1973), page 66. Bunker got the messages from the log book of the *Samuel Chase,* but the Ghost Ships' radios would have picked up those messages too.

My description of the *Ayrshire* crewmen's visit to the *Silver Sword* is based on pages 53–55 of Baker's *The Convoy Is to Scatter.*

The account of the castaway breaking out into an Al Jolson standard came from Irving's *The Destruction of Convoy PQ-17,* page 235.

The captain of the *Pan Kraft*'s candid explanation for abandoning his ship came from Commodore Dowding's final report in the files of the U.K. National Archives. Dowding added, "It is to be regretted that . . . several ships were abandoned 'without just cause,' and lack of determination, although the odds were very heavily against them." Dowding pointed out in the mariners' defense that many of them had never experienced combat before being thrust into the crisis of convoy PQ-17. In addition, he wrote, "The length of time some of these ships spent in Iceland, without shore leave, was not conducive to keeping up a very high standard of morale."

The abandonment of the *Paulus Potter* and of the Germans' subsequent boarding and search of the ship was described in Dowding's report in the U.K. National Archives and in Paterson's *Steel and Ice,* page 110.

My brief account of the doggedness of the *Daniel Morgan*'s Armed Guard crew is based on documents in NARA Records Group 38. David A. Schwind's *Blue Seas, Red Stars: Soviet Military Medals to U.S. Sea Service Recipients in World War II* (2015) contains a detailed account of the ship's Armed Guard gunners' heroics before and after the sinking of their vessel.

The description of the *Olopana*'s unsuccessful efforts to pick up lifeboat survivors was pieced together from several sources, including NARA Records Group 38; S. J. Flaherty's *Abandoned Convoy* (1970), page 27; Lund and Ludlam's *I Was There,* pages 96–97; and Irving's *The Destruction of Convoy PQ-17,* pages 231–32. The detail about the captains of two sunken ships agreeing to take their lifeboats in different directions came from Irving, page 231.

The harrowing story of the sinking of the *River Afton* and Commodore Dowding's subsequent efforts to rescue shipmates came from Dowding's final report on convoy PQ-17 in the U.K. National Archives.

The Admiralty's unusual message to the escorts that their main duty was "to avoid destruction" came from the Admiralty files in the U.K. National Archives. Captain Lawford's struggle over whether or not to release the corvettes to go back and hunt for survivors was described by several sources, including Irving's *The Destruction of Convoy PQ-17,* page 206; Lund and Ludlam's *I Was There: On PQ17, the Convoy to Hell,* page 100; Paul Kemp's *Convoy! Drama in Arctic Waters* (2004), page 84; and Godfrey Winn's *PQ-17* (1948), pages 113–15.

Lund and Ludlam's *I Was There: On PQ17, the Convoy to Hell* describes the decision by the commander of the *Lotus* to go back in search of survivors, page 100. Dowding described the results of that decision—including how it saved his own life—in his final report on the convoy, which is in the Admiralty files at the U.K. National Archives.

Dowding noted the importance of an Arctic mirage in the rescue of the survivors of the *River Afton* in his final report on the convoy in the U.K. National Archives.

The Soviet submarine's unsuccessful attack on the *Tirpitz* and the subsequent sightings of the battleship by British forces are described in David Brown's *Tirpitz: The Floating Fortesss* (1977), page 26; various documents in NARA Records Group 38; and Zetterling and Tamelander's *Tirpitz,* pages 137–38. My account of the various German reactions to the *Tirpitz's* turning back from the attack came from several sources, including Martienssen's *Hitler and His Admirals,* pages 152–53. The story of the German sailor who deserted the *Tirpitz* and his fate came from page 111 of Peillard's *Sink the Tirpitz!* The German Navy's final report on convoy PQ-17, contained in the U.K. National Archives, explains the reasoning behind the Germans' decision to turn the *Tirpitz* around.

The anonymous *Ayrshire* diarist's comment about the increasing difficulty of breaking the ice came from his diary at the Imperial War Museum in London.

Lieutenant William Carter described reaching a dead end in the ice field and his men's adventure with the makeshift canoe on pages 177–79 of *Why Me, Lord?* (2007).

CHAPTER EIGHT: NOVAYA ZEMLYA

My description of Novaya Zemlya is based on a number of sources, including the *Arctic Pilot,* pages 23, 37, and 313–14; McCann's *A History of the Arctic,* pages 244–45; and David McGonigal and Dr. Lynn Woodward's *The Complete Encyclopedia of Antarctica and the Arctic* (2001), page 181. I also visited the Rijksmuseum in Amsterdam in 2017.

Ensign Howard Carraway described in his diary how the change in the wind prompted the decision to leave the ice field. Dr. Victoria Hill, the Arctic researcher at Old Dominion University in Norfolk, Virginia, described to me in an interview how a wind shift can suddenly trap ships in the ice.

Walter John Baker described his strange feeling of disappointment at the pleasant Arctic weather on page 56 of *The Convoy Is to Scatter* (2011).

Ensign Howard Carraway described in his diary the shock of hearing the *Pan Kraft* explode and seeing the black smoke rise in the distance. North also described the experience to me in my interviews with him, and Baker mentioned it on pages 56–57 of *The Convoy Is to Scatter.* I found details about the *Pan Kraft's* cargo in NARA Records Group 38.

Lieutenant William Carter described the offshore fog bank on page 179 of *Why Me, Lord?* (2007).

Several mariners on the Ghost Ships described the German plane passing overhead in the fog. My account is based mainly on interviews with James Baker North III, on Carraway's diary, and on page 180 of Carter's *Why Me, Lord?* Baker quoted the Bible verse on page 59 of *The Convoy Is to Scatter.*

Carter provided the most detailed account of the ships nearly slamming into the ice salient, on pages 180–81 of *Why Me, Lord?* Francis Brummer also described it in *Eyewitness Accounts of the World War II Murmansk Run 1941–1945* (2006), edited by Mark Scott, page 50.

My description of the *Troubadour's* struggles to keep up with the other ships came mainly from Carraway's diary. North, in my interviews with him, vigorously defended the crew and laid the blame on the *Troubadour's* boilers.

Baker described the seals on page 59 of *The Convoy Is to Scatter.* Brummer's quote came from his diary in Donald Vining's *American Diaries of World War II* (1982), page 135. Carter's comment came from page 181 of *Why Me, Lord?*

Carraway described arriving at the bay at Novaya Zemlya in his diary. Baker's reference to the woolly mammoth came from page 61 of *The Convoy Is to Scatter.* Carter's evocative description of the bay and the polar bear fishing came from pages 181–82 of *Why Me, Lord?*

I based my account of the captains' conference in the bay on Carraway's diary. Carraway suggests Captain Colbeth of the *Silver Sword* felt strongly about going no further, which seems out of character for Colbeth, who according to records in Ancestry.com sailed cargo ships throughout the war after his experience in convoy PQ-17. Carraway writes that Captain Moore of the *Ironclad* initially "didn't object" to going no further. Exactly what he meant by that is unclear. Carter, who admired Moore, does not mention any reluctance by Moore to continue with the voyage in *Why Me, Lord?* Lieutenant Gradwell refers only vaguely to the American captains' growing nervousness in his report to his superiors on the voyage. A copy of that report was provided to me by Gradwell's daughter, Mary Corrigan.

The description of the ersatz commando raid on the weather station is based mainly on Carraway's diary, which provides by far the most detailed account of that adventure. Carter wrote a briefer account on pages 183–86 of *Why Me, Lord?* The accounts vary only in that Carter seems to suggest he came up with the idea of the raid, while Carraway credits Gradwell with the plan. Gradwell takes credit for the idea in his report to his superiors, although he leaves out the details. His first officer, Richard Elsden, in his oral history on the website of the

Imperial War Museum in London, reflects that "it's damn silly what one decides to do."

Gradwell's report does not mention his recovery of bodies in the shallows of Novaya Zemlya, but his daughter told me he spoke to her about it and that the experience disturbed her father's sleep for years after the war.

My account of the *Fairfield City* survivors' ordeal came from documents in NARA Records Group 38, and from Robert Carse's *A Cold Corner of Hell*, pages 185–88. Carse, whose book was published in 1969, reviewed detailed accounts of the *Fairfield City* survivors before NARA, infuriatingly, destroyed many of those accounts to create space for other records.

The Soviets most likely would not have appreciated their Pioneers youth organization being compared to the Boy Scouts, although the organizations were similar. According to U.S. Merchant Marine captain John Le Cato's entry in Scott's *Eyewitness Accounts,* pages 190–91, Soviet propaganda held that the Boy Scouts were "a bourgeois group . . . trained to oppress the people of the working class."

Carraway's diary described his shock at seeing the Liberty ship *Benjamin Harrison* in the Matochkin Shar, and his subsequent reunion with his fellow Armed Guard trainees. Gradwell's description of his shore visit with the trappers and their dogs came from his handwritten, unpublished account of the latter stages of his convoy PQ-17 voyage.

The information that the crew of the *Benjamin Harrison* painted their ship white for camouflage came from several sources, including Mark Llewellyn Evans's *Great World War II Battles in the Arctic* (1999), page 80. I hesitated to include it because the ship's Navy Armed Guard commander did not mention it in his report of the voyage, which I found at NARA, but I decided the weight of the evidence supported it.

My information about the crowd of British escorts in the Matochkin Shar with four merchant ships, and Commodore Dowding's attempt to lead them to Archangel, came mainly from Dowding's final report on convoy PQ-17 at the U.K. National Archives.

The German radio and press accounts of the dismantling of convoy PQ-17 came from the U.K. National Archives. Those archives, as well as NARA Records Group 38, contain a number of documents showing the initial confusion by Allied authorities over which ships had been sunk, which had survived, and which were missing.

Admiral G. J. A. Miles's account of his conversation with Soviet admiral Nikolay Kuznetsov came from the U.K. National Archives. Admiral Arseny Golovko's story that British rear admiral Douglas Blake Fisher refused to look him in the eye after convoy PQ-17 came from Golovko's memoir, *Together with the Fleet* (1988). I suspect Admiral Fisher would have disputed Golovko's account.

The description of the fate of homebound convoy QP-13 is based primarily on documents in NARA Records Group 38 and the U.K. National Archives.

CHAPTER NINE: "WE THREE GHOSTS"

Lieutenant Leo Gradwell described his nagging doubts and his exploration of the eastern end of the Matochkin Shar in his handwritten account.

My description of Ensign Howard Carraway marking time in the strait came from his diary. My account of the seaplane visit by Captain Ilya P. Mazuruk came from Gradwell's written account; David Irving's *The Destruction of Convoy PQ-17* (1968), pages 345–47; and other sources. Gradwell did not appear to know that Mazuruk was a famous Russian polar aviator when the two met.

Gradwell's daughter, Mary Corrigan, described to me her father's observations of how the Royal Navy treated officers who disobeyed orders. His description of his thought process in deciding to disobey the order came from the handwritten report he gave Mazuruk to take to British authorities in Archangel.

The updates on the status of the ships in convoy PQ-17 came from files at the U.K. National Archives and from NARA Records Group 38.

The exchanges of messages after convoy PQ-17 between Churchill and Roosevelt and between Churchill and Stalin came from files at the U.K. National Archives. Those messages also are contained in *Roosevelt and Churchill: Their Secret Wartime Correspondence,* edited by Francis L. Loewenheim, Harold D. Langley, and Manfred Jonas (1975); and in *My Dear Mr. Stalin,* edited by Susan Butler (2005).

Yury Alexandrov told me the story of his being sent to the roof as a fourteen-year-old boy to shovel incendiary bombs off his apartment building when I interviewed him in St. Petersburg, Russia, in August 2017. Alexandrov is a retired Russian Navy captain of 1st Rank and the leader of the Polar Convoy Social Group, which organizes reunions of Arctic convoy survivors and historians interested in the subject of the convoys.

My information about Shostakovich's Seventh Symphony and its symbolic significance is based mainly on Brian Moynahan's *Leningrad: Siege and Symphony* (2013), which tells the parallel stories of the composition of the symphony and the siege of Leningrad.

Carraway's account of the ships' deeper exploration of the Matochkin Shar and his missed opportunity to celebrate his half anniversary came from his diary.

The new Russian arrivals in the Matochkin Shar were described in Gradwell's handwritten account and in Ensign Howard Carraway's diary. Carraway described the dinner visit from the *Ayrshire* crewmen; Gradwell described his and Richard Elsden's visit to the Russian icebreaker, his enjoyable visit with the Russian captain, the propaganda film that elicited only nostalgia from Gradwell, and the viewing of the "glossy magazines."

The account of the *Troubadour* and *Ironclad* running aground in the Matochkin Shar and the Soviet trawler's white-knuckle effort to pull the *Troubadour* free came from Carraway's diary and from my interviews with James Baker North III. North was not aware at the time that the depth charge bouncing across the ship's deck had not been armed and thus could not explode.

Lieutenant William Carter's praise of Commodore Dowding came from page 185 of *Why Me, Lord?*

Dowding described leading a second small convoy out of the Matochkin Shar in his official report on convoy PQ-17 at the U.K. National Archives.

Frankel matter-of-factly described his assignment to retrieve the grounded freighter *Winston-Salem* on page 87 of *Eyewitness Accounts of the World War II Murmansk Run 1941–1945* (2006), edited by Mark Scott: "The Russians got word to the British that this ship had particularly valuable cargo, that the cowardly Americans had deserted the ship . . . and that the ship was there at the mercy of any planes or submarines pursuing the ships in the convoy. I was asked if I would go up there."

My account of Gradwell joining Commodore Dowding for a drink and chat came from Gradwell's handwritten account of the voyage. Gradwell's expression of relief tinged with worry came from the same account.

Carraway's diary described the *Troubadour* falling behind yet another convoy. My information about the *Pozarica*'s salute to Captain Izotov on the *Azerbaijan* came from Winn's *PQ-17*, page 185.

My description of the small convoy entering the White Sea is based primarily on Carraway's diary. Walter John Baker described the mirages on page 103 of

The Convoy Is to Scatter (2011). On my own voyage to Archangel, I saw the most dramatic Arctic mirages in the same place Baker did.

Baker described the ships' arrival in the Archangel area on page 105. Carraway's diary described the arrival in more detail and also recounted how he and other mariners gave the *Troubadour, Ironclad,* and *Silver Sword* the nickname "the Ghost Ships." The Navy's message announcing the Ghost Ships' arrival came from NARA Records Group 38. Paul Lund and Harry Ludlam's comment about the Ghost Ships came from *I Was There: On Convoy PQ-17, the Convoy to Hell,* page 184.

Carter described the appearance of the Archangel area and the commissar's inspection of the *Ironclad*'s cargo on pages 187–90 of *Why Me, Lord?* Carraway described his observations of Molotovsk and the inspection of the *Troubadour*'s cargo in his diary. North described the scene to me in interviews.

Russian admiral Golovko described the U-boat's attack on the Soviet settlement on Novaya Zemlya and the subsequent raid by the German cruiser *Admiral Scheer* in the Kara Sea in his memoir, *Together with the Fleet* (1988). Robert Carse also quotes Frankel describing the U-boat attack and its aftermath in *A Cold Corner of Hell* (1969), page 209.

My account of the ordeal of the *Honomu* survivors came mainly from NARA Records Group 38.

CHAPTER TEN: ARKHANGELSK

My description of wartime Archangel is based on conversations by phone and email with Dr. Mikhail Suprun and on a detailed paper by one of his former students, Elizaveta Khatanzeiskaya, "Everyday Life in Wartime Archangelsk: The Problem of Starvation and Death During the Second World War" (2015). Khatanzeiskaya conducted interviews and scoured official documents, memoirs, and news accounts.

Kemp Tolley's description of starving Russians stealing food from the docks at great risk to their lives came from page 115 of his book *Caviar and Commissars* (1983), a lively and often darkly humorous account of Tolley's years as an assistant U.S. naval attaché in North Russia. Tolley, remarkably, had been the U.S. Naval Academy instructor who advised Carter to join the Navy Armed Guard. Tolley summed up why the theft of food in North Russia was a problem without a solution: "Wartime Russia was simply too desperately hungry and ragged for one to expect some of the less highly motivated individuals to pass up an unguarded case of Spam or a bundle of Red Cross sweaters from the Ladies Aid of Kansas. It was not a matter of mere cupidity; it was often a question of human survival." Ambassador Averell Harriman described the Soviet practice of forcing thieves to sit naked in the snow in his entry in *Eyewitness Accounts of the World War II Murmansk Run 1941–1945* (2006), edited by Mark Scott, page 97.

Carraway's description of the food centers in Archangel came from his diary. My descriptions of the city in general came from numerous sources, including Ensign Howard Carraway's diary; interviews with James Baker North III; Brigadier General Boswell's account in *Eyewitness Accounts of the World War II Murmansk Run 1941–1945,* edited by Mark Scott, pages 115–18; and Tolley's *Caviar and Commissars,* pages 57 and 127. Godfrey Winn described the "pagoda-like" opera house in *PQ-17* (1948), page 164.

My information about the labor camps near Archangel and the types of prisoners who were held in them came mostly from Dr. Suprun. North's observations about the prisoners and particularly the POWs came from my interviews with him. S. J. Flaherty's description of the frostbite victims in the Archangel hospital came from his book *Abandoned Convoy* (1970), pages 68–69.

The description of Lieutenant Leo Gradwell's unease about the silence from the Royal Navy came from my interview and subsequent emails with his daughter, Mary Corrigan. Mary also sent me copies of the letters by various people praising Gradwell. The description of Gradwell as "a brave and eccentric barrister yachtsman" came from the account by John Beardmore on the Flower-class corvette website, www.cbrnp.com/RNP/Flower/ARTICLES/Poppy/Beardmore-1 .htm. Mary Corrigan provided me with a copy of Gradwell's post–convoy PQ-17 letter to his mother.

Gradwell's son Christopher Gradwell and his daughter, Mary Corrigan, told me about their father's experiences in Archangel.

The description of the Intourist Hotel in Archangel is based on accounts from a variety of sources. Almost every Allied mariner in the convoy spent at least some time in the place. Winn described the band's eclectic offerings on page 165 of *PQ-17;* Captain John Le Cato described being lectured about Marx while dancing, in *Eyewitness Accounts of the World War II Murmansk Run 1941– 1945,* edited by Mark Scott, page 125. Lieutenant William Carter described his visits to the hotel and the nearby club on pages 197–200 of *Why Me, Lord?* Carraway also described the hotel and club in his diary.

North described the club with the propaganda movie in my interviews with him.

Carraway's reflections on the Soviet Union's ability to focus everything on the war effort came from his diary.

My description of how the Soviet Union was able to recover from the Nazi onslaught and turn the tide are based on my interview with Dr. Suprun, who also provided me with an academic paper he wrote in 2015 entitled "Strength and Weakness of the Totalitarianism in Wartime Soviet Union." I also learned a great deal about the Soviet Union's recovery from Richard Overy's *Russia's War* (1998) and Catherine Merridale's *Ivan's War* (2006). Surkov's angry poem came from page 124 of *Ivan's War,* which also offers a good description of Stalin's Order No. 227 on page 156. Tolley described General Zhukov's demotion of the Soviet officers in the jeep on page 123 of *Caviar and Commissars.*

My description of the unloading of the *Troubadour* came from Carraway's diary and my interviews with North. The account of the unloading of the *Ironclad* is based on Carter's *Why Me, Lord?,* pages 189–90.

The details of the *Ironclad*'s cargo came from NARA Records Group 38. My description of where the cargo was sent by train is based on my interviews with Dr. Suprun and with Sergey Aprelev, a retired Russian Navy captain of 1st Rank who is now a historian and filmmaker, whom I interviewed in St. Petersburg, Russia, in August 2017.

Carter expressed his misgivings about the American level of commitment to the Arctic convoys on pages 193–96 of *Why Me, Lord?*

North described his adventure with the Gum-Gum Boys and in the women's dormitory in my interviews with him. Other mariners described less tense encounters with the Gum-Gum Boys. Dr. Suprun said all-women dormitories such as North described were common in wartime Archangel. North described his friend's fights and arrests in my interviews with him.

Carraway's diary described the return of the Uruguayan coal passer to the *Troubadour.* Tolley described the arrests on the *Israel Putman* on page 94 of *Caviar and Commissars.*

Dr. Suprun told me about how Stalin's anger over the Allies' reluctance to open the second front prompted him to refuse to let a British hospital ship anchor in Archangel, and about Admiral Golovko's clever diversion of the hospital ship to Murmansk.

Frankel praised the merchant mariners in his recollection in Scott's *Eyewitness Accounts,* pages 88–89. Many of the mariners and Navy Armed Guard men who came in contact with Frankel had a good impression of him. My account of Frankel's speech to the hundreds of mariners stranded in Archangel came from Robert Carse's *A Cold Corner of Hell* (1969), pages 213–16.

Churchill described his visit to Moscow to deliver the bad news to Stalin in detail on pages 472–502 of *The Hinge of Fate* (1950). His reflections on what he would say to the Soviets came from page 475. His "Stalin had become restless" quote came from page 479 and his description of Stalin's "rough and rude" remark about convoy PQ-17 came from page 497. Churchill's letter to Roosevelt about the meeting with Stalin came from *Roosevelt and Churchill: Their Secret Wartime Correspondence,* edited by Francis L. Loewenheim, Harold D. Langley, and Manfred Jonas (1975). Roosevelt's letter to Stalin about American airplanes came from *My Dear Mr. Stalin,* edited by Susan Butler (2005). Dr. Suprun told me about Stalin's subsequent, unsuccessful overture to Hitler.

My account of the first German bombing of Archangel came from Dr. Suprun (who says most Russian accounts wildly overestimate the number of bombers involved in that raid). The U.S. naval attaché's messages came from NARA Records Group 38.

Carraway's diary described his homesickness and his tense encounter with the Soviet sentry outside the air-raid shelter.

CHAPTER ELEVEN: THE KNIFE-EDGE

Lieutenant William Carter described the problem of mariners stealing lifeboat rations, as well as his latest encounters with the Kid, on pages 203–9 of *Why Me, Lord?* (2007). Ensign Howard Carraway wrote in his diary about the mood on the *Troubadour* and the steps leading up to its departure from Archangel.

I found manifests of the Ghost Ships' cargoes for the return voyage to the United States in NARA Records Group 178.

My description of the German pattern of bombing Archangel is based on information from Dr. Mikhail Suprun and Carter's account on page 201 of *Why Me, Lord?*

Bob Ruegg and Arnold Hague's *Convoys to Russia 1941–1945* (1992) contains particulars about the ships comprising homebound convoy QP-14. The details about the Ghost Ships' cargoes for the return voyage came from NARA Records Group 178. The detail about the *Ayrshire*'s smuggling of butter out of Archangel came from Lieutenant Leo Gradwell's daughter, Mary Corrigan.

My description of the apparent sabotage of the *Ironclad* came from documents in NARA Records Groups 38 and 175, and pages 215–16 of Carter's *Why Me, Lord?* Carter blamed the sabotage on Nazi sympathizers in the ship's crew, but I think it's more likely that crew members set out to disable the *Ironclad* because they thought they would be safer sailing home on a different ship. Carraway's diary contains his disparaging view of the *Ironclad*—a verbal stone cast from the glass house of the *Troubadour*.

Carraway described in his diary the *Troubadour*'s homebound voyage and the narrow escape from a U-boat near Svalbard. James Baker North III also described it to me in detail in our interviews. Details about the *Silver Sword*'s voyage came from NARA Records Group 38.

My broader account of convoy QP-14's voyage and the sinking of the *Silver Sword* came from NARA Records Group 38 and the U.K. National Archives. I liked the narrative account by Richard Woodman on pages 284–95 of *Arctic Convoys, 1941–1945* (2004).

Ruegg and Hague's *Convoys to Russia* describes the makeup of convoy PQ-18 and its escort force. My account of Raeder's aborted plan to attack the convoy with cruisers came from Anthony Martienssen's *Hitler and His Admirals* (1948), page 154.

The assessment by the senior British naval officer in Archangel that the small escorts of convoy PQ-17 should have protected merchant ships after the scatter order rather than clustering together to run to Novaya Zemlya is contained in the U.K. National Archives as well as in NARA Records Group 38. The other officer's comments about the lessons of convoy PQ-17 came from a message I found in the U.K. National Archives.

Churchill and Roosevelt's exchange of letters about Operation Torch and its impact on the Arctic convoys can be found in *Roosevelt and Churchill: Their Secret Wartime Correspondence* (1975), edited by Francis L. Loewenheim, Harold D. Langley, and Manfred Jonas, on pages 254–57.

I heard both Russian jokes about the second front while I was visiting North Russia in 2017. Kemp Tolley also mentions them on page 119 of *Caviar and Commissars* (1983).

Carraway's diary describes the *Troubadour*'s rough voyage down the East Coast of North America. North described his unpleasant shift as a coal passer to me in our interviews.

Rick Atkinson provides a detailed account of Operation Torch in *An Army at Dawn: Volume I of the Liberation Trilogy* (2002). My description of the war news in *The New York Times* on November 3, 1942, came from microfilm files of the paper.

My information about Carraway's wartime experience after convoy PQ-17 came from my interview and subsequent communications with his son Mac.

North described his careful exit strategy from the *Troubadour* to me in our interviews.

Captain Salvesen never took the *Troubadour* back to sea, but he sailed Allied merchant ships for the rest of the war with distinction. According to a feature article in the *Times-Union and Journal* of Jacksonville, Florida, on December 12, 1976, one of Salvesen's vessels caught fire in 1943 while taking on a cargo of bombs at a wharf in Red Bank, New Jersey. The captain quickly mustered enough crew members to sail the ship out to sea and scuttle it before the fire could reach the bombs and cause a disastrous explosion at Red Bank.

The description of the *Ironclad*'s ill-fated voyage out of Archangel is based on Carter's account on pages 220–32 of *Why Me, Lord?* and on documents in NARA Records Group 178. The U.S. Navy document suggesting the *Ironclad* be turned over to the Russians and the ship's crew be repatriated to the United States as quickly as possible came from NARA Records Group 38.

My account of Carter's account of his relocation to the Liberty ship *Richard Bland,* his witnessing of the aftermath of the Soviet guards shooting an injured prisoner, and other rigors of his life in Archangel are based on his descriptions on pages 233–39 of *Why Me, Lord?*

CHAPTER TWELVE: REINDEER GAMES

My description of Roosevelt and Churchill's meeting at Casablanca is based on Churchill's detailed account in *The Hinge of Fate* (1950) on pages 674–94. Churchill includes Stalin's letter expressing his regrets on pages 665–66.

The letters between Roosevelt and Stalin can be found in *My Dear Mr. Stalin: The Complete Correspondence of Franklin D. Roosevelt and Joseph V. Stalin*

(2005), edited by Susan Butler. Stalin's letter to Roosevelt about the second front came from *The Hinge of Fate,* page 667.

My account of the *Richard Bland*'s horrific homebound voyage is based on Lieutenant William Carter's *Why Me, Lord?* (2007), pages 3–29 and 239–56, as well as Bob Ruegg and Arnold Hague's *Convoys to Russia 1941–1945* (1992) and documents from NARA Records Group 38. Carter's description of the "macabre ballet" is from page 18 of *Why Me, Lord?*

I found the poem "Kill Him," credited to Konstantin Simonov, on page 417 of Alexander Werth's *Russia at War* (1964).

Churchill described his letter to Stalin about the resumption of the Arctic convoys, Stalin's terse response, and Churchill's aside to Roosevelt in *Closing the Ring* (1951), pages 264–70.

The description of Sir Dudley Pound's death and funeral is based on Robin Brodhurst's *Churchill's Anchor* (2000), pages 1–7. I found the *Manchester Guardian*'s reference to convoy PQ-17 on page 149 of Theodore Taylor's *Battle in the Arctic Seas* (1976). Churchill's reflections on Pound and the convoy came from *The Hinge of Fate,* pages 262–66.

My reference to Roosevelt telling Stalin at Tehran that he wanted to see the end of the British Empire came from Robert Service's *Stalin* (2005), page 462. Roosevelt's comment that he and Stalin spoke as "men and brothers" came from Dennis J. Dunn's *Caught Between Roosevelt and Stalin* (1998), page 215. It reminded me of former president George W. Bush's comment in 2001 that he had looked Russian president Vladimir Putin in the eye and gotten a sense of his soul.

On pages 373–74 of *Closing the Ring* (1951), Churchill describes his growing sense that the Big Three was becoming a Big Two.

William Bullitt's comment about the need to place Allied troops in front of the Red Army came from Dunn's *Caught Between Roosevelt and Stalin*, page 177. The statistic about the large number of Soviet advisors in American factories came from Tolley's *Caviar and Commissars,* page 100. Harriman's comment about the bear came from page 223 of Dunn's *Caught Between Roosevelt and Stalin.* The footnoted detail about U.S. troops in Korea apparently seeing old U.S. military weapons in enemy hands came from Albert L. Weeks's *Russia's Life-Saver: Lend-Lease Aid to the U.S.S.R. in World War II* (2004), page 121.

I heard about the mirrors and microphones at the hotel in Archangel from Sergey Aprelev during my visit to St. Petersburg in 2017. He also told me the story about the unsuccessful "goodwill" visit to the Soviet warship. Kemp Tolley's account of the vodka-fueled ship inspections came from *Caviar and Commissars,* page 100.

The story of the mariner falling under suspicion for buying a copy of Shostakovich's Seventh Symphony is from Earl Carter's entry in *Eyewitness Accounts of the World War II Murmansk Run 1941–1945* (2006), edited by Mark Scott, pages 154–56.

I heard stories about the gifting of reindeer while I was in Russia, and also found references to the practice in several books. But the best description by far is on page 106 of Tolley's *Caviar and Commissars,* which I have quoted in this book.

Tolley did not mince words in a report to the Office of Naval Intelligence. Soviet citizens, he wrote, "are ruled body and soul by a bureaucracy maintained by power and fear. It may appear trite to mention the huge numbers of Russians now in concentration camps or dismal outposts in the Far North or East, but this picture is before every Soviet citizen, affecting his every move." Tolley was stunned by how little the average Russian knew about life outside the Soviet Union. "Few know electric refrigerators, portable radio, string beans, corn, mayonnaise, cigars, chewing gum, the game of golf."

Aleksandr Solzhenitsyn's description of his cell in the Archangel work camp came from his book *The Gulag Archipelago* (1973).

My account of Jac Smith's experiences in a work camp near Archangel came from Thomas E. Simmons's book about the experiences of mariner Smith, *Escape from Archangel* (1990). The description of Smith's task of unloading the boxcars appears on page 113.

Simmons's description of how Smith eventually escaped from Nazi-occupied Norway prompted me to pick up a copy of David Howarth's *The Shetland Bus: A World War II Epic of Escape, Survival, and Adventure* (1951). It's a fascinating book about fearless Norwegian mariners who guided small fishing boats between Scotland's Shetland Islands and the coast of Norway to deliver British saboteurs and to rescue fugitives from the Nazis. It also describes a commando mission in miniature submarines to try to destroy the *Tirpitz.*

The information about the Germans transferring planes from the Arctic to the Mediterranean came primarily from Adam R. A. Claasen's *Hitler's Northern War: The Luftwaffe's Ill-Fated Campaign, 1940–1945* (2001), pages 203 and 221. The statistics about the reduced dangers of the Murmansk Run came from the

Masters, Mates & Pilots union newsletter of July 1945, and from Ruegg and Hague's *Convoys to Russia 1941–1945*.

My description of the *Tirpitz*'s eventual demise is based mainly on accounts in David Brown's *Tirpitz: The Floating Fortress* (1977), page 43, Leonce Peillard's *Sink the Tirpitz!* (1968), and Niklas Zetterling and Michael Tamelander's *Tirpitz: The Life and Death of Germany's Last Super Battleship* (2009).

The account of the ex-POWs from the *Carlton* and *Honomu* criticizing the British over convoy PQ-17 after their return to the United States came from a story in *The New York Times* on February 23, 1945. Paul Lund and Harry Ludlam's *I Was There: On PQ17, the Convoy to Hell* (1968) contains a thorough account of how the details of what happened to the convoy slowly came to light in Britain, on pages 221–46. The Admiralty files in the U.K. National Archives also contain numerous letters and messages reflecting the Admiralty's efforts to spin the story of convoy PQ-17, even after the war's end removed any real justification for secrecy. Captain Jack Broome's letter to the *Times* appeared on September 23, 1981.

Charles Bohlen's quote about Roosevelt's health at Yalta came from Rick Atkinson's *The Guns at Last Light* (2013), page 498. The point about Stalin's demand for veto power for U.N. Security Council members is from Dunn's *Caught Between Roosevelt and Stalin*, page 233.

The description of Roosevelt's last day and his attempts to smooth over relations with Stalin and Churchill came from several sources, including Michael Dobbs's *Six Months in 1945: FDR, Stalin, Churchill and Truman* (2012), pages 156–57; and Butler's *My Dear Mr. Stalin*, pages 320–22. Truman's comment while he was a U.S. senator about helping the Soviets and Nazis to keep slaughtering one another came from Dobbs's *Six Months in 1945*, page 163.

Khrushchev's disparaging view of Truman came from his memoir, *Khrushchev Remembers* (1970), page 221. Harriman's "Barbarian invasion" comment came from Dobbs's *Six Months in 1945*, page 164.

The descriptions of the final Arctic convoys came from Ruegg and Hauge's *Convoys to Russia 1941–1945*, pages 77–79.

Lieutenant William Carter's account of the Soviets' efforts to honor him for his service and the U.S. Navy's shifting reaction to those efforts came from pages 265–66 of *Why Me, Lord?*

CHAPTER THIRTEEN: RECKONING

My description of what a twenty-first-century ship would encounter in the way of ice along the route of convoy PQ-17 is based on an interview and email exchanges with Dr. Victoria Hill, an Arctic researcher at Old Dominion University in Norfolk, Virginia. She compared a map of the convoy route with 2018 satellite images of the ice field and applied her own experience sailing in the Arctic. Among the resources she recommended to me was the website of the National Snow and Ice Data Center, which is at http://nsidc.org/arcticseaice news.

My reference to the Russian sub planting a symbolic Russian flag in the seabed at the North Pole came from Charles Emmerson's account on page 81 of *The Future History of the Arctic* (2010), a fascinating study of the Arctic's past and likely future. The information on the voyage of the Russian LNG tanker came from *The New York Times,* August 27, 2017. The former Coast Guard admiral's comment came from *The Washington Post,* September 4, 2017.

The description of the transformation of the Barents Sea into a Cold War battleground is based on several sources, including U.S. Navy Captain (Ret.) Peter Huchthausen's book *K-19: The Widowmaker* (2002), which focuses on the harrowing voyage of a single Soviet submarine but includes a broader history of the Soviet nuclear submarine fleet, as well as an appendix listing Soviet submarine accidents. The book served as the basis for a 2002 feature film of the same name, directed by Kathryn Bigelow and starring Harrison Ford and Liam Neeson. One of my Russian sources for this book, Sergey Aprelev, served as technical director for the film, although he often clashed with Bigelow over what he considered the movie's liberties with the facts. Other sources for this section of the book included Emmerson's *The Future History of the Arctic,* pages 111–16, and Sherry Sontag and Christopher Drew's *Blind Man's Bluff: The Untold Story of American Submarine Espionage* (1998).

Most of my information about the Soviets' use of Novaya Zemlya for nuclear testing came from John McCannon's *A History of the Arctic: Nature, Exploration and Exploitation* (2012), pages 244–45; David McGonigal and Dr. Lynn Woodward's *The Complete Encyclopedia of Antarctica and the Arctic* (2001), page 181; and Emmerson's *The Future History of the Arctic,* pages 119–20. The description of the ongoing problems of nuclear waste disposal in the former Soviet Union came from newspaper stories and Huchthausen's *K-19: The Widowmaker.*

In the course of writing this book, I set out to retrace as much of convoy PQ-17's route as possible. In August 2018, I visited Iceland and toured Hvalfjord, the starting point of the convoy, in the company of Richard Carter, the son of Lieutenant William Carter, the Armed Guard commander on the *Ironclad* and the author of *Why Me, Lord?* (2007).

I found helpful information about how World War II had transformed Iceland during my visit there, and in several sources, including an article in *Wall Street International* on December 24, 2013, entitled "Iceland During World War II: The War and Its Impact on the Country," by Katharina Hauptmann. Emmerson's *The Future History of the Arctic* and Michael Booth's *The Almost Nearly Perfect People: Behind the Myth of Scandinavian Utopia* (2014) were full of information about Iceland's more recent history.

I explored several different ways to sail along the route of convoy PQ-17 and was surprised to find a cruise ship sailing from Copenhagen, Denmark, north and east across the Norwegian and Barents seas, stopping at the ports in Norway where the Germans had waited in ambush for the convoy, and then calling at both Murmansk and Archangel. The cruise was scheduled for almost the exact time of year that convoy PQ-17 had made the trip, and in the same twenty-four-hour daylight. I booked passage on the cruise ship—the M/S *Nautica,* operated by Oceania Cruises—and was delighted with the results. The master of the ship was a Russian, Captain Maksym Melnikov, who had studied the Arctic convoys in school and was gracious enough to share with me his views about them and his knowledge about sailing the northern latitudes. My fellow passengers included half a dozen people with a keen interest in the Arctic convoys. I was able to help a man from Savannah, Georgia, figure out that his father had sailed in convoy PQ-18; a computer whiz from New York with an encyclopedic knowledge of the Arctic convoys helped me find crew manifests for the *Troubadour* and other convoy PQ-17 ships online at www.Ancestry.com. I arranged my shore visits during the cruise so that I could make contact with archivists at museums in Murmansk and Archangel.

My description of twenty-first-century Norway is based on my visits to cities along the coast, where Norway's investment in and profits from the oil and natural gas industry are obvious. Emmerson's *The Future History of the Arctic* and Booth's *The Almost Nearly Perfect People* provided helpful background information about Norway's fossil-fuel industries. I did not set out looking for the underlying scars of the German occupation of Norway, but found them almost everywhere I went. Some of the most striking included the ruins of a Gestapo execution post in a park in Trondheim; and the Museum of the Reconstruction in Hammerfest, which uses film clips, photos, and artifacts to show how the retreating Germans burned the city to ashes in 1944, giving residents only hours to flee with whatever they could carry. I have not been able to get some of those images out of my head.

The descriptions of modern Murmansk and Archangel are based on my visits to those cities. The size of the "Alyosha" statue overlooking Murmansk's harbor is nothing short of amazing. When I first saw it while approaching the city from the sea, I mistook it for an enormous lighthouse. Alyosha is a nickname for Aleksey, a common Russian name, and the statue is meant to represent all Russian military personnel in the same way "G.I. Joe" represents all U.S. soldiers. During my visit to Murmansk in July, the temperature was balmy, although several locals assured me the warmth would not last long. One of them told me a Murmansk weather joke: An out-of-town visitor asks, "What was it like in Murmansk last summer?" A local replies, "I don't know, I had to work that day."

My visit to Archangel led me to the Northern Maritime Museum and the Merchant Yard Museum, both of which are located in the city, and ultimately to Dr. Mikhail Suprun, whose research informs many of the latter chapters of this book.

The statistics about the death tolls for various nations in World War II came from the National World War II Museum in New Orleans, Louisiana.

My information about the 2017 Russian public-opinion poll showing Stalin's resurgent standing came from *The Washington Post* on June 26, 2017. One Russian explained to me that for all the terror Stalin inflicted on his people, "He made Russia strong." He added that Stalin, unlike Putin and other modern Russian leaders, never used his power to enrich himself financially. Whatever demons drove Stalin, they apparently did not include greed.

The Churchill Museum in London contains numerous exhibits with information about his life and career before, during, and after World War II. One exhibit recalls his and his wife's conversation after his electoral defeat in 1945, and his rejoinder. The museum is connected to the fascinating Churchill War Rooms, the underground nerve center from which he oversaw the prosecution of the war.

Kemp Tolley's analysis of the Arctic convoys came from *Caviar and Commissars* (1983), page 98.

My tally of the accomplishments and losses of the Arctic convoys is based primarily on the research of Bob Ruegg and Arnold Hague's *Convoys to Russia 1941–1945* (1992) and Albert L. Weeks's *Russia's Life-Saver: Lend-Lease Aid to the U.S.S.R. in World War II* (2004). I found an editorial about the Ford Motor Company's River Rouge tire plant being dismantled and shipped to Russia in *The New York Times* on November 3, 1942. Dr. Weeks, a historian and author, has examined the newest Russian research on the Arctic convoys. But even he concludes that obtaining an exact picture after the fog of the Cold War is "clearly an impossible task."

Samuel Eliot Morison's comment about convoy PQ-17 came from page 186 of his *The Battle of the Atlantic, 1939–1943, Vol. 1 of the History of United States Naval Operations in World War II* (1947). I found the comment from the Seafarers International Union on page 147 of Theodore Taylor's *Battle in the Arctic Seas* (1976). Churchill's "melancholy" assessment came from page 266 of *The Hinge of Fate* (1950).

Milan Vego's article, "The Destruction of Convoy PQ-17," appeared in the *Naval War College Review,* Volume 69, Number 3, published in the summer of 2016.

My description of Leo Gradwell's life after World War II is based on interviews with his three children. I also drew on documents Mary Corrigan sent me about her father. I researched the Profumo case in back issues of *The Times* of London, and in Christine Keeler's lengthy obituary in *The Washington Post* on December 5, 2017. Gradwell's obituary in *The Times* of London appeared on November 11, 1969.

My account of North's life after convoy PQ-17 is based on interviews with him at his home in Santa Barbara, California, in 2016, and subsequent phone conversations with him.

Howard Carraway's son Mac Carraway described his father's postwar life to me in an interview in Bradenton, Florida, in 2017, and later communications by phone.

My description of William Carter's life after World War II is based on interviews with his son Richard Carter, as well as a retrospective of William Carter's life that Richard wrote.

Both Richard and I were invited to St. Petersburg, Russia, in 2017 by the Russian leaders of the Polar Convoy Social Group, which organized the Dervish 2017 celebration. The event consisted of three days of activities, ranging from a ceremonial wreath laying to a tour of an icebreaker to an academic conference—where I gave a talk about the perspective of the American mariners who sailed to North Russia in the Arctic convoys. The other attendees included five feisty ninetysomething British veterans of the Arctic convoys.

The account of the political scuffle over the anniversary gathering in Red Square in 2015 came from the *Daily Mail,* May 23, 2015, as well as from some of the British convoy veterans I met in St. Petersburg. The *Guardian*'s editorial about the 2016 Arctic convoy memorial ceremony in Murmansk appeared on August 29, 2016.

My description of the evolution of Russian attitudes toward the Arctic convoys is based on my interviews with Dr. Suprun and the remarks of Russian rear admiral Alexander Konayev, who spoke at the conference I attended in St. Petersburg. I also found Weeks's *Russia's Life-Saver* helpful in understanding how Stalin and his Soviet successors downplayed the role of the convoys for political reasons.

The story of the Soviet kindergarten teacher introducing the merchant mariners to her students came from an entry by John Le Cato in *Eyewitness Accounts of the World War II Murmansk Run 1941–1945* (2006), edited by Mark Scott, page 191.

Finally, my account of the docent in the Northern Maritime Museum in Murmansk telling the story of the Ghost Ships and thanking her listeners for helping to keep her family alive came from my visit to Murmansk on the cruise ship. My wife, Kema, who helps me with research and photography, took the tour of the museum while I visited a different museum. Kema videotaped the docent's talk and suggested afterward that I might find something valuable on the tape. As usual, she was right.

ILLUSTRATION CREDITS

BIBLIOGRAPHY

BOOKS

Arnaldur Indridason. *The Shadow District.* Translated from the Icelandic by Victoria Cribb. New York: Minotaur Books, 2017.

———. *The Shadow Killer.* Translated from the Icelandic by Victoria Cribb. New York: Minotaur Books, 2018.

Atkinson, Rick. *An Army at Dawn: Volume I of the Liberation Trilogy.* New York: Henry Holt & Company, 2002.

———. *The Guns at Last Light: Volume III of the Liberation Trilogy.* New York: Henry Holt & Company, 2013.

Baker, Walter John. *The Convoy Is to Scatter.* Morrisville, NC: Lulu Press Inc., 2010.

Blair, Clay. *Hitler's U-boat War.* 2 vols. New York: Modern Library, 2000.

Booth, Michael. *The Almost Nearly Perfect People: Behind the Myth of the Scandinavian Utopia.* New York: Picador, 2014.

Bradham, Randolph. *Hitler's U-boat Fortresses.* Westport, CT: Praeger, 2003.

Brennecke, Jochen. *The Hunters and the Hunted: German U-boats, 1939–1945.* Annapolis, MD: Naval Institute Press, 2003.

British Ministry of Defence. *The U-boat War in the Atlantic.* London: Her Majesty's Stationery Office, 1989.

Brodhurst, Robin. *Churchill's Anchor.* Barnsley, England: Leo Cooper, 2000.

Broome, Captain Jack. *Convoy Is to Scatter*. London: Kimber, 1972.

Brown, David. *Tirpitz: The Floating Fortress*. Annapolis, MD: Naval Institute Press, 1977.

Browning Robert M., Jr. *United States Merchant Marine Casualties of World War II*. Jefferson, NC: McFarland & Company, 2011.

Bunker, John. *Heroes in Dungarees*. Annapolis, MD: Naval Institute Press, 2006.

——. *Liberty Ships: The Ugly Ducklings of World War II*. Annapolis, MD: Naval Institute Press, 1972.

Butler, John A. *Sailing on Friday: The Perilous Voyage of America's Merchant Marine*. Washington, DC: Brassey's, 1997.

Butler, Susan, ed. *My Dear Mr. Stalin: The Complete Correspondence of Franklin D. Roosevelt and Joseph V. Stalin*. New Haven, CT: Yale University Press, 2005.

Carse, Robert. *A Cold Corner of Hell*. New York: Doubleday & Company, 1969.

——. *The Long Haul: The U.S. Merchant Service in World War II*. New York: Norton, 1965.

Carter, William. *Why Me, Lord?* Ashland, OH: Bookmasters Inc., 2007.

Churchill, Winston. *The Second World War, Volume. I: The Gathering Storm*. Boston: Houghton Mifflin, 1948.

——. *The Second World War, Volume IV: The Hinge of Fate*. Boston: Houghton Mifflin, 1950.

——. *The Second World War, Volume V: Closing the Ring*. Boston: Houghton Mifflin, 1951.

Claasen, Adam R. A. *Hitler's Northern War: The Luftwaffe's Ill-Fated Campaign, 1940–1945*. Lawrence: University Press of Kansas, 2001.

De Hartog, Jan. *The Captain*. New York: Atheneum, 1966.

De La Pedraja, René. *The Rise and Decline of U.S. Merchant Shipping in the Twentieth Century*. New York: Twayne Publishers, 1992.

Dimbleby, Jonathan. *The Battle of the Atlantic*. New York: Oxford University Press, 2016.

Dobbs, Michael. *Six Months in 1945: FDR, Stalin, Churchill, and Truman*. New York: Vintage Books, 2012.

Doenitz, Karl. *Memoirs: Ten Years and Twenty Days*. Annapolis, MD: Naval Institute Press, 1959.

Dunn, Dennis J. *Caught Between Roosevelt and Stalin: America's Ambassadors to Moscow*. Lexington: University Press of Kentucky, 1998.

Dupra, Lyle E. *We Delivered: The U.S. Navy Armed Guard in World War II*. Manhattan, KS: Sunflower University Press, 1997.

Edwards, Bernard. *The Road to Russia: Arctic Convoys, 1942*. Annapolis, MD: Naval Institute Press, 2002.

Elson, Robert T. *Prelude to War*. New York: Time-Life Books, 1976.

Emmerson, Charles. *The Future History of the Arctic*. New York: PublicAffairs, 2010.

Evans, Mark Llewellyn. *Great World War II Battles in the Arctic*. Westport, CT: Greenwood Press, 1999.

Fairbanks, Douglas, Jr. *A Hell of a War*. New York: St. Martin's Press, 1993.

Felknor, Bruce L. *The U.S. Merchant Marine at War, 1775–1945*. Annapolis, MD: Naval Institute Press, 1998.

Flaherty, S. J. *Abandoned Convoy*. Jericho, NY: Exposition Press, 1970.

Frank, Wolfgang. *The Sea Wolves*. New York: Rinehart & Company, 1955.

Fredriksen, John C. *International Warbirds: An Illustrated Guide to World Military Aircraft, 1914–2000*. Santa Barbara, CA: ABC-CLIO, 2002.

Freeman, Robert H. *The War Offshore*. Ventnor, NJ: Shellback Press, 1987.

Gatty, Harold. *The Raft Book: Lore of the Sea and Sky*. New York: George Grady Books, 1943.

Gessen, Masha. *The Future Is History: How Totalitarianism Reclaimed Russia*. New York: Riverhead Books, 2017.

———. *The Man Without a Face: The Unlikely Rise of Vladimir Putin*. New York: Riverhead Books, 2012.

Glantz, David M. *The Battle for Leningrad 1941–1944*. Lawrence: University Press of Kansas, 2002.

Groom, Winston. *1942*. New York: Grove Press, 2005.

Hamilton, Nigel. *The Mantle of Command: FDR at War, 1941–1942*. Boston: Mariner Books, 2014.

Harriman, W. Averell, and Elie Abel. *Special Envoy to Churchill and Stalin 1941–1946.* New York: Random House, 1975.

Hemingway, Ernest, ed. *Men at War: The Best War Stories of All Time.* New York: Bramhall House, 1955.

Herbert, Brian. *The Forgotten Heroes: The Heroic Story of the United States Merchant Marine.* New York: Tom Doherty Associates, 2004.

Hoehling, A. A. *The Fighting Liberty Ships.* Kent, OH: Kent State University Press, 1996.

Howarth, David. *The Shetland Bus: A World War II Epic of Escape, Survival, and Adventure.* Guilford, CT: The Lyons Press, 1951.

Huchthausen, Captain Peter. *K-19: The Widowmaker.* Washington, DC: National Geographic, 2002.

Kaplan, Philip, and Jack Currie. *Convoy.* Annapolis, MD: Naval Institute Press, 1998.

Kemp, Paul. *Convoy! Drama in Arctic Waters.* Edison, NJ: Castle Books, 2004.

Khlevniuk, Oleg V. *Stalin: New Biography of a Dictator.* New York: Yale University Press, 2015.

Kotkin, Stephen. *Stalin: Waiting for Hitler, 1929–1941.* New York: Penguin Press, 2017.

Khrushchev, Nikita. *Khrushchev Remembers.* Boston: Little, Brown, 1970.

Labaree, Benjamin W. *America and the Sea: A Maritime History.* Mystic, CT: Mystic Seaport Museum, Inc., 1998.

Land, Emory Scott. *Winning the War with Ships.* New York: Robert M. McBride Co., 1958.

Loewenstein, Francis L., Harold D. Langley, and Manfred Jonas, eds. *Roosevelt and Stalin: Their Secret Wartime Correspondence.* New York: Saturday Review Press and E. P. Dutton & Co., 1975.

Lund, Paul, and Harry Ludlam. *I Was There: On PQ17, the Convoy to Hell.* London: Foulsham and Company Ltd., 1968.

MacLean, Alistair. *HMS Ulysses.* London: William Collins, 1955.

Manchester, William, and Paul Reid. *The Last Lion: Winston Spencer Churchill.* New York: Bantam Books, 2013.

Mann, Chris, and Christer Jörgensen. *Hitler's Arctic War.* New York: St. Martin's Press, 2002.

McCannon, John. *A History of the Arctic: Nature, Exploration and Exploitation.* London: Reaktion Books, 2012.

McCoy, Samuel Duff. *Nor Death Dismay.* New York: Macmillan Company, 1944.

McGonigal, David, and Dr. Lynn Woodworth. *The Complete Encyclopedia of Antarctica and the Arctic.* Willowdale, Ontario, Canada: Firefly Books, 2001.

McPhee, John. *Looking for a Ship.* New York: Farrar, Straus & Giroux, 1990.

Martienssen, Anthony. *Hitler and His Admirals.* London: Secker and Warburg, 1948.

Meacham, Jon. *Franklin and Winston.* New York: Random House, 2004.

Merridale, Catherine. *Ivan's War: Life and Death in the Red Army, 1939–1945.* New York: Picador, 2006.

Moore, Arthur. *A Careless Word, a Needless Sinking.* New York: American Merchant Marine Museum, 1998.

Morison, Samuel Eliot. *The Battle of the Atlantic, 1939–1943. Volume. 1 of History of United States Naval Operations in World War II.* Annapolis, MD: Naval Institute Press, 1947.

Mosier, John. *Hitler vs. Stalin: The Eastern Front, 1941–1945.* New York: Simon & Schuster Paperbacks, 2010.

Moynahan, Bryan. *Leningrad: Siege and Symphony.* New York: Atlantic Monthly Press, 2013.

Mulligan, Timothy. *Neither Sharks nor Wolves: The Men of Nazi Germany's U-boat Arm, 1939–1945.* Annapolis, MD: Naval Institute Press, 1999.

Nisbet, Robert. *Roosevelt and Stalin: The Failed Courtship.* Washington, DC: Regnery Gateway, 1988.

Ogden, Graeme. *My Sea Lady.* London: Bene Factum Publishing, 2013.

Overy, Richard. *The Dictators: Hitler's Germany, Stalin's Russia.* New York: W. W. Norton & Co., 2004.

———. *How the Allies Won.* New York: W. W. Norton & Co., 1995.

———. *Russia's War.* New York: Penguin Books, 1997.

Paterson, Lawrence. *Black Flag: The Surrender of Germany's U-boat Forces.* Minneapolis, MN: Zenith Press, 2009.

———. *Steel and Ice: The U-boat Battle in the Arctic and the Black Sea, 1941–1945*. Annapolis, MD: Naval Institute Press, 2016.

Pearce, Frank. *Running the Gauntlet*. London: Fontana, 1989.

Peillard, Leonce. *Sink the Tirpitz!* Translated from the French by Oliver Coburn. New York: G. P. Putman's Sons, 1968.

Perlmutter, Amos. *FDR & Stalin: A Not-So-Grand Alliance, 1943–1945*. Columbia: University of Missouri Press, 1993.

Pielou, E. C. *A Naturalist's Guide to the Arctic*. Chicago: University of Chicago Press, 1994.

Pitt, Barrie. *The Battle of the Atlantic*. Alexandria, VA: Time-Life Books, 1977.

Reminick, Gerald. *Patriots and Heroes, Volume 2*. Palo Alto, CA: Glencannon Press, 2004.

Richards, Phil, and Richard Banigan. *How to Abandon Ship*. Baltimore: Cornell Maritime Press, Inc., 1942.

Riesenberg, Felix. *Sea War*. New York: Rinehart and Company, 1956.

Rigge, Simon, with the editors of Time-Life Books. *War in the Outposts*. Alexandria, VA: Time-Life Books, 1980.

Rohwer, Jurgen. *Axis Submarine Successes, 1939–1945*. Annapolis, MD: Naval Institute Press, 1983.

Roskill, Captain S. W. *The War at Sea 1939–1945, Volume 2*. Uckfield, England: Naval & Military Press, 1956.

Ruegg, Bob, and Arnold Hague. *Convoys to Russia 1941–1945*. Kendal, England: The World Ship Society, 1992.

Ruge, Vice Admiral Friedrich. *The Sea War: The German Navy's Story, 1939–1945*. Annapolis, MD: Naval Institute Press, 1957.

Salisbury, Harrison E. *The 900 Days: The Siege of Leningrad*. New York: Da Capo Press, 1969.

Schofield, B. B. *The Russian Convoys*. Philadelphia: Dufour Editions, 1964.

Schwind, David A. *Blue Seas, Red Stars: Soviet Military Medals to U.S. Sea Service Recipients in World War II*. Arglen, PA: Schiffer Publishing, 2015.

Scott, Mark, ed., *Eyewitness Accounts of the World War II Murmansk Run, 1941–1945*, Lewiston, N.Y.: Edwin Mellen Press, 2006.

Sebag-Montefiore, Hugh. *Enigma: The Battle for the Code*. New York: John Wiley & Sons, 2000.

Showell, Jak P. Mallmann, ed. *Fuehrer Conferences on Naval Affairs, 1939–1945.* Annapolis, MD: Naval Institute Press, 1990.

———. *Swastikas in the Arctic: U-boat Alley Through the Frozen Hell.* London: Fonthill Media, 2014.

Simmons, Thomas E. *Escape from Archangel.* Jackson: University Press of Mississippi, 1990.

Smith, Jean Edward. *FDR.* New York: Random House, 2007.

Snow, Richard. *A Measureless Peril.* New York: Scribner, 2010.

Snyder, Timothy. *Bloodlands: Europe Between Hitler and Stalin.* New York: Basic Books, 2010.

Solzhenitsyn, Aleksandr. *The Gulag Archipelago, 1918–1956: An Experiment in Literary Investigation.* New York: Harper Perennial, 2007.

Sontag, Sherry, and Christopher Drew. *Blind Man's Bluff: The Untold Story of American Submarine Espionage.* New York: PublicAffairs, 1998.

Spufford, Francis. *I May Be Some Time: Ice and the British Imagination.* New York: St. Martin's Press, 1997.

Starnes, H. Gerald. *Torpedoed for Life: World War II Combat Veterans of the U.S. Merchant Marine.* New York: CreateSpace, 2013.

Starostin, Maksim I. *Krigsdagbok fra Murmansk (War Diary from Murmansk).* Oslo, Norway: Orkana Akademisk, 2017.

Taylor, Theodore. *Battle in the Arctic Seas.* New York: Sterling Point Books, 1976.

Tolley, Kemp. *Caviar and Commissars.* Annapolis, MD: Naval Institute Press, 1983.

U.S. Hydrographic Office. *Arctic Pilot: The Coast of Russia from Voriema or Jacob River in Europe to East Cape, Bering Strait, Including Off-lying Islands, Volume 1.* Washington, DC: U.S. Hydrographic Office, 1917.

U.S. War Shipping Administration. *The U.S. Merchant Marine at War: A Report of the War Shipping Administration to the President,* January 15, 1946. Washington, DC: U.S. Government Printing Office, 1946.

Vining, Donald, ed. *American Diaries of World War II.* New York: Pepys Press, 1982.

Walling, Michael. *Forgotten Sacrifice.* Oxford, England: Osprey Publishing, 2012.

Weeks, Albert L. *Russia's Life-Saver: Lend-Lease Aid to the USSR in World War II*. Lanham, MD: Lexington Books, 2004.

Werth, Alexander. *Russia at War*. New York: E. P. Dutton & Co., 1964.

Wherrett, David. *From Yorkshire to Archangel: A Young Man's Journey to PQ-17*. Kibworth Beauchamp, England: Matador, 2017.

Williamson, Gordon. *U-boat Tactics in World War II*. Oxford, England: Osprey Publishing, 1990.

Winn, Godfrey. *PQ-17*. London: Hutchinson, 1947.

Winton, John. *Ultra at Sea*. New York: William Morrow, 1988.

Woodman, Richard. *Arctic Convoys, 1941–1945*. Barnsley, England: Pen & Sword Maritime, 2004.

Wynn, Kenneth. *U-boat Operations of the Second World War, Volume I: Career Histories, U1–U510*. Annapolis, MD: Naval Institute Press, 1998.

Zetterling, Niklas, and Michael Tamelander. *Tirpitz: The Life and Death of Germany's Last Super Battleship*. Havertown, PA: Casemate Publishers, 2013.

DOCUMENTARY

I recommend a 2014 documentary featured on the British Broadcasting Corporation entitled *PQ-17: An Arctic Disaster*.

WEBSITES

I also found these websites helpful:

www.usmm.org

www.ancestry.com

www.convoy.web

www.naval-history.net

www.uboat.net

www.pq17.eclipse.co.uk/

www.cbrnp.com/RNP/Flower/ARTICLES/Poppy/Beardmore-1.htm

www.uboatarchive.net

INDEX

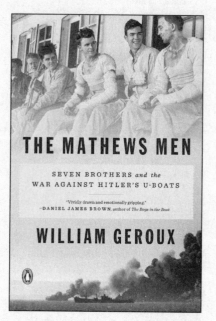